Cherry

'Mary has talents I aspire to. She's a poet and there are passages in her writing that glitter . . . And her references are universal, she just has to dip into her capacious memory'
Frank McCourt, author of *Angela's Ashes*

'Readers seduced by Karr's uncanny memoir of a childhood spent under the spell of a volatile, defiantly loving family can look forward to more exquisite writing in this sequel . . . moving effortlessly from breathtaking to heartstabbing to laugh-out-loud raucous, the precision and sheer beauty of Karr's writing remains outstanding'
Publishers Weekly

'[Karr's] language is assertive, thick with sensation, swarming with memory, in love with its own effect. She's fantastic and a bit repellent, a show-off blazing with pleasure at her remembered self, the girl she once was and the woman she's become'
Observer

'Gorgeously funny, sexy as hell, heartachingly poignant and terrifying'
Eve

'Absorbing and beautifully written, it's a summer must-read'
Shine

'An uncompromising and honest account written with considered detachment . . .[Karr] is her own best critic, best analyst, best observer, best spokesperson'
Irish Independent

A smart, searing memoir . . . Romance, in all of its wondrous and heartbreaking incarnations, is Karr's great subterranean subject, the ground upon which her witty, whip-smart writing catches root . . . [a] wildly intelligent, searingly funny, and suprisingly tender book'

Elle

'A brilliant and unforgettable memoir about growing up female in America . . . Mary Karr's follow-up to her memoir *The Liars' Club* is told with the same painful honesty, sparkling self-deprecating wit and acute insight . . . One of the most inspiring and devastating books about coming of age around'

Metro

'Sassy, perfectly paced prose'

Literary Review

'This dazzling account of female adolescence in search of an authentic self is the truest and funniest I've read'

The Tablet

'An ideal book for anyone who ever slammed their bedroom door'

Sunday Express

'The best depiction of being high I have ever read'

Diana Athill, author of *Stet*

Mary Karr's memoir, *The Liars' Club*, won the PEN/Martha Albrand Award. A poet and essayist, she has won Pushcart prizes in both genres. She is the author of the poetry collections *Abacus*, *The Devil's Tour* and *Viper Rum*. She lives in New York State and is the Peck Professor of English at Syracuse University.

ALSO BY MARY KARR

AUTOBIOGRAPHY

The Liars' Club

POETRY

Abacus

The Devil's Tour

Viper Rum

Cherry

a memoir

MARY KARR

PICADOR

First published 2000 by Viking Penguin,
a member of Penguin Putnam Inc., New York

This edition published 2002 by Picador
an imprint of Pan Macmillan Ltd
Pan Macmillan, 20 New Wharf Road, London N1 9RR
Basingstoke and Oxford
Associated companies throughout the world
www.panmacmillan.com

ISBN 0 330 48576 8

A portion of this work first appeared in the *New Yorker*.

The acknowledgments on page viii constitute an extension of
this copyright page.

5 7 9 8 6 4

A CIP catalogue record for this book is available from
the British Library.

Printed and bound in Great Britain by
Mackays of Chatham plc, Chatham, Kent

To Bob & Vanette,

Mary Ellen & Patti,

and Doonie

And to St. Jude,

the patron saint of lost causes

PERMISSIONS ACKNOWLEDGMENTS

Acknowledgments

Courtney Hodell first bought this book for Viking, then spent years cajoling it into existence. Her customarily brilliant edits were indispensable. So were the ongoing confidence and readings of my friend and agent Amanda Urban, the final pass by Paul Slovak, and the tireless appraisals in this and all efforts from my assistant, Betsy Hogan. Plus Don DeLillo.

My son, Dev Milburn, endured the writing process while acing junior high with a grace that threw my own adolescence into stark relief. As a kid and an anthropological presence, he was (and is) a wonder.

During several long winters, three families welcomed and sustained us—specifically John Holohan's clan, Jack and Mary Hogan, and all the Pascales (Chuck and Lynn, Neal and Deb, Tony and Millie). Childhood friends who shared stories and pictures along the way were Vanette Atchley, Cindy Cannon, and Bob Perry.

Finally, three pals served as constant touchstones: Mary Ellen Blade, Patti Mora, and Kent Scott.

—To all these, I bow my head.

Contents

PROLOGUE * California 1972

Time's march is a web of causes and effects, and asking for any gift of mercy, however tiny it might be, is to ask that a link be broken in that web of iron, ask that it be already broken. No one deserves such a miracle.

—Jorge Luis Borges *A Prayer*
Translated by Andrew Hurley

NO ROAD OFFERS MORE MYSTERY than that first one you mount from the town you were born to, the first time you mount it of your own volition, on a trip funded by your own coffee tin of wrinkled up dollars—bills you've saved and scrounged for, worked the all-night switchboard for, missed the Rolling Stones for, sold fragrant pot with smashed flowers going brown inside twist-tie plastic baggies for. In fact, to disembark from your origins, you've done everything you can think to scrounge money save selling your spanking young pussy.

It's best if you set out on this quest with friends equally young, because then all of you will be carried through several days' sleepless drive and infrequent pee-stops across massive scorched desert by a collective hallucinogenic insomnia that turns the gigantic cacti into (alternately) first a guitar-toting mystic and then a phantom hitchhiker and finally into a spangled matador cutting veronicas above the sand floor. You will be carried past these metaphorical monsters by the fire and wonder of your collective yearning toward your chosen spot, the black dot on the map at which your young-muscled bodies will be fired. In this case, Los Angeles.

Los Angeles. You've never been there, never been to any city that newscasters mention on TV. Still, in the three months since you've decided to head for California, you like to lie on the bare floor your mom let you yank the carpet out of and then lacquer black while you say the city's name over and over as in prayer. Los Angeles, Los Angeles. You know almost nothing about the place, so while you're waiting for your friends to come in a blue truck to ferry you off, you stare at its spot on the map, as though peering close enough will split the small dark seed of your future and reveal whatever self you're fixing to become.

You know this won't happen, of course. You're not exactly stupid. You're only standing in your shitty yard on the brink of what will be a vaporously hot morning waiting for the blue truck with questionable fuel pump and worn brakes to take you the fuck out of there. You look up the road. Nothing: a pink sky, the same warped curve of blacktop leading to the stop sign. The map you got in a neat rectangle at the Fina station now surges in your hands under the light wind.

So much comes from California, and now you're going there, to the origins of things. The LSD you call orange sunshine looks like baby aspirin and comes (in name if not in fact) from Orange County, California. It's just one more totem of the Golden State that set you yearning for it.

If you had your druthers, you'd all be setting out for northern California, San Francisco specifically. That's where Haight-Ashbury is (The Hate, your right-wing sister calls it). On TV and in *Rolling Stone* magazine and in books like *Electric Kool-Aid Acid Test,* you're told this place is aswarm with longhaired boys—blond and anorectic looking. These boys are not like the meat-eating, car-disemboweling, football-watching, squirrel-murdering boys you grew up dodging spitballs from. These west coast boys subsist on brown rice and ceramic bowls of clear broth in which sheer ideograms of seaweed float. Unlike the boys of your town, who (for the most part) read nothing but the football scores, or (for the surfers anyway) the tidal charts of the newspapers in order to paddle out just before the best waves break, these California boys have rooms lined with books. They know their astrological rising signs and the names of constellations and how to weave plain old string into beaded macramé belts that you can sell outside rock concerts for some bucks apiece.

These boys occupy more and more of your conscious thought. Lying on your Sears trundle bed with the Mexican throw you picked up on a surfing expedition, you picture their long torsos and shirtless chests above their low-slung Levis.

San Francisco has other myths that recommend it, other draws besides the bead-bedecked boys. The only two books you own by living poets come from San Francisco's City Lights Books—a dwarfish little pamphlet by Allen Ginsberg and its companion text by Lawrence Ferlinghetti. They fit neatly in the cardboard box you're taking to Los Angeles.

Meanwhile, you're waiting for courage. You hope to marshal enough of it to go inside and say goodbye to your daddy, who has decided to deal with your final departure as he's dealt with the past three years' occasional departures. He ignores it. There's nothing so dire that Daddy can't let it slip by with a stoical stare. Before you have to meet that gaze and turn from it so the weight of it is borne on your back for all the days you live away from this house, you try to get your hope-machine pumping.

The map usually does it, staring at it. You drag your ragged thumbnail along the trajectory you'll follow across the state of Texas (*ear to ear,* as your daddy says), the whole yellow desert you'll pass through ending finally in a vast wash of royal blue. The Specific Ocean, you call it, for you've learned there's often a slanted truth in words you blur like this.

You finally sit your bony ass down on the concrete porch where the night's chill of heavy dew seeps through the butt of your jean shorts. You try for a few minutes to refold the map as it was in the wire cage at the Fina station. But it's a dismantled mechanical bird in your hands with no Tab B or Slot C to make sense of. You mean to write a poem about that, too, but it keeps coming out all wrong in the ticker tape that clicks through your head. You very much dread saying goodbye to your daddy, who has, in fact, ignored your upcoming trip so well that even your emptied room and the plates you stood wrapping in *Leechfield Gazette* classifieds escaped comment.

There Daddy sits in his straight-backed posture, all right angles on the faux leather chair in clean khakis and shiny black shoes. Six in the morning: all dressed and no bar to go to. He is not smoking. Not smoking for him is a form of pouting. He'll also turn down food when he's mad. Say, Y'all go on, I'm not hungry. It's his way to say that nothing anybody has interests him one sliver.

When you bend over to hug him, he smells of coffee dosed with whiskey. His mere presence in its dogged absence makes you cry, and the tears fall from your face to his khaki back where they hit and darken the weave. Behind him there's an entire wall of books that first set the engine of your yearning in motion and over many years of reading and study led to this disapproved-of departure. Next to the wall of books is a painting of the seacoast at High Island that your mother did in the early fifties before you were born.

Maybe it's no accident that you have camped at that very spot a hundred nights, sleeping-bagged under Meekham's Pier, so you could be there when the good waves rolled in with the main tide just before dawn. Maybe that painting of Mother's kick-started this longing for the sea that your readings of *Moby Dick* only augmented.

You dab the back of your hand against your eyes so you can better see the wrinkled majesty of your daddy's profile against the white wall. He's looking off into the painting like old Ahab scanning for whale, but the corners of his mouth pinch down. And while you know it's his standard look—nothing personal—the innate distance in it fuels your own diffidence. It's what keeps you from talking to him overmuch or questioning his whereabouts or offering details of your own. You sense his actual, upcoming geographic distance from you as a keening whine in the base of your skull.

What you crying about, Pokey? he finally says. (Probably there was tenderness in that voice, but you first heard it as annoyance.) He roots through his pockets for a handkerchief. You just stand there, your face wet. You finally say that you're gonna miss him.

Where you going? he asks. The question's posed with that airy wonder that makes you puzzle over what the whiskey has left unsinged from his head.

When you say California, he winces at you in disbelief.

He says, Who told you that? Who told you you could do that? As if anybody has told you much of anything related to your comings and goings for years. You've long since stopped slithering in and out of the house through your window screen. You've come and gone at all hours, weekends and weeks at a time.

Suddenly, the threads that tie you to your daddy seem frail as spider's silk. You fumble for something that will impress on him your earnest competence in planning this trip. The work ethic usually gets him, and in spurts you will work hard. You tell him how much money you've saved. You mention the two factory jobs you have lines on—one silk-screening T-shirts, another fiberglassing catamarans. He doesn't ask you where you'll stay, so you don't have to lie about the friends of friends who vaguely agreed to let you park the truck in their driveway. But you lie anyway.

In your lie, you build a rolling assortment of town houses on the beach. There are boats listing on the bay and sleek polished cars in numbered slots. You don't even fully believe such a world exists off TV shows, but still you tell your daddy about it. Then you decide it belongs to Beth Ann Guidrey's uncle. You choose her because your daddy's especially fond of her, but he never runs into her divorced parents who might disavow the story.

The TV is on some rerun, but your daddy stares past it. He's off inside his own head, where he goes to wander—you imagine—some solitary rows of low-growing peanuts or fat watermelons still held to the vine, which rustly world hasn't existed since 1920, when he was a boy in the fields around the logging camp trying to hide from work in the far, low furrows. You have been wiped from his consciousness in one clean swipe.

He stares and stares as if by looking away from you like this, he could, after a minute, look back to find the girl in pigtails you once were and whose plate he still composes with piles of black-eyed peas and cornbread slathered with oleo.

He finally says to the TV screen, You want me to make you some breakfast?

He asks you every morning. And every morning you say you're not hungry.

From the far juncture, you'll imagine you can see inside his heart better. Your daddy is tired with a generalized alcohol-soaked heaviness that has nothing to do with any body. Later, you'll hear he has a mistress much younger than he is, a waitress, whose husband—once he discovers this betrayal—will put a bullet first through her skull, then his own. This will cause your daddy to weep like a child and curse at anyone who tries to hold him and flail out as if to strike you, which you know he would never do.

You will also someday realize the impossibility of your daddy's dilemma with regard to you. Sure, by not forbidding you to go, he silently endorses an insane plan whereby you leave home with little more than a hundred dollars for an unknown region with this gaggle of boys whose chief recommendation is that they've all so far managed to evade—despite the cops' best efforts—serious jail time. In fact, your older sister, Lecia, likes to say, If the law don't want them, why should Mary? If, however, your daddy had forbidden you to go, you may well have damned him for that. The truth is, for whatever reasons, you've become strange to each other. He stormed the beach at Normandy, drives a truck, hangs out at the American Legion or the VFW with other men in work clothes. You're embracing the skittery surface of surfing and psychedelia. The atmosphere between you has gone muddy. You are a mere scarecrow in his telescope lens, and he in yours.

Maybe it's only after your daddy's been dead fifteen years that you create this longing of yours for him and his denial of it, because it's easier to bear the notion that he rejected you than vice versa.

Goddamn lying bastards, your daddy finally says. And you see he's fixated on the TV. Then he says, You don't need to go to California. His reasoning for this judgment is so ancient he doesn't even bother repeating it. Like all his advice, it's endured in the same form for seventeen years. The grooves it's worn in your young head have been played too often. They produce only static: His parents rented him out to Kansas sharecroppers for field work when he was just a boy. He never wants you to feel turned out that way, and since the only bona fide reason for going anywhere is (as he sees it) either a war they make you fight or a financial flamethrower on your butt, you don't need to go.

He says, You need to stay right here at forty-nine-oh-one Garfield. California's ass.

For him that's the end of it. The television starts the chirpy music from *Dialing for Dollars,* a show he used to watch with reverence, shushing all talk and waving off phone calls while he waited each day for the phone to ring. Not long ago, he noticed that the chopped up phone books they drew numbers from weren't just Leechfield but included other towns, even other counties.

Hell that's not local, he said the first time he noticed that they were calling Beaumont.

Lecia was teasing her platinum hair for a date. The can of Aqua Net she fanned around made your eyes burn. She said it was local to the broadcast area. You know for a stone fact that she tells people your parents aren't her parents because she'd rather be an orphan raised among distant-cousin-type lunatics than someone who shared up-close your family's tainted genetic material.

Your cheeks are cool from the tears. You're shocked again by how little room you take up in this house. You turn to the small blue screen, where this year's Oil Queen is slipping her small hand into the chicken-wire barrel of sliced up phone books. Her flipped-up hair is dyed Elvis-black. She wears a small tiara pinned over her bangs. Her organdy prom dress rustles when she hands Cowboy Dan the Weather Man today's number.

This is the moment your daddy waits for each day, when the exchange is revealed so he'll know exactly what town it is. He says, Hell that's long distance! That's Jasper County. He beams a righteousness worthy of Abraham at the goddamn lying bastards on the TV.

You have been dismissed again.

In truth, you dismissed him long before, but you won't be able to face that for years. You shrugged off his hand when he tried to hug you. When he nagged you about breakfast, you waved him away. You can't admit to yourself that you first turned your back to him. So you invert the rejection—this distance, your scorn. They're now his attitudes aimed at you. In reality, he's an old man in his sixties whose raggedy-looking daughter refuses his every word and whose flight from him seems—no, is—unimaginable.

Suddenly you can't bear to stand in the same room with him another instant. Part of you expects him to stop your leaving. You can well imagine the blue truck chugging into your driveway, then your daddy's ropy arm reaching inside its window to draw out that long-haired surfer boy you fancy in order to tear him the proverbial new asshole. Your mother promised this wouldn't happen. But the seed in you that fears it is also—in the most locked box of yourself—the part that wishes your daddy to claim you back. Of course, you wouldn't stand still for such restraint of your freedom, but part of you yearns for the old order and his old self—possibilities currently sliding by. Intuitively you know that years of wandering lie ahead for you.

In the kitchen, your gray-haired mother is reading a massive book on art history and digging into a grapefruit half with a serrated spoon. You ask her, Is he gonna stop me going?

This gets her attention, for your exasperation with your daddy is a mirror of hers, which makes this a moment of conspiracy that already feels like betrayal. She looks up and sets the spoon down. She says, What'd he do?

He told me I couldn't go, you say.

She rolls her eyes. Asks what you expect. Finally, she says, I wish I was going with you. She tells you how she feels like a sinner abandoned to the purgatory of this black sucking bog where everybody but her gets to leave.

Years later, you'll learn to respond to your mother's complaints about Leechfield with the useful information that she did leave, and then came back. Sometimes, in moments of fury you'll say, *Leave now if you're that miserable.* That sentence hasn't yet been formed, much less has it gathered the weight of long-studied conviction you'd need to speak it aloud. But on this day, in the yellow light of your kitchen, her unhappiness loads you down with unnameable guilt.

In the living room, your daddy's talking to the TV again, this time to a Sabine Pass car salesman who puts his freakishly homely daughter on a kitchen stool for all his commercials. That girl is ugly, your daddy tells the TV. He says, Have to tie a pork chop around her neck to get the dog to play with her. Make a freight train take a dirt road.

You study your mother's beautiful clear face under its dandelion of white hair and see she's clearly tired of the green world and only loves what she can draw through her eyes from a page. For years you'll only come back to her when you get a ride or plane fares go down or the weather's good enough to hitch. In your chest, a chasm is opening.

Your mother still somehow cannot fathom your leaving her in this madhouse, though she groomed you for it and urged you to it.

She finally tells you that he'll be fine, your daddy. She says, He won't make a scene, I promise. You make her swear, and she hooks your pinky with hers like a kid. She goes back to art history, while you go back to the dim cloud of guilt at escaping this place she finds so wretched. You feel like a prisoner whose reprieve sparks despair in the remaining inmates. She starts digging in her grapefruit again as if she'll find in its pith the wisdom she wishes for.

You say, That's all I need, for him to snap and hit somebody.

She says, I told him we couldn't stop you. You'd just go anyway, and then we wouldn't know where you were.

Actually nothing could be further from true. In fact your mother's unbridled enthusiasm for this half-baked enterprise of yours sets a cold wind blowing through you. You're waiting to think up something revelatory and definitive to say when the black cat jumps up on the counter and starts nosing in her saucer.

Your mother says, Ever see anybody else's cat like grapefruit?

The doors between you are closing. It's true you've brought all the rhetorical tricks you learned in ninth-grade debate club to selling your mother on this idea for the better part of a year. (It's only when you're grown that you know how blatantly you lied with your resolve to leave: you were scared.)

Your mother rolls her eyes at the cat lapping grapefruit juice, says, Everything that comes into this house is crazy—whether we choose them for that or they get that way, I don't know.

When you go to pick up your surfer pal Doonie, his mother stands by the silver garbage can holding a dripping paper bag of trash. She's got on her bank-teller's dress with its black-and-white houndstooth check, her glasses hung from a gold chain around her neck. She's watching the boys strap the surfboards tighter to the racks and rearrange bags and boxes of albums in the truck bed. Worry pinches at her intelligent face, so you feel prompted to speak to this undisguised horror that you've halfway prompted.

You say, I'll look after them, Miz Deets.

She shakes her head, comes back with, And who's gonna look after you? She drops the garbage sack into its place, then stoops to pick up the lid. She stands there holding it a second like a shield before she fits it to the can.

Then she turns to you and says: Your mother's actually letting you do this?

This type of question sometimes obliges you to invent stuff—some scene of parental concern with your mother bribing you to stay while your father storms in the background. But you lack energy for any more deceit about your family's actual nature. On another coast, in another town, you plan to exist free of such duplicity about family and self. You'll drive from this place and through some transforming aperture into a world where your new self—golden and unalterable—will gleam.

So to Miz Deets you just say yes, your mother is letting you go, and this admission feels like a personal blight. It somehow speaks ill of you that your own parents can relinquish you with such ease.

Doonie hops off the truck-back to hug his mother goodbye as hard as she'll let him. She tilts her head to one side saying don't get my lipstick all over. Doonie has the angular body of a praying mantis, and she holds him by the elbows and kisses the air in his direction while wind whips his curly hair around their faces. When she pulls away, you can see her eyes have filled. Don't worry, Miz Deets, you say. Your face assembles itself into National Honor Society certainty, this expression that says: I'm a by-God American. Bring it on.

But Miz Deets seems unmoved from her doubt and worry. She says, Mary, I was your mama, and you getting in that truck with all them boys, I'd tie you to the bedpost.

This is not meant to hurt. It's just flat reportage.

You wedge into the truck with your so-called brothers and pull away from the last parental outpost, the vehicle rattling down the narrow road toward the interstate. The boys fire up a goodbye joint, and you suck down more than your share. Your young body is instantly a fresh-lit arrow notched and drawn back and about to be loosed. There's even a poem about this you intend to write, but in the little notebook you carry you just set down some drifty lines about flaming arrows fired at the sun.

One of the surfboards bolted onto the truck roof is way longer and thicker than all the others. Its underbelly sports a wicked rectangular scar. And in fact surgery was done on it. Following an idea copped from this Jimi Hendrix movie, Doonie cut a window into the fiberglass, then hollowed out a niche in the foam. The resulting hole was filled with an unbroken brick of moss-green pot and various baggies of pharmaceuticals.

Add to those substances your fiercely clung-to ignorance and your need for velocity, and you have a dangerous cocktail.

Someone should stop that truck and the future it chugs toward. Though Miz Deets looks worried, she's ultimately like other parents and lacks faith in her own powers to control your leaving. You pull away from her feeling naught but hope, though before those six bodies in your company have hardened into adulthood, several will be cut down by drug-related obliterations. Two will take their own lives. Two will pull time in jail.

Who saw it coming? Not you, certainly. Not the friends who follow soon in their own frail vehicles. Casualties to jack up the tally. There's the young heart cloven with a switchblade so deep the boy was dead, the coroner said, before he hit the barroom floor. There's the square-off with well armed drug dealers that ends in a boy tied to the chair and beaten. (The biblical phrase Doonie used for these first reports: Live by the sword, you die by it.)

Not to mention the so-called self-inflicted wounds: the car wreck that led to quadriplegia. The brain damage. The overdoses (plural).

Innumerable types of custodian will manifest: parole officers and trustees and court-appointed whoevers. Cops who'll cuff a fella inside the paddy wagon and drive reckless all the way to the station till his wrist breaks. Cops who'll peel off a bill on the street if they see a man jonesing too bad. Methadone supervisors and urine checkers; hair analyzers and body-cavity searchers.

With the AIDS virus comes the adage you first hear by phone in the late nineties: *Just get me high and let me die*—this followed by a sepulchral cough.

In Los Angeles, drugs work these transformative magics till the place stands as a geographical epicenter of grief, a city as sacked and ruined for you as Troy. Well into your forties, any time business forces you to fly there and you watch the airport tarmac unfurl from your cabin's glinting oval, it will feel like the wrong side of some psychic track.

Nobody tries to stop you. Maybe no one could. When the blind seer in *The Odyssey* foretold the loss of all companions, that portent went unheeded. The captain had turned to the horizon by then. The ship's ropes had been loosed, and the sails filled.

You wouldn't have listened. Wedged bare-legged in the banged-up truck with your fellows, you are still immortal, and that coast across the yellow map of the richest country on earth is beckoning to you with invisible fingers of hashish smoke.

PART ONE * **Elementary's End**

. . . We sense there is some sort of spirit that loves
birds and animals, and the ants—
perhaps the same one who gave a radiance to you in
your mother's womb.
Is it logical you'd be walking around entirely
orphaned now?
The truth is, you turned away yourself,
and decided to go into the dark alone.
Now you are tangled up in others, and have forgotten
what you once knew
and that is why everything you do has some wierd
failure in it.

—Kabir *The Radiance (13th century)*
Translated by Robert Bly

I want to make a noise with my feet
I want my soul to find its proper body.

—Nicanor Parra *Piano Solo*
Translated by Miller Williams

Chapter One

Violet Durkey has a hamster and a miniature turtle who lives in a shallow plastic bowl under a palm tree with snap-on fronds, and an albino rabbit named Snuffles with pink ears from Easter. It's the hamster I'm thinking about here.

One night he nosed out of his poorly latched cage and scampered across the glowing iron surface of the gas heater, blistering the bottoms of his tiny pink feet, the same feet whose weensy, lizard-like nails Violet had wanted to lacquer Sashay Pink. (Her mom said oh no Violet.) The vet prescribed a greenish antibiotic balm Violet was meant to smudge on with a Q-tip every morning. This balm, deemed icky by Violet, was so tasty to Hamster that he not only licked it up but ultimately (unbelievably) came to nibble off the digits (fingers? toes?) on all four of his feet, which act left him—when Violet burst in from school that day—with bleeding stumps so painful for everybody to look at that he had to be put to sleep.

Violet told this tale of woe in the skating rink's tiny toilet—her blue eyes misting over and her Earth Angel Pink mouth quivering while

Ruth Ann, Sherry, and Suzy Torvino gathered around. The skating rink was a hurricane-fence cage with a brown canvas roof and vinyl flags like those you see in a used car lot strung whapping around its perimeter. From box speakers mounted at the tent's four corners, the Beatles sang that she loved us yah, yah, yah. This song was warped by coming through the pink plywood door to where we stood at a makeshift sink with little blue packets of Wash-'N'-Dri for after you got done peeing. (Actually, because I never overtly peed on my hands, I never bothered with hand washing anyway.)

In the tiny mirror that hung from a nail poked in fiberboard, Violet's round, clear face was flushed under her pale freckles. This was the year before we all hit sixth grade. Violet straightened her curly brown hair not with bouts of Curl Free, which her mother said she was too young for, but by having her big sister steam iron said hair under a towel, using clouds of Aqua Net after to hold it. But in the close humid air of that bathroom, the hair spray was failing. From Violet's otherwise glossy pageboy, small ringlets were breaking loose at the hairline, seizing up in a way that evoked Renaissance paintings (Hans Somebody the Elder) that my mother praised for their delicacy. (The fact that Mother, who was a painter, kept art books deemed our entire clan somewhat suspect.)

In short, Violet was beautiful, and much beloved by the general populace. Her parents and two teenage sisters pampered her, yet she managed to represent herself as both entitled to that pampering and somehow surprised by it. The skates she owned (not rented) had held no one's feet but hers and did not leave her socks smelling like goat turd. They fit exactly. They were fresh-polished nurse white and had pink pom-poms laced to the toes. The pom-poms matched her gingham clam-digger pants with the knee ruffle, and those matched her crop-top. She and her mother had stitched this outfit up themselves from the Simplicity pattern that morning. When, during school, I whined out loud about my lack of wearable dresses (I had scads but only deigned to wear four of the least babyish ones, and so had to repeat my Monday dress each Friday), Violet always asked why I didn't just stitch something up. She recommended me to Sigona's dry goods, where a bin of mod print remnants cost just fifty cents each. More than once she told me that a dress for me probably wouldn't take a yard.

She might as well have asked why I didn't slay a zebra for its hide for all the interest I had in sewing.

Violet smelled like grated lemon peel and baby powder. Her Snoopy box purse, balanced open on the sink edge, held a miniature packet of pink tissues for just such weepy moments. There was also a pink rat-tail brush, and a minuscule glass vial of perfume that reminded me of nothing so much as a cyanide capsule from *The Man from U.N.C.L.E.*, my favorite TV show about international spies.

I poked my head past the elbows of girls encircling her while she dabbed under her lashes with the Kleenex wad. I asked to borrow her brush, hoping that this begged favor might buy me entry to their circle when gawking outside it for fifteen minutes had failed to.

"I'm *sorry,* Mary." Violet talked in italics sometimes when addressing me, the way you would to a deaf person or foreigner you were pretty sure otherwise wouldn't twig to what you were saying. "My mother *won't* let me loan it *out.* I'd get in *so* much *trouble.*" It seemed that Mrs. Durkey feared Violet's glossy head would wind up squirming with head lice if she passed her brush around (a not unfounded fear). With that, I was dismissed. She drew back into the comfort of her friends. In a nonitalicized voice, Violet told Ruth Ann and Sherry and Suzy Torvino that they needed to bring their own pillows to her sleepover that Friday.

My expression must have altered, for Violet's eyes in the tiny mirror clicked in and then detached from Sherry's and Ruth Ann's in turn. We'd all been on a cobbled-together track team that summer, myself the relay alternate, and I'd fancied myself somehow welded into Violet's good graces by a meet we all traveled to in Houston. But Violet's gaze, which had lit on the floor, said otherwise.

"You're having a sleepover?" I finally said.

This kind of overt angling for invitations was part of what kept me outside the elbows of those girls. I seemed destined to blunder into conversations nobody else cared to have. Most girls knew better. If Mavis Clay had overheard her own omission from such a party, she would have skated out without a word. But I had to pipe up, to worm the mystery of the event into the air. (Counterphobic, some shrink will later call it, being magnetically drawn to whatever one fears most.)

"See my mom only told me I could have five girls, and Ruth Ann's my best friend, and Sherry's my second-best, and Suzy's my third. And if I don't invite Joettie Bryant, she won't invite me to her trampoline party. And if I don't invite Lynda Delano, her dad will yell at my dad at work. And if I don't invite Jasmine Texler, Joettie can't come because her mom goes to Church of Christ and doesn't know my mom." Violet gaped at my ignorance of these complex barters in social currency, and all the girls but Ruth Ann mirrored that gaping. (Ruth Ann was someone whose calm blue eyes tended to fall on me at such moments with something like care.)

"But that's six girls," I said. Violet looked puzzled, her head cocked itself a notch to the right. I held up my hand and counted them off each finger. "Ruth Ann, Sherry, Suzy, Jasmine, Joettie, Lynda." With Lynda I stuck my thumb into the air and let my jaw hang.

"Well okay." She looked imperiously at me. "My mom said I could only have six girls then."

Such was the early logic of exclusion, as explained to me by Violet Durkey—who, in all fairness, committed no crime other than being adorable enough that I wished to be her. I don't remember if I actually told Violet Durkey at that instant that she was a snotball and her hamster probably ate his feet off as part of a suicide plan to get loose from her. At some point in my social career, I did let such a comment fly. Which is precisely why I didn't get asked to sleepovers. Other girls from families weird as mine managed to overcome their origins. Lecia got invited out by popular girls. So did Jasmine Texler, who'd moved to our town after her mom drank a bottle of laundry bluing and died. Jenny Raines even got elected cheerleader though her mom lived in the state loony bin.

Without the company of other girls, the summer became the first of many vastly vacant summers, a long white scroll of papyrus onto which something longed to be writ. Unless I'd found some book to lose myself in (the ferocity of my appetite for books rivaled a junkie's for opiate), the idleness was stultifying.

That summer I fell into reading as into a deep well where no voice could reach me. There was a poem about a goat-footed balloon man I recited everyday like a spell, and another about somebody stealing somebody else's plums and saying he was sorry but not really meaning it. I read the Tarzan books by Edgar Rice Burroughs and fancied myself running away to Africa to find just such an ape man to swing me from vine to vine.

I read *To Kill a Mockingbird* three times in one week, closing it on the last page, then cracking it open again to the first till the binding came unglued and had to be masking-taped back on. In it, a girl my age got rescued from a lunatic trying to kill her by the town bogey man, who'd years before stabbed his daddy with scissors while cutting paper dolls. She actually took this guy Boo by the hand and made friends with him, showing a courage and care beyond anything I could ever muster. (When our town maniac, a massively fat man named Otis, came shuffling down the road talking in whispers about Jesus and the Blessed Virgin and the good elves of this world, I always crossed to the other side.) In the second or third grade, I'd seen the movie of this book, and always superimposed my own face over that of the puckish Scout, while also picturing for myself the chiseled resolve of the young Gregory Peck playing her daddy. Inside their story, I could vanish from myself.

But books have last pages. The instant I finished one such page, I'd be forced to look up at whatever soap opera I had on. In the overacted, melodramatic gestures of those black-eyelined actresses I felt my own day's heaviness even more keenly. They flung their wrists to their foreheads in torment, or clutched their own heaving bosoms, or pitched their black-veiled selves across glossy coffins. In short, they moved through dramas of consequence far beyond any I'd ever be called to act in.

Mostly, the house was empty. When Daddy wasn't pulling shift work at the refinery, he either tried to cadge some sleep or stayed off on mysterious rounds. At thirteen, my sister Lecia had already manufactured a persona for herself that ranged free of the family and its unspoken stigmas. She filled out a 36C cup and dated a variety of football stars. When she climbed the bleachers at a game with legs a yard long in cut-off jeans, her blond flip sprayed into a form no wind could alter, high schools boys stood up by the row.

Mother was only in her studio one afternoon a week, not painting, but teaching painting to various Leechfield housewives. In response to an ad she'd run in the *Gazette,* women came to set up easels there Wednesday afternoons. To keep them from baking alive, Daddy installed a secondhand window air conditioner that leaked icy water into a pie tin with a steady drip that marked those otherwise timeless afternoons like a conductor's baton. I was supposed to be exiled to the house for these sessions, for which the ladies paid good money to have Mother stare with furrowed concern bordering on horror at their canvases—muddy-looking peaches and grapes, stiff-backed sunflowers stuck dead center lackluster vases. The worst were the portraits—kids and grandkids mostly, with massive hydrocephalic foreheads and wall-eyed expressions. ("One eye's looking at you and one's looking for you," Daddy said of one.)

The percolator would burble up the burnt coffee smell under the pine resins from the turpentine, a heady mixture that drew me from the solitary house's endless black-and-white soap operas. Mostly, I'd just sit outside the door on the hood of Mother's yellow station wagon in the dark garage, listening to the ladies' endless complaints about their husbands. I specifically recall one lady saying she wouldn't let her husband touch her pocketbook (a word I'd somehow always known was a euphemism for pussy) till he'd bought her a dishwasher.

"Hell, you might as well sell it down on Proctor Street, if that's the deal," Mother said. You could hear the intakes of breath all around, and pretty soon the offended lady came bumping out the door, wet canvases in hand. Once or twice I'd stand in the doorway and wheedle for my own sketch pad and charcoal and one of those giant beige gum erasers that I liked to eat when I was littler.

Other days, Mother was at college studying for her teaching certificate—a real oddity back when few moms worked outside the home. But she wanted a higher standard life than the local average and feared destitution at every turn. (Ironically enough, it was her own extravagant habits that tended to edge us to that brink. During a few screaming matches over debts she ran up, my daddy accused her of far outspending anything she earned teaching, but I wouldn't swear this was true.) Her college work seemed to me like yet another escape route from the banality of time at home with us.

Mother also had a secret history of hasty marriages and equally hasty dissolutions. Pretty much if you pissed her off good, you could expect to hear her tires tearing out the driveway. Within days, the knuckles of a process server would rap on your door. But I'm writing about the 1960s, when Lecia and I didn't yet know about all her pre-Daddy adventures. She ultimately racked up seven marriages in all, but we'd only witnessed the two to my daddy—with the short, nearly negligible blip of my stepfather. (He'd appeared after my grandmother's death, after Mother had been briefly carted off to the hospital for—among other things—the vast quantities of vodka she'd managed to guzzle.)

Such events kept our household from drawing much traffic. Kids loping straight through the yards on Garfield Road tended to cut an arc around ours as you might a graveyard. Probably this was more habit than any deliberate shunning, but the effect was the same.

With the house carved of human life, I took undue interest in the occasional chameleon that slithered from the tangle of honeysuckle through the vents of the air conditioner in my room. Once I spent a whole morning at the bathroom mirror trying to get one such unfortunate lizard to serve as a dangly earring by biting my earlobe. (If you squeezed his soft neck just right, his mouth would open like a clasp.) But he'd only bite down for a second or so before his jaw opened and he fell down my shirt front or into the sink and I'd have to catch him again. His tail finally broke off, and our Siamese—then hugely pregnant—wolfed him down her gullet in two quick swallows.

The house held me in a kind of misty nether-time. The air conditioner hummed. The refrigerator kicked on and lapsed off. I waited a lot, though for what I don't know. Nothing whatsoever seemed to be approaching from any direction. *I wait like an ox,* Franz Kafka wrote and Mother underlined in one of her college books. The sentence was copied down like an axiom into one of the dozen or so Big Chief tablets I bought that summer, then let stay blank after a few scribbled pages.

But if it's great literature you're after, Big Chief tablets seem gray-paged and flimsy, too pale to inscribe with genius of the caliber I aspired to. So I pilfered a black leather sketchbook from Mother's studio. To disguise my theft, I glued green and red Christmas glitter on the cover in a swirly pattern meant to be hypnotic. I never ripped out her pencil sketches of fishing boats, or the advice on portraiture she'd dated 1964: "Details of features not as important as mood, character, or manner etc. Artist must be proficient enough to work intuitively. Relatives or friends may not see person truly." Under this, I wrote in baroque cursive: "Me too—Mary Karr 1966."

To hold that book in my hand—its simple bulk and being—is to grasp onto the hard notch from some faintly erased time line and draw myself back there. Opening it, I breathe old air.

Any fable I've told about who I was then dissolves when I read that loose-jointed script I wrote. We tend to overlay grown-up wisdoms across the blanker selves that the young actually proffer. (When my son was born, I remember staring into his blue, wondering eyes, then asking the obstetrical nurse what he might be thinking. "You know the static channel on your TV?" she answered.)

So in actual written artifacts from my past, I sound way less smart than I tend to recall having been. My poems clip-clop doggedly along, less verse than trotting prayers, wishes to become someone other than who I found myself to be, to feel other than how I felt. The diary entries don't differ from any eleven-year-old's, though the pathos I found in them makes me wince: "I am not very successful as a little girl," I wrote. "When I grow up, I will probably be a mess." The Sharp family had dragged me to two tent revival meetings that summer in a town called Vidor (famous, by the way, for its Ku Klux Klan fish fries). On those steamy nights where people fanned their dripping faces with funeral fans on which a blue-robed Jesus knocked on a gleaming golden door, I never followed the weeping line of believers to the altar to dedicate my life to the Lord. But the rhetoric stayed with me. My writings are rotten with it. Mountains crumble and rivers run dry, etc. Rainbows come out after floods worthy of Noah. Every cheek is rosy, every cloud silver-lined. Reading those pages, you can almost hear the tambourines shaking in the background and a surge of ballpark organ music as the preacher asks you to testify.

Unfathomably, the career path I drew was the strange one I wound up undertaking, "to write ½ poetry and ½ autobiography." Though I never managed to wrest for myself a career as "philosipher," whatever I thought that meant, I also longed also to become "a real woman, a hardworking woman with a pure soul. Not just a perfumed woman on the outside."

I also wrote a lot of poems for the star of a cowboy show on TV called *Branded*, on whom I'd developed a wicked crush. In fantasy, he was interchangeable with Marshal Matt Dillon from *Gunsmoke* and Paladin from *Have Gun Will Travel*—cowboys who would soon magically transform into knights in armor after I discovered tales of chivalry. Jason McSomething, I think they called him. He'd been falsely convicted of treason during a Civil War battle and sentenced to hang before escaping. Most episodes, he galloped around the West looking for folks who could prove he wasn't a big sissy who ran out on his regiment. But somebody who thought him guilty would always pop up, so he'd have to slink out of town—hiding under some wagon straw or holding onto the side of a train. Always he left behind some widow schoolteacher or banker's daughter he was just fixing to get frisky on. I devoted more than a few pages to praising Jason's long suffering. (The stoicism I favored was less in the mode of Marcus Aurelius and more reminiscent of the donkey Eeyore from *Winnie the Pooh*.) I imagined him hoisting cups sadly in the air, saying goodbye to folks he'd never see again. One reads, "Faithful companions we may be./ But, Soldier, fill no glass for me!" That sort of thing.

When the pencil lead wore down and faded to slate gray, I'd sometimes walk to remote neighborhoods and knock on the doors of strange houses. If someone answered, I'd claim I was trying to sell Christmas cards, though I lacked any samples or other convincing evidence that this was so. I don't recall trying to extort actual dollars. (I had money, and there was nothing to buy anyway.) I just had nothing better to do.

People were damn nice about it. They handed me sugar cookies and Rice Krispie Treats in waxed paper, foil-wrapped kisses and hard candy by the fistful, but no Christmas card orders got totted down, even though I copied some random names from the phone book to convince everybody how well cards were selling.

Once a middle-aged woman in a pale blue duster hovered in the doorway a minute before bursting into tears. She put both hands on her jowly face. The tears rivered between her knobby fingers while I tried to figure out how to flee. Cool air spilled from her house as I stood melting in the heat.

"It's okay, baby," she said, into the damp palms pressed over her mouth after I'd said I was sorry for about the fifteenth time. "You just put me in mind of my boy. He's passed over—" She choked off a sob, a body-wracking convulsion that really made me wonder if people could break in half with grief.

Finally she gathered herself up. For a heartbeat's space, neither of us said anything. Then her shoulders relaxed a whit. "Do you want to see?" she finally asked, in a voice hardly above a whisper. She didn't even say see what. Nor did I run through any of the dire warnings I'd heard about getting in cars or houses with strangers. Maybe that's odd. Doubtless a more regular kid would have cobbled up a dental appointment to bolt off to. But the weight of her grief drew me to her. She held open the aluminum screen an extra notch for me to pass through.

The living room was cold as a meat locker and smelled like a pot of cabbage left too long on the stove. The light was muddy as gloom, all the shades being drawn flush to the sills. She'd also laid down plastic runners along the most traveled paths to keep the carpet naps fluffy. So plastic paths led from the door where I stood to a mossy-looking plaid sofa, then zigzagged to what must have been kitchen and bedroom and bath. Tables that would have hit you at knee level or shin level in the dark crowded every inch of available floor space, and were themselves packed with little porcelain figurines. A more useless assemblage of objects I've never seen—hoop-skirted shepherdesses with pilgrim's staffs, guys with powdered wigs, dinner bells, and gilt-edged snuff boxes. I remember specifically a disembodied female hand with rings and bracelets and red nails. The hand seemed to be reaching up from under the wood grain.

The dead boy's pictures lined one whole wall. Of his face, I remember almost nothing. He was blond when little, and his hair got darker as he grew. What's stuck with me in those staggered pictures' advance through his short life were the costumes marking any boy's inching toward manhood—a toddler with suspendered shorts; a school-age boy with a homemade birthday hat; then a Little Leaguer's striped knickers; baptismal robes; and finally a gangly teen in a white dinner jacket holding a corsage box.

"He shot himself," she said. Her face told me it was on purpose. Up till that day, he'd been the perfect boy, she said. Then he went to a dancing party and asked a girl onto the floor. And she said no. He came home miserable, opened up the Bible to the Twenty-third Psalm, and shot himself, right in the head. They were in the next room at the time watching Lawrence Welk's Champagne Music Hour.

What she did next is the kind of gesture I've since learned that I somehow invite. (After I stopped thinking of such moments as my fault and began to regard them as an odd form of privilege, I handled them better.) She steered me by my shoulder along another plastic path to the coffee table. I did not shrink from her touch. I both longed to see and dreaded what we were headed for: the worn black Bible on the rectangular laminated wood. A laminated card stuck out of the pages to keep the place.

Hefting up the Bible worked some tranquilizing voodoo on her. She became strangely calm, as if getting to the heart of some matter she'd been circling all day. She'd done it before and often. Her ease told me that. Some passing assemblage of milkmen and water-meter readers and Avon ladies had stood where I was standing and sought to arrange their faces into tolerable expressions, as I then did. Certainly I wanted to stay upbeat, but grinning like a monkey was way wrong. I settled on the look of earnest expectancy, but pleasant.

She opened the massive Bible and held it out for my study. A stain the color of burnt chocolate took up most of the pages' deep valley. The paper had puckered from the wet. Still the words were legible. "The Lord is my shepherd . . . ," I read in my head.

Then I was saying a hasty goodbye, for only a few years before, my own wild-assed mother had threatened suicide. Part of me believed the notion was contagious, a germ I could pick up that might reinfect Mother. I didn't consciously ponder this, but it flitted through me strong enough that before the lady could say diddly, I was shaking her leathery cold hand on the porch in waves of heat. Then I was running home full tilt as if the house wouldn't be empty when I burst in. The tedium there was suddenly preferable to the terror of those houses I loped past, inside which were unknown losses.

Sometime that summer I stopped prowling around strange houses and concocted a real job shining shoes at the barbershop. This act of mine thwarted Daddy's vow that his daughters never work for pay while under his roof. Still, I defied that order by taking his shoeshine box to the shop and weaseled myself a post in the red leather shine chair.

The shop held special allure that week since I'd overheard somewhere that John Cleary was going in for his annual crew cut the next day. I watched in worshipful silence as, under Mr. DePello's humming clippers, hanks of John's shining yellow hair fell in slow strips to the linoleum, where it was swept into the copper dustpan. Afterward, his shaved and knobby skull floated in Mr. DePello's hand mirror. There'd been around his ears that strip of untanned scalp we called "white sidewalls." John's hand ran over the stubble real slow, as if it held for him a great mystery. The gesture was one that drifted back to me in my bed at night, such puzzled tenderness as he touched that bristle. Maybe he even caught a mirrored glimpse of my figure in the giant red vinyl shine chair, for my awe must have been palpable. Mr. DePello untied the apron and shook it so short hairs fell to the floor in cuneiform patterns. John handed the mirror back and said *yessir looks good, thank you.* To me he said *seeya at school,* though school was months off and our paths till then crossed practically every day.

The bell jangled as he left. I watched him swing his leg over his bike and shove off down the sidewalk in a strip of sunlight. Long after he'd gone, I resisted the urge to snatch a handful of his clean yellow hair from my suddenly growing collection of John Cleary memorabilia.

Probably this unlikely brush with his grooming habits kept me coming back to the barbershop another day or so. But he never showed up again. No one my age did. Nor did I ever have a single customer. And I was, if not overtly lazy, quick to bore. The slow turning of *Field and Stream* pages (they allegedly hid the *Playboys* in a drawer when I showed up) and the repetitive, metallic snip of Mr. DePello's slender scissors on some bald guy's tonsurelike fringe eventually wore me down to my natural, nail-biting state.

After I watched *Song of Bernadette* on TV that summer, I drew in my glitter-spackled book a picture of Jesus. For a while, I prayed ardently on my knees by my bedside—not yet for titties or for John Cleary to ask me to the couples' skate, but for a best friend.

Only one girl showed outlaw tendencies nearly as wild as mine: Clarice Fontenot, who at fourteen had three years on me, which discrepancy didn't seem to matter at first. The only obstacle to our spending every conceivable second together that summer was her Cajun daddy's tight rein on her, which consisted of seemingly innumerable chores and capricious rules he ginned out.

The Fontenots lived in a celery-green house on the corner that seemed to bulge at its seams with her wild-assed brothers. They all slicked back their hair on the sides and walked with a sexy, loose-hipped slouch. If they looked at you at all, the glance came from the sides of their faces. Like their tight-lipped father, they barely spoke, just radiated a sly disapproval.

Clarice's role in that Catholic household seemed to be serving their needs. While they ran the roads, she scrubbed and hung laundry and baby-sat a variety of black-eyed cousins whose faces (like hers) were spattered with freckles as if flicked from a paintbrush. Her blights and burdens put me in mind of Cinderella's, though Clarice rarely whined. Still, her circumstances defined her somehow, for her jittery, electric manner seemed to have formed itself solely to oppose both her station in life and her brothers' quiet surliness.

Clarice would have hung out at my house every day for the abundant food and the air conditioning if not my somewhat peculiar company. But her daddy's strictness was the stuff of neighborhood legend. A compact, steel-gray man, he was about the only guy on our block who didn't do refinery work (I think he worked for the gas company). That he wore a tie to work made him not exotic but peculiar. No one's daddy knew his schedule or ever heard him say more than a passing hey. Usually, Clarice could only play at my house an hour or so before she'd be called home for chores. I didn't take these partings lightly.

Once she was back home, I'd patrol the strip of road before her house, skateboarding past palmettos and the dog run and back again, trying all the while to predict her return by the advance of her work. Window by window, the glass she was washing would lose its grease smears and begin to give back blue sky and flickers of sun when I rolled by. Or I'd watch through those windows while Clarice unhooked each venetian blind. I'd try to measure how long it would take for her to lower those blinds into the Clorox-fuming bathtub, to wash each slat, then towel it off and reappear to hang the blind, giving me an exasperated wave before moving to the next.

Sometimes her daddy just summoned her home for no reason. Which infuriated me. She'd joke that his fun-meter had gone off, some invisible gauge he had that measured the extent of her good time and sought to lop it off. He'd insist she stay in her own yard, and forbid me to cross over the property line. I'd pace their yard's edge for an hour at a pop, or just sit cross-legged along their hurricane fence line reading while their deranged German shepherd loped and bayed and threatened to eat my face off. From my lap I'd flip him the permanent bird using a Venus pencil to keep my fingers cocked in place. A few times, Clarice joined me in this border-holding action. She'd loiter in the heat on her side of the fence, glancing over her shoulder till her dad's gray face slid into a window or his gravelly voice shouted her in.

Doubtless her daddy meant this all as some kind of protection. Plenty of girls her age "got in trouble," and there were countless lowlife characters circling like sharks to pluck any unwatched female into libidinal activity in some hot rod or pickup truck. But my own parents were so lax about corralling me at all ("You can do anything you're big enough to do," Daddy liked to say) that I found Mr. Fontenot's strictures mind-boggling. In my head I engaged in long courtroom soliloquies about him, at the ends of which he and his feckless sons were led away shackled while a gavel banged and Clarice and I hugged each other in glee.

Clarice bridled against her daddy's limits but never actually broke the rules. She lacked both the self-pity and the fury I had in such abundance. She laughed in a foghorn-like blast that drew stares in public. She could belch on command loud enough to cause old ladies in restaurants to ask for far tables. I never mastered this. But thanks to her, I can whistle with my fingers, execute a diving board flip, turn a cartwheel, tie a slip knot, and make my eyeballs shiver like a mesmerist. While other people worried what would come of Clarice if she didn't calm down, for me she had the absolute power of someone who fundamentally didn't give a damn, which she didn't (other than toeing her father's line, which she seemed to do breezily enough).

My first memory of her actually comes long before that summer. It floats from the bleached-out time before we'd passed through the school doors, so we had no grade levels by which to rank ourselves.

A cold sun was sliding down a gray fall sky. Some older boys had been playing tackle football in the field we took charge of every weekend. In a few years, they'd be called to Southeast Asia, some of them.

Their locations would be tracked with pushpins in red, white, and blue on maps on nearly every kitchen wall. But that afternoon, they were quick as young deer. They leapt and dodged, dove from each other and collided in midair. Bulletlike passes flew to connect them. Or the ball spiraled in a high arc across the frosty sky one to another. In short, they were mindlessly agile in a way that captured as audience every little kid within running distance of the yellow goalposts.

We could not help watching. Even after I stepped accidentally in a fire-ant nest and got a constellation of crimson bites on my ankles. Even after streetlights clicked on and our breaths began to spirit before us and to warm my hands I had to pull my arms from my sweatshirt sleeves, then tuck my fingers into my armpits so the sleeves flapped empty as an amputee's. In fact, even once the game had ended, when the big boys had run off to make phone calls or do chores, we stayed waiting to be called for supper. I can almost hear the melamine plates being slid from the various cupboards and stacked on tile counters. But having witnessed their game, we were loath to unloose ourselves from the sight of it.

It was before the time of stark hierarchies. Our family dramas were rumored, but the stories that would shape us had not yet been retold so often as to calcify our characters inside them. Our rivalries had not yet been laid down. No one was big enough to throw a punch that required stitches or to shout an invective that would loop through your head at night till tears made your pillowcase damp. Our sexual wonderings seldom called us to touch each other, just stare from time to time at the mystery of each other's pale underpants or jockey shorts, which we sometimes traded looks at under a porch or in the blue dark of a crawl space. For years our names ran together like beads on a string, Johnand-BobbieClariceandCindyandLittleMary (as opposed to Big Mary, who was Mary Ferrell). With little need to protect our identities from each other, we could still fall into great idleness together—this handful of unwatched kids with nowhere to be.

At some moment, Clarice figured out as none of us had before how to shinny up the goalpost.

That sight of her squiggling up the yellow pole magically yanks the memory from something far-off into a kind of 3-D present. I am alive in it. There's early frost on the grass, and my ant bites itch. Clarice's limbs have turned to rubber as she wraps round the pole. She's kicked off her Keds, so her bare feet on cold metal give purchase. About a foot at a time she scoots up, hauls herself by her hands, then slides her feet high. And again. She's weightless as an imp and fast.

At the top of the pole, she rises balletic, back arched like a trapeze artist. She flings one hand up: *Ta-da,* she says, as if she were sheathed in a crimson-spangled bathing suit with fishnet hose and velvet ballet slippers, then again *ta-da.* We cheer and clap, move back to the ten-yard line to take her in better. This is a wonder, for her to climb so far above us. And there we align ourselves with the forces of awe that permit new tricks to be dreamed up on chilly fall nights when nothing but suppers of fried meat and cream gravy await us, or tepid baths.

For a few minutes, Bobbie Stuart tries to weasel up the other pole, but he's too stiff. His legs jackknife out from under him, and his arms can't hold his long thin body.

Then Clarice does something wholly unexpected for which she will be forever marked.

She sticks her thumbs in the gathered waistband of her corduroy pants with the cowgirl lassos stitched around the pockets. With those thumbs, she yanks both her pants and her undersancies down around her bare feet. She then bends over and waggles her butt at us as I later learned strippers sometimes do. Screams of laughter from us. John falls over and rolls on the ground like a dog, pointing up and laughing at her bare white ass, which still holds a faint tan line from summer.

We've just about got used to the idea of her butt when she executes another move. She wheels around to face us and show us her yin-yang, a dark notch in her hairless pudendum. Her belly is round as a puppy's jutted forward. Then our howls truly take on hyena-like timbre. And there across the ditch, which marks the realm of adult civilization, appears the fast moving figure of Mrs. Carter through leaf smoke of a ditch fire. She's holding the spatula in her hand with which she intends to blister our asses, Clarice's most specifically.

But she's a grown-up, Mrs. Carter. Her steps on the muddy slope are tentative. Not wanting to funk up her shoes with mud, she hesitates before she leaps across. And in that interval, Clarice slithers down the yellow pole and tears off in a streak. And the rest of us flee like wild dogs.

Decades later, I asked Clarice point blank why she did it. We were in our forties then, living two thousand miles apart, and talking—oddly enough—on our car phones. Her voice was sandpaper rough with a cold, but it still carried the shimmer of unbidden amusement. I'd only seen her every two or three years—the occasional holiday, at my daddy's funeral, and after Mother's bypass surgery when she kept vigil with me. Still, there's no one who'd be less likely to tell me a flat-footed lie. Across the hissing static, I asked why she took her pants down that day, whether somebody had dared her to and I just didn't remember.

The answer that she gave remains the truest to who she was and who I then so much needed her to be: "Because I could, I guess," she said. "Wasn't anybody around to stop me."

Chapter Two

MOTHER'S OLD POWERS CAME BURBLING up in her again that interminable summer, for the first time in years. She tore around so fired up about her schoolwork she left an almost visible trail of energy. She pored over books the way a thirsty person sucks down water. Even poking at a pot of mustard greens, she'd have some paperback on the Russian Revolution getting damp on the counter beside her. When I staggered out from sleep before dawn, I often found her studying calculus at the kitchen table, held in a cloud of Kool smoke like some radiant, unlikely Buddha.

"It's a language," she said of the math one morning, tapping her legal pad with the tip of the mechanical pencil. "I've never understood that. It's a language that describes certain stuff really precisely." Before I'd even rubbed the crust from my eye corners, she was prattling on about some old Greek named Zeno who fired an arrow at a target. Trouble was, he was trying to measure how it traveled in this really stilted way. So he cut up the line between the bow and the target—first into feet, then into inches, then half inches, then quarter inches, and so on till the whole infinitesimal universe unfolded in that strip of air, multiplied. This didn't seem like a language anybody would bother to talk. You want the butter passed, you don't talk about arrows shooting. I said something to that effect.

But Mother was incandescent with the idea. Her green eyes shone. She ran her hand through her thick hair and left brief rows in the new white streaks. "You do if you're trying to measure this line."

"Why not just say it's a line, thus and such long?"

"Because that doesn't describe the whole thing. The rate of change. It's a language for motion, speed. Like in those Pollock paintings. Movement." Her hand cut arcs in the air. The number of pieces Zeno cut the line into approached infinity. The size of the pieces approached zero. Didn't I see the beauty of that? I didn't. I only wondered if the waffle iron was scrubbed out from the day before, and what manner of interest I'd have to feign in this before she'd whip up some batter.

"It's called taking the limit. As *x* goes to zero and *n* to infinity. Get it? One's going one way big forever, and the other's going one way little forever?" I still didn't. Her words washed over me as the words of every math teacher I'd ever had, like the blat of a flat-noted trombone. (Years later, a college math tutor would pick up this dropped thread, and I would let out a delayed belly laugh of understanding at the punchline of some ten-year-delayed joke.)

Some time after her calculus final, she bought roller skates like mine, the metal kind that clamped around your shoes, to go skating with me. She wobbled to a stand holding my arm. When she hung the key threaded on a brown shoestring around my neck, I briefly felt something like pride.

While Mother and I tested our balance on the front walk, Lecia hovered inside the door screen, threatening to hide in the bathroom so nobody would associate her with an activity so dopey as this. "You're not my sister," she said, her shapely form withdrawing a foot deeper into the murk of the house. "I mean it. No take-backs. Stick a needle." She crossed her heart with one square finger. "You set off down that road, I'm an only child. I swear."

Lecia's just thirteen and heading into eighth grade, but already she can hardly stand to live here, for we are liable to say or do any damn thing that strikes us. Daddy once asked a square-shouldered date of hers, "Did you poot, young fellow?" His name was Gaylord or Ray or Daryl, and when the content of Daddy's question finally dawned on him, his mouth slung open.

"Why no, sir!" Gaylord/Ray/Daryl blurted out.

"Well somebody cut one," Daddy said. He narrowed his eyes. "It was a silent one, but deadly. And it wasn't me." He turned my way, "Was it you, Pokey?"

"No, sir."

"Well keep that butt closed for business," he said to the boy with a tight nod. And I held my face still as a plaster mask.

That's why Lecia sailed around all the time on some imaginary parade float, and why that day before Mother and I went skating, she was firing invisible daggers at me. She felt stranded in our household as in a bad Okie movie, orphaned from her real kin amid us feral types.

"You ready?" Mother said. I was. Though I was too old to need help, she grasped my hand, and her touch injected a kind of warm, familiar syrup along my arm. Linked that way, we went rolling down the bumpy sidewalk toward the road. My feet shivered clear up to my knee bones. If I put my teeth together loose, they chattered like those joke teeth you sent away for from the backs of comic books. Once we hit newly tarred asphalt, we got flying. My hair blew back from my head like wings. Kids lined the ditches, for a mother skating was a noteworthy event. She kept her arms wide like a ballerina's. It was dusk. The refinery gases pumped into the atmosphere left us manufactured psychedelic sunsets: the sun was a Day-Glo ball in the poisoned sky.

That night when it came time to go to sleep, I padded out of my room to ask Lecia was she coming to bed. She sulked on the tweed couch reading. The lavender bedroom she slept in was officially mine. Still, no matter how epic in scale our fights of the day had been, she usually corked off in there, both of us rolled into the same saggy puddle of mattress.

Lecia just lay there silent, the Siamese cat, Sally, stretched out along her sternum, ink-dipped paws between those mountainous boobs. This seemed a particular betrayal, for I thought of Sally as mine. (A lie under which many cat owners labor.) The times I jammed that cat into lace pinafore, she'd never once bit or scratched me. Oh she'd struggle. I could feel her sinews tighten in my hand. Only once did she lose her temper though. When I'd tied her into my baby carriage with an elaborate web of Christmas ribbon, she managed to gnaw through her restraints and wound up under an azalea bush hissing in her white bonnet.

Lecia didn't even look up from her detective magazine when she told me that nobody's mother skated.

"Oh come on. Who cares what nobody does?" Truly when it came to convention, I had a lot of double-dog fuck-you in me by then.

"You'll care when you hit junior high and you're the new Becky Smedley." This prompted a thin layer of concern, for the comparison had been made before. One of those chip-toothed boys with ringworm scabs on his arms had likened me to Becky after I wouldn't let him copy my math one morning. She was certainly no skinnier than I was, and I'd watched her in the cafeteria suffer the scapegoat's fate of sitting alone among cubed carrots and peas shot from various straws.

What she'd done to warrant this was a mystery. She was gawky, sure. Plus she was a good head taller than most of the boys but for a few who'd been held back a lot.

What she did to encourage it, though, was plain: she took it—every flipped paper clip, every sign pasted to her back, every foot slipped out sideways into the aisle so she'd trip and her avocado-green tray would sail from her hands. Thus the cube steak and sliced peaches would become airborne with the milk carton whose red-and-white presidential faces we failed year after year to memorize. Into this slop and other slops like it Becky went sprawling. And she did not rise up. Her passivity in the face of such acts became a magnet for them. Even second- and third-graders would trail behind her like bad goats bahhing. Over the years her sticklike form curved in on itself—head bent down another millimeter each day, shoulders pinched forward—till her whole body became a sort of living question mark, the punctuation with which she responded to every mean sentence we could construct.

"Becky Smedley is too big a spaz to go skating," I said. The cat sighed, her eyes at half-mast. From Mother and Daddy's room, the TV chittered.

"No but if she did go, she'd take her mother. And they'd hold hands." I looked down at Lecia. Surely her hair hadn't been in curlers all day, but that's how I recall it—in giant wire rollers under a lacy net. She kept her hair set that way for so long that the pink spikes fixing the curlers in place worked permanent dents into her head.

"What's wrong with that? There's nothing wrong with that."

"If you don't know, there's no help for you," Lecia said. Her voice was flat. The cat pushed her nose against Lecia's chin, then tipped her triangular head to rub her face there.

"You don't know everything," I said. Actually I doubted the veracity of this.

"No but I know that. Goddamn sure do." Not once since I'd stood there had our eyes met.

"So you coming to bed?" I finally asked. My invitation was close as I could get to an apology.

"I'm sleeping out here," she said.

It was my wrongness she meant to convey, and ultimately to correct—to save me from my own self, to protect me from the fate of Becky Smedley and her ilk. But the condemnation of her sleeping on the sofa felt like more than I deserved.

Not everybody branded by difference suffered Becky's fate. The town tolerated affliction with more grace than most places I've lived. They had to, for we were, as populations go, teeming with chemical and genetic mutation. Toxic air, I suppose, cooked up part of the human stew. Plus there was inbreeding galore. People disapproved of marriage between first cousins, but it happened, and at least one boy I knew was rumored to have knocked up his sister. Three kids in my grade school contracted and later died from leukemia and bone cancer. (What are the odds of that?) Before we lined up at the elementary school for sugar cubes in paper cups, the polio bug ran through us, for there were stagnant ponds a plenty, and we worried little about wading in ditches to catch crawfish after a heavy rain, even times you could see the encephalitic mosquito eggs afloat on the surface.

Lecia's best friend, Caroline Forman, had actually logged time in one of those notorious iron lungs we saw pictures of in *Life* magazine. Her thin legs inside braces bent in too much to bear her weight. She used steel crutches with double arm cuffs. When she slept over, I swung on them from room to room.

Add to polio victims the hunting accidents—one boy lost his leg below the knee—the falls from high places, cuts never stitched, concussions never X-rayed for, the minimal dental care and complete absence of orthodonture, and you had a population so maimed and mutilated, bucktoothed and listing, that we had to dole out insults and blows to each other, for it was the closest contact many got.

Far more deadly than overt physical handicap was social wrongness of some sort. Its markers were way more subtle. Knowledge of it came slower. For me, it started with a slow-wincing awareness of my bodily flaws.

Mostly I didn't feel that way, of course. Mostly I was a child, infused with the mindless joy that a girl who's been taught to swing a bat and catch pop flies is blessed with. The fact that my father doled out these lessons was a win. Most girls never saw their dads, and mine doted on me in a way neighbors found peculiar but which I relished.

Plus odd as Mother was, she was beautiful, which had seemed an upside deal till my own form went starkly angular and my skin started blotching up. Then her beauty became a sideways indictment of sorts. She tried to buoy me up by telling me how adorable I was all the time, but her certainty about this in the face of contrary evidence sometimes made me doubt she saw me at all.

I remember running to her vanity table with my first pimple. Surely I'd had a few before. But this one was smack in the center of my forehead. Mr. O'Malley, the swimming pool manager who'd one day have the impossible job of teaching me algebra, had pointed this one out. Loudly. "That where the Indian shot you?" he'd said, smirking down with the sunburned face of the ex-jock he was, someone who'd grown used to pom-poms being shaken at his every victory. Every kid lined up for the high board had doubtless heard him. My hand moved between my eyes and touched the sore spot I hadn't noticed before.

Mother was creaming makeup from her face when I showed up with it. Regarding O'Malley's comment, she said, "He's an asshole. You can't even see it with your bangs." The silvery cream being patted along her jawline was glossy as meringue.

But my wet bangs had been pushed back at the pool, for Clarice and I had been playing a kind of water ballet where you hiked your butt up and dove far enough down for your ears to throb inward. Then you shot back up to the surface head first, hair slicked back like an otter's pelt.

"Lemme see it," she said. Her thumb pressed the edge of the sore place with fingers smelling of eucalyptus. She said the sun probably helped it, and the chlorine. "It looks better than yesterday," she said.

"This was here yesterday?" I said. My jaw unhinged. I felt the black world outside our windows whirl as I tried to gauge the implications. And why hadn't Mother told me? If she was heading out to college classes with the back of her skirt tucked into her girdle, I'd by God let her know. That's what family was for, to help cut back the extent of your unabashed fooldom so it didn't spill out all down the streets and avenues and leave you shoved and spat at like poor Becky Smedley.

While Mother tissued off her Noxzema, I tried to reconjure yesterday. Had I played Otter? No. Clarice was the only girl I did that with, and her grandma had come to visit from Louisiana, so Clarice spent yesterday splitting field peas and peeling new potatoes for supper.

This mental skitter for mastery of my public self rose up from nowhere as I scrambled to reimagine yesterday. Then incidents started to unpack from a simple image as days are wont to do if you ponder them with sufficient anxiety. I'd had a horse-fight against none other than John Cleary. From my post on Carol Sharp's back, while her water-shriveled hands held my knees, my skinny arms had locked the whole length of John Cleary's muscly brown ones. At one point toward the end of the match, John had actually reached around to grab my hair from behind. I'd hit the surface laughing, nasal passages stung with sucked-in chlorine. Visualizing that very instant, I felt another trapdoor in my quivery sense of self fling open. My bangs had fallen aside then, so this massive boil in the center of my forehead had been right in John Cleary's face. He probably saw my pulse in it.

Such rushes of physical shame came more often that summer before sixth grade, for my once idle crush on John had been intensifying. My collection of related memorabilia—scant a year ago—now filled my jewelry box's every compartment and forced the lacquered lid with the cherry tree to gap.

Open that lid. A slender ballerina with a pink crinoline tutu spins before a rectangular mirror no bigger than a gum packet. There's John Cleary's school picture about twice as big as a postage stamp. His thick blond hair is slicked over to one side in an odd triangular thatch that looks ready to sprong up at any minute. On the back, he's unceremoniously written "John Keith Cleary," in a slanting script I could probably still copy today. That everybody in Miss Boudreux's class got the same picture didn't lessen its value for me. In the ring nook are inch-long slips of oxford cloth torn off the back of John's dress shirts—fruit loops, we called them. Finally there's the green army soldier who lies horizontal, rifle shouldered as if over sandbags, ever awaiting the invasion of unseen attackers into the jewelry box. I pocketed it from the eight-jillion such soldiers John fixed in battle configurations in his room. Most treasured of all, though, are the few straws from various drugstore malteds, candy-stripe papers I could put my mouth on to deliver to John discreet, unfelt kisses.

I had first declared my love for John at six with littly subtlety: I walked the road before his house with I LOVE JOHN CLEARY in black magic marker on the back of my T-shirt.

It was the same year that John handed me my first ever mash note, which, once the fat-lined page was unfolded, read like this: *If you play nasty with me, I'll like you for one year.* This was such an obvious ruse as to be insulting. Worse than that, the note was dog-eared. Other hands had unfolded it before it reached me. With the cold fury born of scorn, I sneaked the note back in John's Superman lunchbox, where that afternoon his mother drew it out from amid wax-paper leavings and the gnawed-out apple core. As a result John was introduced that evening to the flat side of his daddy's cowhide belt.

Since John was a boy, the world permitted him these lapses into such sharp callowness, but mostly he was sweet. If I flew into Carol Sharp for crowding me under the basketball hoop, it was John who pulled us apart. *She didn't mean anything,* he'd say to her while from behind me he hooked my arms. The straight shot of the ball from John's chest level to my stinging hands was the arrival of certitude. It said something like I did belong, and everybody was really okay if you thought about it first thing in the morning before it got too hot.

The rest of us in the neighborhood were still unformed, our characters fluid. Our alliances followed tidal shifts we could neither predict nor chart after the fact. We swore to God to keep secrets we later blurted out. We pledged fealty to sleepover companions who later served as targets for our bulging water balloons. John was more substantial. When in the football huddle he was drawing a play in his palm, I jostled to stand near him. So did everybody.

He was also wicked cute. There was this adorable gap between his front teeth you could fix the pointy end of a pencil in. Plus in a town where phone book listings tended to Mexican or Cajun names, John's hair bleached near-white every summer, and his blue eyes stood out amid the mostly black-eyed populace. He was fair enough to freckle and Catholic enough to blush through those freckles if one of the girls who circled him like buzzards at the rink rolled over to ask him to couple skate.

Besides being commonly adored, he'd that summer been kind to me in ways I chose to interpret as chivalrous. In a savage game we played called Hide-the-Bat, he'd actually left base to lure the predatory "it" (the guy swinging a ball bat) away from me so I could dash untouched to safety. Just before he'd done this, our eyes had met. He was beaming an unspoken *Get ready* to me. But I felt that gaze differently. That was the instant a tensile line stretched between us. Some silk actually seemed to spin invisibly in the summer air from him to me. I pictured at its end this silver hook flying—unseen by others—into my chest to lodge in the meat of my heart and forever tether me to him. From then on, in fantasies I derived from all the King Arthur stories I was soaking up, John Cleary became the pious but ardent Sir Lancelot defending my honor before barbarians. In his presence, words like *destiny* and *evermore* flickered through my head. I inked his name on every random slip of paper—or even on palms or foot soles—in elaborately curlicued script.

First loves take us like that. But because they rarely have any consequence (few marry the sixth-grade sweetheart), people slight them. They exist in the thin cliché of bad country tunes, thus becoming generic, sandblasted of peculiarities. Our own features in youth have not yet been sharply carved. So in some way, we don't exist yet. Thus we mock ourselves for loving so easily and in the process choke the breath from our first darlings.

Which denies their truth, I think, for my inner life took full shape around such a love. I learned to imagine around his face. Before such enchantment takes us, there are only the faces of parents, other kin. Those are doled out to us; they *are* us in some portion. These first beloveds are other. And we invent ourselves by choosing them.

The pimple episode catapulted me into a painful new vigilance toward myself, for I knew I needed to ready myself for John Cleary now, to change into one of those junior high girls who could make him go quiet as Lecia could do.

One thing I definitely needed was a bra, the wearing of which might urge my chest to grow some titties. In Sigona's dry goods store, there was a terraced altar of Playtex bras I'd been sneaking looks at. But I had to ask Daddy for the money. And he, of course, had to say what for. When I told him, his face broke in a grin. "Baby," I remember him saying one night, "you want a bra, hell I'll buy you a little bra." We were shelling pecans at the time, and I had to use both hands to squeeze the cracker, which only smushed the nut in two, and sent shards flying sideways in the rug.

"I don't just want a bra, goddamn it, Daddy."

"Lemme do it, Pokey," he said. After a quick crunch with the nutcracker, the husk fell into the bowl in large, neat pieces.

My head was down. I was using my fingernail to grout out the bitter part in the nut's tight furrows. What did I want, he asked, if not a bra.

What I wanted formed in my head for a good instant before I said it: "I want titties, goddamn it, Daddy. Not some bra."

His eyes widened slow at what I'd dared to say. "You want titties?" He threw back his head and hooted with laughter, howling up at the dusty light fixture.

I hurled a handful of pecan husks into the bowl and stood up. Mother came in wearing a nightgown and rubbing lotion into her hands. "What is it?" she said. Her head was wrapped in a towel like a swami.

I tore into my room and power-slammed the door into its molding. The window glass shivered. I hurled myself down on the lavender-flowered spread. Part of me knew I'd crossed the border into some country where he didn't—or wouldn't—tread.

I instinctively knew the rules laid down for girls' comportment, but I wasn't yet resigned to them, for to place my head into that yoke was to part with too much freedom. One day I sat on my porch sucking the long ears of my Bugs Bunny popsicle into a syrupless white dunce cap when a herd of boys my age on bikes pedaled into view. They were shirtless, sailing down the street in careless whooshing speed.

One blond boy named Corey was somebody's cousin down from Houston for the summer. He was slim and brown and expressionless in a way that let me manufacture complex thoughts for him. (Was it Chekhov or Tolstoy who complained about what deep personalities we can manufacture behind "some little scrap of face"?) His surfer cut hung in a bright wing across his forehead. He stood stock still in his pedals for the entire strip of road past my house like the figurehead on a ship's prow, and his thoughtless beauty dragged from me the faint tug of something like desire. His body was thin-muscled as a greyhound's. Maybe his hurtling motion made enough wind to cool him off, but he didn't look to suffer from the heat I felt so squandered in.

This wasn't desire as it would become. Not yet. The cool fire circled more in my abdomen than between my legs, and it was vague and smoke gray. I pictured no boy yet—not even John Cleary—gathering me into his arms. Despite what Nabokov's Humbert wanted to think, I've never met a girl as young as I was then who craved a bona fide boning. But glowing nonspecifically from my solar plexus was this forceful light. I wanted John Cleary or Corey or some other boy to see that light, to admire it, not to feed off it for his own hungers. When I closed my eyes at night, I did not manufacture naked bodies entwined. Mostly I didn't even venture into kissing. Rather my fantasies at that time were all in the courtly mode. I pictured John Cleary/Corey taking my hand for the couples' skate at the rink, how we'd cut a slow circle together in a spotlight, with his gaze inventing me in the stares of those we passed.

But the boys' bicycle pack also sent a stab of envy through me. If I couldn't yet capture John Cleary with my feminine wiles, then surely I deserved to enjoy the physical abandon he got, liberties I instinctively knew were vanishing. (I know, I know. Psychoanalytic theory would label this pecker envy and seek to smack me on the nose for it. To that I'd say, o please. Of actual johnsons I had little awareness. What I coveted was privilege.) Boys did not have to sit like miserable statues alone on their front porches. They could be swooped up and carried by the force of their compadres before idleness had sucked all momentum from the day.

This lodged a bad idea in my head, unignorable as any pebble. I went into the air-conditioned kitchen to confer with Mother. She was pouring cornbread batter from a crockery bowl into a cast iron skillet. The cold compound hit the bacon fat greased pan with a hiss. A pot of volcanic-looking chili must have been burbling on the stove, for in memory all the scents of seared meat with four kinds of pepper and cumin made glands in my throat go tight.

Did Mother think I was too old to go outside without a shirt? She didn't.

The bowl returned to the counter, and I swiped a bit of the gritty batter onto my index finger (not sweet like Yankee cornbread, but serious with salt and lard). Asking Mother was a formality, for she seldom saw much reason not to do anything you thought up.

That's how at age eleven I came to peel off my T-shirt, mount my pink-striped Schwinn, and set off down the oyster shell of Taylor Avenue wearing only red shorts.

By the time I reached the first porch where a line of ladies in their rockers were sipping iced tea, it was clear I'd made a terrible mistake. Their eyes widened, and their heads turned rigidly to one another and back at me as if on poles. After I rounded the corner, I felt their stares slide off my back. A different kid would have gone hauling butt back to her garage. She would have stayed inside till some car wreck or church supper had drawn the local talk from her escapade. But I was not bred to reversals. I only had to make it one loop around the block to finish.

On the second block, Mr. Hebert was elbow deep in his truck engine, his son Gerald Lee holding the caged mechanic's light. The heavy man's body unbent quick from the truck's bowels. He shouted toward the house. A screen door popped open, and there was Mrs. Hebert, a startled jack-in-the-box-type figure in sponge curlers, her mouth a tight o. Gerald laid down the light he'd been holding and ran the same direction I was pedaling to alert other kids, slanting off across the Ferrells' backyard to try to head me off. He vaulted over the far fence, dodging their chained-up mutt before he vanished from view.

The Clearys' house stood as the final gauntlet. It was also the vortex from which the most intense judgment could emanate. Sure enough, under the pin oak, all the neighbor women sat in low-slung green folding chairs doing some kind of lap work that involved huge silver pots. It was only a short streak past them to my yard.

I felt the shining whiteness of my chest, wholly untouched by sun since I was three or four—so different from the sleek, tanned chests of the boys. It blared out my mistake in pale flesh.

Mrs. Sharp reached a thin arm out to touch Mrs. Cleary's elbow. Mrs. Cleary's hand flew to her mouth just as I sailed past. Behind the hurricane fence, Gerald Lee's witnesses were galloping, sharp-faced boys who had no fear of pointing and hollering at my near naked self. I surged into my yard. Somebody called my name. The bike dropped in the grass and took something of me with it as I hurdled the five porch steps in just two leaps.

Chapter Three

Mother was missing, and I stared out the back screen after her absence. Vapor ghosted up the patio bricks and made skeletons of the rusted furniture we never sat out on. Her figure-drawing class at the local college had let out hours ago. Now I tried to divine her presence on those roads that webbed out from our crackerbox house.

Maybe her disappearing had to do with the fight my parents woke me up having last weekend. They hadn't gone at it full bore like that in so long, I almost didn't believe the voices were theirs. I eased out of bed all smoky-headed and tiptoed into the dining room, clinging to the shadow of the bookcase.

Mother had said, "It doesn't have to be like grandpa did it for it to be worth investigating. Now the *I Ching*—" She cut off her sentence as if she'd thought better of it. "Fuck you," she finally said. For extra measure, she shot Daddy the finger with both hands from down low, about hip level.

Daddy leveled his stare at her. "You know in the state of Texas, 'fuck you' is interchangeable with 'Please hit me.'"

She jutted her jaw out. "Go ahead! Go ahead and hit me, you ignorant sonofabitch." But Daddy was picking up his truck keys, saying she wasn't worth it.

When I slid under the covers next to my sister, you could hear his truck tires roll out on gravel. "You awake this whole time?" I asked her.

"Who could sleep. Jesus. World War Three," she said. Mother slammed the bedroom door. The air conditioner's compressor kicked on, so the porch light surged like a beacon signaling some far off ship.

"You ever worry Mother's gonna start drinking again?" I finally said.

"She doesn't have to drink, she's so loaded up on pills." And it was true that her bedside table was a forest of prescription bottles, some with dates going back to Kennedy. In the distance, Daddy's truck engine wound down to nothing, but I still clung to the silence for the noise. The air conditioner chugged like bad diesel. In the back bedroom, Mother put on Mozart's *Requiem*. "Great," Lecia said. "Dead man music. Lullaby and good-goddamn night."

We lay listening to the weaving angelic chorus till it gave way to this deep-throated war march sound—the hounds of hell rising up from some hole in the earth to chase Mr. Mozart's ass to the grave.

"Where does Daddy go all the time?" I asked after a while. "I mean, there's nowhere to go this late. The package store's closed. The Legion's closed. You can't even get a tank of gas."

"Who knows?" Lecia said, and I said Mother must. "Mother doesn't know shit," Lecia said with certainty. Till right that instant, I'd clung to the notion that Mother somehow colluded with Daddy in not explaining his whereabouts.

"You ever ask her?" I said, for there was a thread of hope that Lecia had only presumed Mother's ignorance on this.

"Hell yeah. She says if he wanted her to know, he'd tell us, and if he didn't, he'd just lie." By the time the luminous dials on the clock read midnight, Lecia was breathing deep.

Daddy was so far off in those days, even when he was there, he was gone. In every room I occupied, he was just passing through. One night that summer, I'd decided to wait up for him. When it got late, I'd fetched a quilt to wrap around me and a pillow. No sooner did my cheek settle into that softness than sleep had come. In the next instant, I'd felt Daddy scooping me up from my seat into his arms.

"You smell like Tennessee whiskey," I said. "Where you been?" He said just making rounds. Cradled against his chest, I felt the cold of his shirt snaps on my cheek. The whole house was dark. Our reflections moved across glistening windowpanes. I asked what time it was, and he said time for my narrow ass to get on to bed. "They's school tomorrow." I rolled out of his arms onto the covers with a plop like a meal sack. "You getting long, Pokey," he said. And when I asked him when I'd get too old for him to carry, he said not as long as he could walk.

Only a week had passed since then, and I was at the same back door, staring out into the same dark after Mother. Hell is repetition, somebody once said, and this backyard never altered. Its orders were dull. Nothing would move but the occasional cockroach unless wind hit the foliage.

The Siamese shoved her chin against my ankle. I banged the aluminum screen open so she could snake out. The noise must've jolted Daddy up, for down the narrow hall where he'd been asleep the bed creaked. "That you, Joe?" he said, by which he meant Mother. There was a wire of joy in his voice that nobody but Mother could get from him. After I said it was just me, he stayed quiet. I stood in the doorway a minute before asking was he awake enough to play some rummy. His silhouette just lay back down. "Get on back to bed, Pokey," he said. "She'll roll in directly."

On the white pillow, his black hair was a crow's wing. A pair of headlights swam slow past the windows. I made out his beaked profile, like the calm, farsighted Indian on old nickels. (His mother was from some tribe we never figured out.) There was no crisis so dire that Daddy couldn't sleep through, particularly if he'd pulled two nights of double overtime at the refinery, as he just had. I came to stand by Mother's side of the bed. Still he didn't open his eyes.

"What if she's dead?" I said.

"She'll stay dead," he said. "She'll still be dead come morning." He folded his hands on his chest like a corpse himself. (I'd later picture him again in this posture when I read a poem by Bill Knott: "They will place my hands like this./ It will look as though I'm flying into myself.")

"She's all right," Daddy finally said. I wasn't so sure. Her bedside table was still scarred with leftover circles from a series of vodka-full tumblers. On the lacquer surface, moons in various stages of eclipse overlapped. From inside one of those moons came a glint, a dime I figured to pick up.

But what I felt between thumb and forefinger was a ring, the platinum star sapphire Daddy had presented to Mother in a velvet box at Christmas. For months after she first came home from that other short marriage to our stepfather, she'd steer Lecia and me past the jeweler's at the tail end of any errand to ogle that ring. Daddy paid a month's salary for the mossy black stone with a six-pointed star that seemed to emerge on the oval surface as if through seawater from uncharted fathoms. Come Christmas morning, Mother clicked open the box and sighed like a burden had been wrested from her. It did not augur well that Mother would slip off that ring, which she'd sworn never to remove, till death do us part and all that.

I didn't want Daddy to know and so hid it under a pack of cigarettes in the standing ashtray, a bronze Viking ship poised to sail off the earth's edge.

When Mother had first come back to Daddy and us, she'd contracted to do mechanical drawings of appliances for repair guides, exploding dishwashers and outboard motors and Waring blenders so every unscrewed washer floated distinct in a lavender cloud. Somehow in moments of fear, I felt myself to be mechanically bolted together like that. The more real the threat of her absence became, the more I felt all the bolts and lug nuts of who I was loosen.

"I'll stop by the bookstore at the college," she'd said that afternoon, keys in hand. "Y'all need anything?" Lecia wanted a *True Detective* magazine. Even at fourteen, she had the authority required to ask for such a thing.

Since my driving Mother away always stood as possibility, I reviewed my morning with her in the laundromat. While she body-blocked acres of wet sheets into the industrial dryer, I played pinball. Bells dinged, and lights flashed under me. The silver ball zigged and zagged, fell into holes and popped out, flew like a bullet if I whacked it right in a rare instant so it either ricocheted between poles to rack up thousands of unearned points or fell hapless into the slot between the machine's forward-stretched flippers. My score never hit what I was after. The melon-breasted blond on the glass facing me stared down at the mechanical landscape I'd failed to master with what I took to be a sneer. Behind me, a line of washing machines jogged. In the dryer on the wall, the snaps of my jeans were clicking. An odor of bleach-scented cotton hung in the air.

Mother stood at the plate glass looking out on Leechfield's sparse main street. Over black capris, she'd buttoned one of Daddy's massive white shirts, from which she'd torn the sleeves. She'd jammed her feet into brown cowboy boots caked with mud and run down at the heel.

"Wonder how far we'd have to drive to get some provolone cheese," she said. "Houston maybe." She moved to the formica folding table and started matching up Daddy's banlon socks. I didn't right off recollect what provolone was.

"You know those hoagies we used to buy in Colorado," she said, "across from the hotel." (I did remember them.) "I'm talking about that kinda white cheese they used, thin as paper." She peered through the giant red O in the word LAUNDROMAT and said, "I'd kill for some provolone cheese."

I hadn't much liked it and said so.

"Sure you did," she said. She lowered the pink sheet she'd held before her like a purdah veil. I fingered a cool metal coin return just in case some change got overlooked. That whole row of coin returns just waiting had started to look to me like hope, and there were two rows of washers after that.

She said, "Point is, you can't buy any cheese but Velveeta in this whole suckhole." When she leaned over the table to grab the sheet corners, I could make out her bra through the shirt's thready arm holes. That wouldn't have bothered Mother one bit.

"Parmesan," I finally came up with. "You can get that at Speir's. Chef Boy-Ar-Dee brand. Right next to the pizza mix."

"In a can," she said. "And it's *Parmigiano*—this hard cheese that comes in a wheel you need an ax to cut into. You grate it. The stuff you get in the can tastes like foot powder." The sheriff's car rolled down the road. I looked at Mother's muscly arm coming out that thread-ragged hole through which her Playtex Cross-Your-Heart was still visible—half a cream-colored nipple's worth.

"When were you eating foot powder?" I said.

"You'd worry the bark off a tree's what you'd do," she said.

"I mean it," I said. "How did you get expert in the flavor of foot powder?"

"It tastes like it smells. Don't get all philosophical on me," she said. She was patting around for matches among used-car swap sheets on the window seat. An unlit Salem tipped down from her lip.

That night she was gone, I wondered if I'd helped Mother match up Daddy's banlon socks and embraced the folding of the Wisk-scented towels and the scorning of boxed cheese instead of trying to defend its uncertain beauties, her morning would have gone better, and I wouldn't be staring after the emptiness her absence cut. But the cheese Mother mocked as low-rent I secretly longed for. Melted Velveeta with chopped jalapeños in it could be scooped onto a broken tostada and crunched down on, salty smooth and sharp at once. Mother's scorn for Velveeta mirrored her scorn for Leechfield in general and for my daddy in particular, which had led to her running off from us the year before.

The patch of sky between our chinaberry tree and the garage roof had wheeled around so that some archer Daddy always saw assembled from star points forever drew back his bow. But no matter how many times Daddy used his index finger to sketch Orion, I couldn't make it out. My eyes just saw a random pattern of buckshot. And for my way of thinking, there wasn't any God up there behind the black scrim steering things. I'd long since ceased to be a dumbass about that. In lieu of some beaded giant in the sky arranging the nail-headed stars, I put my dubious faith in the power of human will.

That's where Lecia came in. At fourteen, she was will incarnate. If I worshipped anything at that time, it was her canny intelligence. Surely she could rout Mother out when I couldn't.

It was three A.M. when I came to stand above her sleeping, curvy form, her body under the chenille bedspread like the princess's in *Sleeping Beauty.* The honeysuckle vines across our windows even threw tangled shadows on the lavender quilt like that movie's thorn vines, which the prince had to hack through when the wicked queen had become a scaly dragon breathing zigzags of fire. *Lecia,* I said. But one word wouldn't budge her. Like Daddy she'd learned to sleep hard. I sat down, so her rolled-up form tilted ten degrees closer to me.

I put my hand on Lecia's shoulder. And even though she usually slept like the dead, her brain must have been so hair-triggered for she surged up, gasping a string of invectives that went something like *What, Goddamn, what is it! Fuck's sake.*

She right away came up with driving around to search for Mother. She poached Daddy's truck keys from the nail by the refrigerator, then we tiptoed barefoot back to our bedroom to unhook the screen and slither out.

There's much to be said for getting in and out of a dark house by window. The physical sneakiness of it has few grown-up corollaries. Maybe burglary buys you such a thrill, or adultery. But to feel your child's thumbs pop up a pair of aluminum window-screen latches from the bubble-headed posts that hold them flush is to know the outlaw joy of escape. Your parents' realm of power has definite borders you can cross out of.

The screen swung out at the bottom. We lay on our bellies looking at the house next door where Peggy Lawrence sat at her parents' brown upright piano pounding away at a movie song about the hills being alive with the sound of music. In the window well a few gray moth corpses were crumbling to dust. I turned around so my feet stuck out the slot and started worming my way backward outside. The sill scraped my belly, but I finally stood ankle deep in wet grass like a thief birthed from my own room. When Lecia hit the ground beside me, she swatted a mosquito on her calf and stared toward the lit window. Peggy's boyfriend turned a page with his long-fingered hand. Her butt in the full skirt of her blue gingham dress took up the better part of the bench. I whispered to Lecia that they proved for every ugly man, there's a woman. And Lecia shot back that was lucky for me.

In the dim garage, the truck's grillework looked like nothing so much as bared fangs. I'd toted a pillowcase with two encyclopedia volumes and *The Complete Works of William Shakespeare* to wedge at the small of Lecia's back so she could inch closer to the floor pedals. Daddy was a demon on any detail relating to his truck, and he might notice the seat hiked to the wrong notch. Since he also kept maniacally close track of the odometer for purposes of standing at the gas pump and boasting about his good mileage, I'd upended a screwdriver in my back pocket for opening the glass over the dashboard and jacking the numbers back.

The driver's side door creaked loud enough to start Lecia and me hopping around flapping our arms at each other. She gave me the finger, and I hissed at her. Afterward we stood in the silence a full three minutes listening toward the house. But Daddy must have been snoring on, for his footsteps didn't crunch down the gravel path.

I was charged with steering backward out of the garage while Lecia pushed on the front bumper. I stuffed the pillowcase of books behind me and still could only reach the clutch with a tiptoe. The shift went into neutral—*the crossbar of a H,* Daddy had told me. Using the rearview, I fixed on Taylor Avenue, which rolled big and bigger out of that oblong mirror as Lecia heaved against the hood. There was one bad bump and a curve I had to cut before the road's slope started the truck rolling faster than I'd figured. Lecia was shout-whispering for me to stomp on the brake. The truck finally seized up with its back wheel a foot out of a wicked ditch.

A low fog covered the road. Our headlights dipped into it as we lurched along from gear to gear.

"Not the smoothest ride I ever had," I said.

"Then get out and walk," she said.

We bobbed along in pouting silence a few blocks. Stop signs reared up, and we edged into the empty intersections past them. At the Fina station on the corner, a long purple sign held a psychedelic lightning bolt down it—Pflash! The James Brown Package Store was long since closed, but in its parking lot sat a squat, pumpkin-shaped vehicle with its amber parking lights on and a pair of sockless feet in loafers jutting out the back window. It was Adam Phaelen's car we crunched up beside on the oyster shell gravel.

He reared up blinking, his hands raised up like we were the law. I hopped out, ostensibly to ask had he seen Mother. But in truth, his pale blue shirt was unbuttoned, and I wanted to cadge a closer look at the narrow patch of curly hair on his otherwise smooth brown chest, for Adam Phaelen was my Elvis. He bore before him along the otherwise gray avenues of Leechfield one of the handsomest faces in Christendom. He had black curly hair and china-blue eyes that crinkled up in a know-something-about-you-that-ain't-public grin. When he made a rare appearance at a football game or the town pool, I made it my business to elbow my way through the gaggle of teenage girls that comprised his orbit. He wore English Leather cologne that I'd seen him draw out of his glove compartment in a wood-top bottle.

It was that silvery odor of cologne that wafted to me from the open window of the pumpkin-mobile that night. He squinted at me and lowered his hands, then paused to look back at Lecia behind the wheel of Daddy's chugging truck.

"What y'all doing out this late, squirt?" he said. I told him while he fished a broken Kool from the green-and-white pack in his breast pocket. "Ain't that the shits," he said. "Last damn one too. Y'all don't smoke, do you?" I shook my head and halfway figured to start. On the off chance that Adam Phaelen'd ever again require from me a Kool cigarette, I would manage to produce one with a flourish.

He hadn't seen Mother, of course. He'd been playing poker with some old boys for nearabouts two days and had a dim memory of heading out for more smokes. How he'd wound up in the parking lot of the dead-bolted package store was a mystery. He leaned over the front seat, then wondered aloud what fucking asshole made off with his keys. "Sorry, baby," he said for swearing. When he called me *baby,* all the molecules in my body listed toward him, but he was lying back down, saying there was no help for it now. He was just gonna stretch out till daylight when his mother'd be up. I stood there while his heavy-lashed eyes sealed themselves against me, and the fine tendons of his sockless feet resumed their post crossed in his loafers out the window.

Back in the truck, I felt my body still vaguely luminous from its brief amble into Adam's vicinity. I could so easily picture him standing on my concrete porch in a powder blue tuxedo, holding a plastic corsage box with an orchid big as my head inside. On the other side of the door, I stood rustling in a black taffeta gown, a diamond choker around my neck, my hair sprayed into an almost topiary form.

But in reality, Lecia was steering us to the highway that led to Mother's art class. The streetlights chopped up the night in a regular staccato, with her face flickering through the bright patches. Her forehead was tight, and there was a hard set to her jaw.

"You think Adam Phaelen's cute?" I finally said.

"Like you read about," she said with just half her attention. "Cute isn't the word."

I kept thinking about his full mouth. At night in bed, I practiced kissing the fleshy part of my hand at the base of my thumb. That's how I trained for the real kiss Adam Phaelen would doubtless plant on me, once he snapped out of his cologne-soaked fog and twigged to the Inner Beauty that Mother swore shone out of my liquid brown eyes.

A red traffic light above an intersection bobbed in the wind. Lecia eased to a stop without a hitch and downshifted to first gear. "Why in hell"—she said—"would they string up this many traffic lights in a town when there're no cars?"

"There are cars here," I said, "just not after it gets dark." I was working my way up to what I thought of as The Big Question. The light slipped to green, and Lecia eased into the intersection. She was getting slick at it.

Finally, I said, "Would you give it up for Adam Phaelen?"

"What do you mean?"

"You know what I mean. Give it up. For Adam Phaelen," I said.

"Don't be ignorant," she said. I looked at her soft profile in the dashboard light, the big bubble of black hair net above her face inflating her head size overmuch.

"Is that a yes or a no?"

"It's a don't be ignorant. Jesus. Adam Phaelen's twenty-one years old."

Actually he was twenty-two. On his birthday, I'd caught sight of him at a high school football game when I'd gone to pee. He was staggering around under the bleachers wearing a black gabardine suit with his tie all unhitched and a crimson red brocade vest, from which he'd untucked a half-pint of cherry brandy. You could make out on his neck above his shirt collar a love bite the size of a half dollar. He'd called me *little sister* in a rusty voice that made the stars lurch.

"You want a guy with experience," I finally said. "Otherwise, they hurt you."

"They hurt you anyways," Lecia said, "the first time anyway. Experience or no."

Many nights, I'd listened through the heating vents to Lecia and Nickie Babin discussing the mysteries of being deflowered. That's how they talked about it. Something you owned was stolen, something of worth ruined. You never could get it back. And your whole market value as a female unit took a subsequent plummet. (Such talk conjured a prickly burr in my own gauzy sexual wonderings, for a long ago evening had left me fearing for the state of my own cherry.) Through the truck window that night, I watched a phone line laze in a low-sloping arc between poles.

"I got news for you," Lecia finally said. "Adam Phaelen wouldn't fuck you with somebody else's dick." Then she asked, "What are you talking like this for?"

"Just wondering," I said. We heaved to a stop by the fried chicken stand, where a pullet hen in a crouched running posture circled all night. Now why didn't somebody flip the switch to turn that thing off when they flipped the closed sign at the glass door?

"Well quit it," Lecia said. "That's all we need. You giving it up."

"I was actually wondering about *you* giving it up," I said.

"Well I'm not giving it up. Not to Adam Phaelen or anybody, anyhow. Jesus. Where do you get this shit?"

"It's natural to wonder, Mother says it's how we're made," I said.

"Speak for yourself," she said. After a long silence she added, "And get unmade that way. You'll be in junior high soon for chrissakes."

We must have driven in silence mostly after that. The gray road came at us in segments through the fog we drove into and out of. Many veils lowered across our windshield were torn away. At no time along the roadside did Mother's yellow station wagon appear. When we reached the college parking lot, it was bereft of cars.

But somehow in the process of driving, the early rushes of terror about Mother had dulled down. Maybe it was the moist air, or that glimpse of Adam Phaelen. But the minute the truck wheels rolled silently back into the dark garage (Lecia had killed both engine and headlights to sneak back), the fear came back again even sharper inside me. ("Like stabbing a stab wound," the poet Thomas Lux once wrote.)

Lecia seemed less worried than disgusted with the whole endeavor. Her hands made a strong stirrup to heave me back up to our window slot, after which she bench-pressed the pillowcase full of books we'd used. I hadn't noticed how fragrant the night was till I slid back in air-conditioned dark, away from honeysuckle and wisteria and cape jasmine. The house smelled of mildew and my sister's sweat. She fell asleep right off. I sat up with Daddy's flashlight thumbing the old Shakespeare for sonnets to learn.

We'd used the volume as a booster seat so I could reach the plywood table as a toddler. Its cover was a weathered navy cloth with a massive water stain on the front. Cardboard showed through the corners. But any speech I learned from there could charm Mother into still attention—a rare state for her. With a sheet draped over one shoulder and a laurel wreath of twisted florist wire, I made an ignoble Mark Antony.

I balanced the book on my pubic bone and pinched the flashlight under my neck. At first I couldn't actually read without Mother's absence rushing back to distract me. Still the book's weight alone anchored me with a strange comfort. I kept thumbing the onionskin pages for the pictures alone. There was a triad of Weird Sisters over a kettle.

There was a dwarf with the face of a frog. The footnotes—absorbed in a glance—began to sink in first.

> COIL: disturbance, ado.
> FORTH-RIGHTS: strange paths.
> OMINOUS PORTENTS: evil forebodings
> URCHINS: goblins in the shape of hedgehogs.

These realms were rife with monsters, but there was odd solace in them. The woods and castles and battlefields seemed to carry definite rules of comport, orders everyone adhered to. But for kings and queens and nobility, everyone seemed to stay put where you'd left them.

Before I even knew it, I was slowing down, starting a kind of blind search, skimming first one passage then another with the urgent attention of a wizard over a book of spells. I wanted some entrance to those dominions, some language to say what I was mute to.

I don't know whether it was that night or some other I found the soliloquy from *Richard the Second.* I only know that finding it let me sail off some blind cliff face into full-blown flight:

> *—Of comfort no man speak:*
> *Let's talk of graves, of worms, and epitaphs,*
> *Make dust our paper and with rainy eyes*
> *Write sorrow on the bosom of the earth. . . .*

Sure the passage was dark. But in my somewhat magical system of thought, pessimism served as a hedge against disaster. Think the worst, and you stave it off.

I read and reread the passage, covering verses with my palm then checking a line at a time what I could remember. Next to me, my sister was sawing metaphorical toothpicks. In the far room my cowboy daddy was equally clean of thought. I was the only one awake, for I was growing into a worrier, a world-class insomniac, what one friend would later call a grief-seeking missile.

Chapter Four

I WANDERED FROM BED ALL sleep sodden and crusty eyed to find Mother sitting placidly at the plywood table over a sketch pad, the charcoal stick in her hand aslant over the paper's rough field. She held out her arms to fold me into a warmth that stilled the body-thrumming worry I'd woken up with.

Daddy shuffled around the kitchen fixing his mess kit and thermos for work while Mother told Lecia and me the truncated version of the night before—how a man on a thruway turnaround had attacked and abducted her in the car. I never understood quite why Daddy only heard certain stories in abridged form, but could predict the expanded version coming by the silence we sat in till he hugged us all and picked up his truck keys. Soon as the engine revved up, Mother reached for her smokes, and it all poured out.

"He just popped up out of the ditch," she said. She'd been idling on the turnaround while headlights passed when the car door yanked open, and he shoved her down. He put his fat knee in her middle, then socked her hard enough to leave a bruise the size of a serving spoon on her left cheekbone. Above it was a small moon-shaped cut that Mother claimed matched the horseshoe ring he wore. (Daddy would say a fella wearing a ring like that was all hat and no cattle.) Then the guy tore open her flower-print blouse before backhanding her again for good measure.

All this was near impossible to picture, and Mother's cool, indifferent tone didn't add to the reality of it. She was flat-eyed as a reptile, as if some screen were lowered behind her irises. The whole deal came out with no more feeling than the average book report.

I pulled my knees up inside my string T-shirt, and the stretched-out neckhole of that shirt showed my own titless chest. The untrammeled view went clear past where boobs should have been to the elastic top of my panties. I quick put my bare feet down on the cool linoleum.

"He choked around my neck," Mother said. Her square fingers went to her throat. Its necklace of red marks looked more like hickies than fingerprints.

"That would've scared me big time," Lecia said. It's her confidential adult voice, intimate but nonchalant. (More and more now, Mother talks to her like she's some sorority sister, and Lecia answers back that way.)

"I fought him and wrestled around and clawed at his face," she said. "He had a fat, wadded-up kind of face. Very German-looking. His big beer belly pressed down in my middle. He said, 'I love it when they fight.'" Mother looked off sideways, as if for intervention from some unseen bystander.

He shoved her over and got behind the wheel. He said his name was Dutch. On his right forearm was the tattoo of a great gear wheel with big square teeth. Dutch was a talker, it turned out. He couldn't stop yakking about all the things he was fixing to do to my mother.

"Like what?" I wanted to know. The back door was open to a noisy summer thunderstorm. All the plants danced and shimmied under the rain.

"You *know,*" Lecia said. But I was a vulture for morbid detail, the result of reading by flashlight under my covers at night *Sergeant Rock* comics, where you could see soldiers flayed and dismembered and blown—as the Sarge said—to smithereens.

"Don't be a dipshit," Lecia said again. A flash of lightning made the backyard surge up in its jungle colors before dimming down again under the gray rain. She stood on one leg like a crane with her other foot propped on the opposite knee.

"He said he'd left women dead in ditches before," Mother said. Thunder clapped, and I felt my forehead clamp onto that thought—*women dead in ditches.*

"I would've just jumped out," I said. "Jumped and rolled and hit the ground running." It was a Batgirl move I could picture executing with catlike grace, cape flapping behind as I loped down the highway toward the cruiser I'd conjured there.

"Never happen," Lecia said. She pulled out a column of Saltines not yet torn into and did we want some. We didn't.

"He was in the fast lane, or I would've, " Mother said.

Lecia tore open the wax paper. She started crumbling that whole tube of crackers into a crockery bowl.

"I knew what he was after," Mother said. "Said he was 'a high octane sex fiend.' That was his phrase." Lecia was pouring buttermilk on her cracker crumblings, mushing them up with a spoon.

Till that moment, my mind had blurred past the sexual nature of the attack. I'd heard the tale as one of a deranged killer. The urge to choke the life out of my mother was somehow more palatable than some oaf wanting to rape her.

Lightning flashed again. "That was close," Lecia said. She started counting out loud to see if the storm was moving toward us or away. *One Mississippi, two Mississippi . . .*

I asked Mother couldn't she just have kicked this guy in the nuts? This was the recommended wisdom when facing rape. Knee him in the cojones. Though I'd never actually witnessed anybody doing it, I'd seen a fastball landing in a little league catcher's crotch bow the fellow up like a cut worm.

"I couldn't get to his balls," Mother said. "I was scared shitless. He was gonna *this,* he was gonna *that,*" Finally she told him she *wanted* to go with him, got him convinced.

This was maybe the most boggling fact in the whole story. How would you convince a man with a gear wheel tattooed on his forearm of your ardor for him, especially when your shirt was torn half off and your face bleeding where he'd popped you? Mother waved her hand as if to shoo something off. "He wasn't exactly the brightest bulb on the tree," she said. She told him she had money for a bottle if he'd just pull over at the package store. When he did, she jumped out and started yelling, and he took off the other way, toward the rice fields. The guy in the liquor store grabbed his shotgun and went after him. Mother got behind the counter with the guy's wife, who called the law.

It turned out Dutch was fast for a fat man. Before the liquor store guy could get his weapon shouldered, he made out Dutch's figure on the other side of the barb wire, scrambling over the top of one of those rice levees. Like a cockroach, the guy said. He'd got that far.

Through the window I watched the knotted honeysuckle and the broad leaf of the banana plant pelleted with fat rain. A hard rain blown in from the Gulf could set all the leaves in the world adance. It was worrisome. Our house lacked real foundations. Like all the houses I knew, it had only squat stacks of brick to prop us a few feet off the spongy ground and keep us dry when water rose. Probably the support beams didn't actually shake with thunder, but I remember it so—the rattle of windows coming unputtied in their panes and the asbestos siding that held us together starting to shiver.

"Thank God they caught him," Mother said. "Sheesh." She wore the abstract half smile of somebody who'd just checked out. (Looking back, I'd wonder if Mother wasn't in some state of shock, though this kind of blunt affect was part of her standard repertoire.)

"Now little titless can sleep at night," Lecia said. She never missed a shot at my sissydom, or the chickenlike nature of my chest. I told her to shut up. "Could he see you in the lineup?" she asked, for we'd watched many an episode of *Dragnet* where the suspects line up before blinding lights while the tearful victim, slouched low in a puddle of dark, lifts a finger at the guilty party.

"It wasn't like on TV," Mother said. "They didn't hold what you'd call a proper lineup." She was just sitting around some guy's spearmint-colored office drinking instant coffee out of styrofoam cups. A deputy led Dutch in uncuffed.

"He was awful beat up," Mother said. "They must have worked him over with a tire iron. Weird thing was him trying the whole time to look bored. Like he was somewhere else." Her mouth winced down, a pair of parentheses at the corners. "I swear to God, he looked embarrassed," Mother said, "like a kid somebody just asked to dance."

"Daddy would have done him way worse," Lecia said. And it's true that I've never seen Daddy walk out of a barroom fight with worse damage than knuckles he cut on some poor fellow's busted dentures.

"God, if Pete had gotten a hold of him," Mother said. Her head wagged, then cocked at an angle like a new thought tumbling inside her skull had rolled it over. She said, "If it had been one of you girls, even the law couldn't have saved him."

This last comment seemed odd, for while Lecia's body always garnered looks in public, the thought that I might warrant sexual attention—even in the warped form Dutch's took—was new. That possibility invited me deeper into the mysterious fellowship between Lecia and Mother. In that way, being worth raping came as a deformed sort of flattery and an actual promotion to womanhood. It carried a twisted kind of thrill.

But something else followed in a backwash. My scary long-dead grandma had once dropped me off at the Saturday movie matinee with a warning not to let any strange man feel under my dress. *Now why would anybody do that?* I'd wondered. I was just six or seven at the time. The idea of some scruffy-handed grown-up taking that liberty in the region of my underpants scared me. I watched all of *The Tingler* with my skirt tucked in hard under my butt. I did not get up once, even to pee, even when the popcorn hitting the back of my head came regular.

Mother picked up her pack of Salems. Thunder hit again, and the lights fluttered. She stood for a moment in that flickering then said we needed to be more careful running around town. Then she walked away from the episode, down her hallway toward her bed, where, I figured, she'd lay up all day washing down valium with Fresca. That was okay by me. So long as I could plot her location within the vectors of our house, I was fine.

PART **TWO** * **Midway**

Was it possible they were there and not haunted? No, not possible, not a chance, I know I wasn't the only one. Where are they now? (Where am I now?) I stood as close to them as I could without being one of them, and then I stood as far back as I could without leaving the planet.

—Michael Herr *Dispatches*

You only love
when you love in vain.

Try another radio probe
when ten have failed,
take two hundred rabbits
when a hundred have died:
only this is science.

You ask the secret.
It has just one name:
again.

—Miroslav Holub *Ode to Joy*
Translated by George Theiner

Chapter Five

I've been sitting in the crotch of this itchy damn tree with my feet dangling down so long they both feel like concrete. I shinnied up here to find John Cleary in the park's spread out fireworks crowd where folks have been gathering since dusk. They've come on foot toting stripey lawn chairs and knitting bags and metal coolers. There are quilts spread out over the stiff grass so babies can lay down without taking in cockleburrs and starting to bellow. My eyes glide over the mess and seem to latch down on everybody in town who's not John Cleary.

Eventually from the swarm of bobbing heads, I find his crew-cut stubble, bleached white into a jagged, low-flying halo. He's astride his banana-seat bike, one foot on the ground while he waits for the mosquito truck to show up so he can pedal behind it with his buddies. There's a cowboy song about ghost riders galloping across the clouds with their faces blurred by dust. That's what I think when I see the truck and John Cleary riding off behind it, leaned over his motorcycle handlebars, his thighs pumping.

John Cleary is what Daddy would call my huckleberry (not that John's agreed to that position yet). So sometimes I get so engrossed watching him, I forget myself entirely. That's how it got dark around me. That's how I wound up with these heavy throbbing feet hung out of the tree, like the elephant feet in the *Textbook of Medical Anomalies* I like to sneak peeks at in the library section marked ADULTS ONLY when the librarian goes onto the steps to smoke.

Meanwhile, John Cleary managed to vanish into the crowd, as did Clarice, who's sleeping over tonight.

Not until the last sparks go out when folks start folding their blankets and collapsing their beach chairs do I finally make them out over by the tilted merry-go-round with Bobbie Stuart and Davie Ray Hawks. They're all squatting over a patch of dirt with their arms dangling inside their knees like something out of *National Geographic*. Maybe somebody's lit one of those caterpillars of ash you can buy at Moak's fireworks stand out on Hogaboom Road. I never purchase fireworks myself, but I often find myself repeating the phrase Hogaboom Road at night to see how fast I can say it without slipping up: *hogaboom road hogaboom road hogaboom road.*

Clarice never does anything like this, and if she's spending the night and hears me prattling like this, she'll roll over and prop up on one elbow and tell me flat out that's why everybody thinks you're weird. It's not your mother or Pete, or the nudes on your walls or the fact that your parents divorced then got back later. It's you chattering to yourself like a gerbil instead of just going to sleep. But Clarice doesn't give a big rat's ass if I say Hogaboom Road till the kitchen kettle whistles for coffee. "You are a marvel," she likes to say, shaking her head and drawing one side of her mouth down in a half frown. But she watches me as if I warrant pondering, and she never doesn't laugh at my jokes.

John and Bobbie sword-fight with sparklers, joist and parry, while dumbass Davie Ray Hawks tries to get his sparkler going with what they call a punk—a little brown straw with a coal on the end that'll light a cherry bomb fuse but is useless on a sparkler. Finally, I get so tired of holding back unspoken opinions like this that I holler, and they come running from the edge of the field in a quick herd.

Clarice looks up at me with her hands on her hips like I'm in trouble. "That's where you've been hiding," she says.

"Ya'll get me down from here," I say. "My feet fell asleep hanging."

"Why should we?" Davie Ray Hawks says. He's the only one who keeps his bangs slung across his forehead in a surfer cut.

"Because we'll let you in our club if you do," I say.

"What kind of club?" Bobbie wants to know. His sparkler's hit a wet spot and sizzled out, so he's holding a bent silver wire in a way that seems forlorn, like a flower with all its petals stripped off.

Clarice pops out with, "A sex club." Which sends the boys into a fit of giggling and punching each other on the shoulder.

Only Davie Ray Hawks is unconvinced. "Y'all don't have any sex club."

"We didn't start it," Clarice says, "but we're in it. It's a junior high thing." To me, she seems to be holding down laughs, but the boys doubtless think she's serious as a heart attack.

John fakes being wholly engrossed in his sparkler, but if he were a dog, his ears would be pricked forward. He says, "Who all's in this club?"

Clarice names Larry Miller, the lifeguard at the pool, whose bathing suit we spend a lot of time trying to look up the leghole of. I shush her, for I spend whole hours hung on the side of his lifeguard stand and don't want these peckerheads to shoo him off talking to me by dragging his name through the mud.

"Uh-uh!" Davie Ray says, with more force than seems necessary. "He's in a fraternity in college. My cousin Janie's gone to dances with him."

"He's not having sex with y'all," Bobbie says.

"We never said he was," Clarice said. "It's all broken up by grade."

"Get me down outa here," I finally say, for Clarice is leading us down a path I no way want to miss by being stuck up a tree. John and

Bobbie come to the tree's base and hold up their arms. I put the heels of my hands where my butt's been in the tree crotch and lower myself till they can each grab a leg. First, it's like a princess being helped down from a carriage by two pages. But when their hands clamp on my thighs, I get a powerful jolt from them grabbing hold. The feeling slides clear up to my middle and lodges just under my rib cage where it presses against my hard-thumping heart.

It's strange. We've known each other our whole entire lives, since we were babies splashing bare assed in the same wading pool. We have hauled each other up on tree house ropes and built human pyramids on each other's backs and red-rovered through each other's joined arms. But this touch is different. Feeling those strong hands on my legs suddenly startles me. Suddenly and deeply, these two boys are not like me.

They must feel it too, because they practically let go at the same time like they grabbed an electric wire or something. They back off and start looking in opposite directions like nothing happened.

Clarice goes into detail about the different levels of the sex club. How at our level you get to practice French kissing and slow dancing. Davie Ray Hawks claims he already knows how to tongue-kiss, a phrase I've never heard that makes the whole thing way too overt sounding. In my head flashes a drawing I had to label and fill in with map colors—the esophagus and sinuses and tonsils floating in some hollow man, whose whole existence is devoted to demonstrating body parts to kids who want to hork looking at them. That said, I lately like watching Clarice's brother French-kiss his girlfriend Peg on the couch when they think we're asleep. By TV sign-off time, it's fairly clear their mouths are open. What I can't figure is if their tongues are slipping around in there the whole time, lapping on each other, or if they just lip-lock and every now and again touch tongues.

The sex club notion causes initiation rites to pop up, and it's an idea we all glom onto. Me and Clarice put our heads together and conjure some pretty good ones too, tests that if you pass, you get to practice kissing with me and Clarice. Here's what we gin up:

1. Pour lighter fluid on your hand and set a match to it.

2. Roll a cherry bomb in peanut butter, then mash a bunch of BBs on it, then drop it lit in the mailbox on Main to see if the whole thing explodes.

3. Take a shit-bomb (paper sack filled with somebody's doo) to the home of the junior high principal, Lead-Head Briggs. Light the sack on fire, then hide in the ditch while he stomps it out.

4. Blindfold Davie Ray Hawks and tell him he's putting his finger up somebody's butt, but really it's just wet bread wadded up in a soup can.

We stand on the edge of the field swatting mosquitoes, not sure where else to go. All around in other fields and neighborhoods, you can hear the sharp pop of fireworks like gunfire from some far off war. Kids are hollering, and Huey Ladette's mama calls him in because goddamn it, it's late, and she's gonna tear him a new asshole.

Somehow we get to my garage by meandering, nothing on purpose. I find the key to Mother's padlocked studio, where we're scared to turn on the light in case my parents look out back and wonder. Something's about to start, and we stand on the brink of it, still pretending to be shadows to one another amid the paint fumes. If I close my eyes, I can almost feel the mountain pines that give off this smell. The air hangs heavy as gauze between us all. Outside, about a zillion crickets have gone into *chirrup, chirrup,* each in a different soprano voice. The toads come back in alto, and they're worse than any choir I ever sang in, if matching up notes is a measure. Still they blend somehow, a kind of curtain of sounds woven together, and the firecrackers go *pop pop pop,* and the bottle rockets whish out sparks then burst.

After my eyes get used to the dark, I make out John's crew cut. He's walked over to a canvas propped in a puddle of moonlight, an old nude Mother never framed. "Lookit this!" he says. There's a slow foot-shuffle in the dark as Bobbie and Davie Ray and Clarice congregate in front of it.

"Get a load of those knockers," Davie Ray says, and there's hissed whispers to shut the fuck up.

"Boy she got some headlights, don't she," Bobbie says.

"Lecia pose for this?" Davie Ray says, which draws stuffed giggles from all the boys. The unsaid comparison to my little ace-bandaged-looking chest pins me like a spear.

"Y'all are gross," Clarice says, and John says that's her sister, chrissake. Then to make sure nobody thinks he's a goodie-goodie, or too much on a girl's side, he reaches a hand up and tickles one painted boob, saying, *Gootchie gootchie goo.*

Somebody comes up with rules for a kissing game, but basically Clarice and me each kiss a boy while one of them sits out. Then we switch. If I had my druthers, Davie Ray Hawks would just go home and let me kiss John while Clarice kissed Bobbie. But the whole point of a game like this is how everybody's kiss is at the same level, so each of us holds the same value, even though in matters of kissing, opinions always run fairly deep. But only by leveling the ground like this does the kiss get possible as activity.

The first boy I kiss is Bobbie, who holds my elbows as if we're about to spin toplike through the dark. His lips are chapped dry as parchment and sweet. Then somebody says switch, and Davie Ray Hawks is on me. His lips are blubbery and wet. He puts his hand in the small of my back and leans into me. But I don't feel danced with. Plus once he gets me arched back a good ways, I can feel what must be his dick hard as a crescent wrench poking my leg. The raw fact of it grosses me out, and this whole scene starts to feel all blunt and greasy.

Then Bobbie's voice says switch, and John Cleary draws me to him, and there's such a surge inside me I can't locate where it's bubbled up from.

I hold my breath, afraid of messing up. That corn dog I ate earlier flashes through my head, and I get a weird urge to draw back, dash out the studio and up the back steps and into the bathroom to brush my teeth, rinse, spit, and rinse again with Lecia's Listerine before blinking myself magically back to John's arms.

None of which I do, of course. I hold my breath and count to myself like during a storm: *one Mississippi, two Mississippi.*

There's a TV commercial for some thick green shampoo that they drop a pearl in to show how rich and heavy it is, the pearl falling through this heavy green goop. And that's what John smells like. Prell, it's called. All the cut grass in the world gets mashed into a bottle of this stuff. And the time we move into is that slow-falling, underwater shampoo time. John does not hold my elbows like he's scared to get too close. He makes a cage of his arms I step right in (colt in a corral, I think). He tilts his head and says with a breath like Juicy Fruit right before he kisses me, "Is this okay?" Before I can say yes, we bump teeth a little, then he's breathing the Juicy Fruit right into my mouth, my lips, and his lips come closer till the softnesses match up.

John's tongue is not hard and pointy like Davie Ray's or plumb absent like Bobbie's. It parts my lips a little as if testing the warmth of water. And after a second I get the idea that my tongue's supposed to do something other than lay there or draw back hiding. I ease it forward so as not to poke at him the way Davie Ray Hawks did me. I taste the coppery flesh of his soft tongue on my wet one. My breathing seizes up again. And I put my hands up and press them flat against his chest because half of me is afraid I'll fall entirely into him if he keeps holding me. And there over his breast pocket, a small embroidered seahorse dips its head down and coils its tail inward till it's a perfect figure for how shy I suddenly feel. Through the shirt cotton is John's own strong heart.

I try to reteach myself to breathe normal, but it comes out in halts and jags. I feel grit in the crook of my elbow and creases in my neck and a single dot of sweat bumping down my spine to the small of my back. Then I feel John's hands tremble on my back, and I try to draw him out of that trembling with my own tongue, and it's like we're drinking from each other.

Suddenly, I know so much. I understand about waves and cross tides and how jellyfish float and why rivers empty themselves in the Gulf. I understand the undulating movement of the stingray on *Sea Hunt* and the hard forward muscle of the shark. Now I know why they call it pet-ting, for even though I'm more still in the plush warmth of his mouth than I can ever get in church, my whole body is purring. I let myself breathe into him a breath that tastes like ashes from a long fire.

Outside there's the bump of a screen door. Maybe my folks letting the cat out. I hear it latch back careful the way Daddy would do. There's the far off whine of a bottle rocket shedding sparks across some field. Then nothing.

Then the crunch of foot on gravel sets us all in a panic. Everybody rears back from kissing and starts mouthing stuff I can't make out. Clarice has her knees squinched together like she has to pee. She flaps her hands like a bird fighting its way out of a nosedive. Davie Ray Hawks sneaks over to the curtain and looks out a sliver. When he wheels around in the moonlight, his face is bug-eyed, his hands held out wide in an expression copied from Frankenstein right when he got zapped in the head with lightning. Daddy's crunching barefoot down the gravel path alongside the garage, closer and closer till the door on the other side of this studio door aches on its old hinge.

I think of explicit threats he's made about using his straight razor to slice up anybody who ever messed with Lecia and me. I think this qualifies as messing. He wouldn't actually use a razor on those boys, of course, or lay a hand on me or Clarice, but they might well catch an ass-whipping. But a whipping would be way better than this waterfall of shame I feel at the prospect of him knowing I've been standing around with boys in the dark letting them put their tongues in my mouth. This is definitely not what he expects me to be doing.

In the hot dark, John Cleary's eyes are blue as struck matches. Plus he's drawn his whole head turtle-like inside his shirt collar, and pulled that up over his nose like Pud in *Bazooka Joe* comics. I start figuring our way out of it.

Wolfman, I could say to Daddy. *We were playing wolfman.* Or better still, *We were gonna make a play about a mummy where lightning knocks out the electricity right before the mummy staggers in . . .*

Daddy's in the garage now, easing the door back flush to the frame. When I hear him talking, at first I think it's aimed at us. I take his sugary tone for a kind of sideways menace. "Poor old fella," he says. Then the black cat Daddy thinks of as his yowls like he's been picked up in the middle. That's when I know we're safe. Daddy's not heading in here at all. The other kids probably don't twig to it, but I wouldn't breathe a word that might spark Daddy's Indian ears into hearing us. Still the air starts to ease back into the room.

We stand like statues in freeze tag listening to him in the dark. "Don't nobody love old Roy like he has coming," Daddy says. Clarice tries to stuff down her giggles at that. Davie Ray's waving his arms and miming *shhh,* John draws an invisible hankie out of his breast pocket and mops his forehead.

Meanwhile, my own daddy is talking out loud to this shiny black tomcat. "Works hard all day being a cat," he says, then, "I know it. Nobody even rubs his chin. He's chasing mice all day. Keeping his whiskers slicked nice." Daddy heaves open his truck door then shuts it. The whiskey bottle clinks against the seat adjuster as he draws it out. I can picture the broken paper seal and the gold twisty lid and my daddy's whiskey throat guzzling under the dome light.

Nobody's folks drink like mine. John Cleary's daddy has had the same case of Lone Star in the garage so long spiders have nested all over it. Knowledge of that difference in my family makes me suddenly alone in the room, though an instant before in John's arms, I'd stood embraced in more warm than I could recall. Now Daddy's drinking has carved me away from everybody else. He's sucking down whiskey and talking to a cat, saying, "Just tell old Pete about it." And maybe Roy does tell him, for the room is a gray velvet tomb we're all buried in listening hard. After a long time, Daddy says, "Dadgum 'em all to hell."

Then the door opens and his steps crunch away, and our exhalings of relief are so loud, I miss hearing the house door.

Outside, the night has grown exponentially larger. The roads to the horizon seem to stretch farther. We're small under the sky's dome. There's mist at our ankles, and the moon is low. I still feel quivery as a rabbit from where John held me. I can barely look at him because I know he possesses that soft mouth that matches up with mine so right.

How can you know such a thing about a person and not lean into it? I squat down and pretend to sift for quartz pebbles in the road gravel till I think his blue eyes glide over my shoulder's curve, but when I sneak a look, he's staring back toward Bobbie's house. Bobbie says, "Old Pete's tough as a boot."

John says, "I wouldn't wanna tangle with him."

Davie Ray makes the sign of the cross. "We damn near died back there," he says. This puffs me up a little, that Daddy's so formidable in everybody's mind. Clarice isn't saying diddly. Like me she's doubtless thinking of all that softness these otherwise scabby-looking boys embody. But she also knows that the whole sex-club idea has swept past us, that interval in the garage gone to ether. We're back on our own separate islands. Nobody could even say "sex club" or mention what happened without being thought of as warped in the head.

Bobbie says, "Let's go back to my house and make Jiffy Pop and watch *Thriller*." Then they're slapping away, no goodbye, no see you later. They practically vaporize before us.

When they're far enough away, Clarice asks me if I felt myself getting hot back there in the studio. "And I don't mean temperature." I say hell yes. We stand there a second, unable to either say more about it or to let the feeling go.

Finally, Clarice says she wants popcorn too, but I don't want to go back in my house now. Just seeing Mother and Daddy would somehow banish how I feel. As long as they're away from me, I can close my eyes and taste John Cleary's Juicy Fruit, feel the unexploded weight of him breathing on me.

Mother harps all the time on how sex and even touching yourself is normal as can be. Her only worry is that I'll get what she calls hot pants and get knocked up. She'll let me look at her erotic art book with folks entwined and rolling around like weasels whenever I want. But while lately I consider cracking it open most every day, I always wait till she and Daddy aren't home.

Somehow even letting Mother and Daddy whiz through my head totally wipes away the girl John Cleary just held. She's long gone, and in her place stands this skinned-up kid again. I want to stave off going home wicked bad.

I ask Clarice if she wants to go over to Bobbie's house to ask the boys to share their Jiffy Pop. She says that, as excuses go, that's really pitiful sounding. To show up there would be asking for it. Since the boys have probably got blue balls from kissing us, no telling what they'd do. Her brothers have explained to her that unchanneled sperm makes your balls swell and somehow backs it up into your brain. "They don't think straight with blue balls," Clarice says.

Because John Cleary's kisses have plugged my body into some unspecified socket still humming on high, I ask Clarice what girls get to have that even approximates blue balls.

"Diddly shit, that's what," Clarice says. Or else you get a Reputation. If you let boys suck hickies on your neck or if you do the shimmy at the skating rink so your boobs slap back and forth like Marilyn Fruget, then you get guys standing around lagging pennies off a wall behind the raceway, talking about how they finger-fucked you and your yin-yang made their hand smell like tuna fish. Clarice is going to high school year after next and has big plans for improving her social standing. She says a novena every night to grow titties, and when that crop finally comes in, the last thing she can have is A Reputation.

Nor, she warns me, do I want one when I start junior high this fall. I tell her that tonight I'm not so sure.

There's a line Mother read me from a book about poor crackers dragging their dead mama across Mississippi or Alabama or some godawful place: "I feel like a wet seed wild in the hot blind earth," the girl says. Just hearing that told me something about being a girl I didn't know. But standing inside John Cleary's breath and body temperature with our mouths melting into each other makes me really know it. *Really really,* as Clarice would say, *down south of your neck.*

Chapter Six

SEVENTH GRADE ACTUALLY STARTS for me the week before it starts, when Mother drives me to Payless to choose shoes from the rows of mud-ugly footwear on industrial display racks that stretch back far as a football field. That they're two pairs for five dollars is still no bargain. The size elevens are grotesquely baby-fied—a slanted array of round-toed Mary Janes with slick-bottomed soles. The straps are stiff as saddle leather. The holes for the buckle-prongs don't even stab all the way through, so the tiny metal stick just pokes at the cheap plastic. If you scuff the patent leather on any of these, it by-God holds the mark. Each style I try deforms my sense of self even worse than those before. In pair after pair, I stump along the cement aisle, straps flapping.

Eventually we go to a department store, but the pricey shoes I wind up setting in my closet are only slightly less babyish than those at Payless. My size is just too small to warrant styling for. One look at the shoes we buy aimed out at me from the closet floor like little gunboats fixing to fire, and I know all about the life I'll lead inside them. That's how seventh grade starts.

That's the year Lecia's hanging out with high school boys, so I walk home every day past football practice alone. Faking I don't see the boys, I keep eyes to the ground while I kick every dandelion in my path baldheaded. Every day I feel more like some defeated matador limping out of the arena after I've been gored, or like some general coming back from a long battle. Mother once read me about how Napoleon in exile used to take endless baths. And I feel like that. Like Napoleon, and some bunch of barbarians has stolen my empire and even my horse. I want to peel off my armor and soak in the tub till my digits prune up and I can wrap myself in thick cotton to sleep for the rest of my life.

Meanwhile, the football drills crashing around me are hard to ignore—all those muscled-up bodies in collision. There's never a scrimmage that soon after school, just clumps of players in clunky white pads and practice helmets repeating movements designed to induce misery in their executors. Boys run wind sprints in threes and fours that end between these poles. When one guy peels out of the group to the sidelines to vomit, a pair of his own buddies actually comes to yell at him. There he is bent double, horking up his macaroni, and his teammates are barking at him like drill sergeants about being a sissy. It strikes me that whatever advantages there are to being a boy—getting to stay out late and having other people wash your clothes and bring you plates of stuff—get undercut by having to play football. (There's also cutting up chickens and changing the oil in the car, but the misery of those things pales next to how football practice looks.)

One day, I'm almost to the ditch behind the Smiths' house when some guy in practice pads comes rattling up who turns out to be John Cleary. He's strapped and laced into his white practice uniform and is saying wait up.

John's face is never far from what I'm thinking, but seeing it manifest so close to mine so suddenly feels like an ambush. I know John can't actually look into my pupils and see his face floating there with red Magic Marker hearts scribbled around it. But having the real John overlap so suddenly with the dreamed-of boy yanks my most fervent secret from its inner cave and into stark sunlight. I try hard to take in his galloping beauty straight on, to stand my ground. (Part of me is also crazily rewinding to play back my whole walk across the field, for surely I did some stupid thing. I wouldn't pick my nose or anything in front of the whole team, but I could have been skipping or singing some goofy song under my breath.)

John Cleary. His face behind the mask's cage is red under its freckles, and the sky's blue looks washed out next to his cobalt eyes. They stare at me from inside the helmet space as Lancelot's might through a visor. "Did you get how to do that thing in Miss Picket's?" he wants to know, for in a stroke of luck, we sit kitty-corner in English.

"You mean the essay? Sure. I finished it in class." I stand back a little, fairly sure I don't smell particularly good. My only hope is that he doesn't smell good either, and his football sweat will swamp my field-walking sweat. But for some reason, I can never smell anything coming off John Cleary but cut grass and Ivory soap.

"You got time to help me with mine? I mean, not now, of course." He looks around all apologetic, as if I could have failed to notice he was in football practice. There's a pair of twin grass stains on the knees of his short britches that somehow make the remaining whiteness of him brighter. "Maybe after supper? I mean, if you're not buried with other work." I suddenly go mute, for the prospect of this arrangement is so foreign, so wholly hard to imagine, it takes a minute to sink in. John Cleary. Asking me over. After sundown. To do homework. What flashes in my head is that night in Mother's studio in summer. I wonder if he ever thinks how soft the tips of our tongues were reaching toward each other from the dark caves of our mouths.

The "sure" I eke out is the only blip my stopped breath can handle. I stand there, heart fish-flopping inside my rib cage. But he just says thanks and jogs back to where the push-up guys are resting. His moving form is the whitest on the field—slim-hipped, muscle-legged, his back broad as a gladiator's.

There's nothing wrong with junior high that a night with John Cleary won't rectify (one of our spelling words). I start to run home but feel my head waggle on my shoulders and have to force myself slower.

Once home, I remember the love spell our voodoo neighbor gave me for John Cleary. LaFaree lives behind us and reads tarot and plays Ouija board with me and Clarice sometimes. This spell involves my laying hold to John's hair trimmings and fingernail clippings to mash into a candle I can burn. That's why I stick a sandwich bag in my pocket before I trot over to his house. For good measure, I also tuck in the plastic mass card she gave me of Saint Jude. The patron saint of lost causes, LaFaree had told me, things despaired of.

In the Clearys' yard, their sprinkler goes *whap whap whap* and throws a huge silver spiderweb above the lawn in the dusk. The plastic card I finger in my back pocket feels like the only smooth, cool thing in a sandpapery world.

I barely knock before Mrs. Cleary answers holding a dish towel. She's got on a blue calico apron that reflects her eyes nice. Her wide smile is a ditto of John's. She stands there wiping her hands off. "Little Mary," she says, like isn't she lucky I'm there. Then she shoves the screen open.

I haven't set foot in the Clearys' house since fifth grade when John and Bobbie and I started a motorcycle gang with playing cards clothespinned to our bike spokes. It's smaller than our house. The ceilings are lower and rooms smaller, but the scale doesn't seem so much cramped as cozy. There's a strong smell of chocolate. "Waiting for a plate of fudge to harden up, Mary Marlene. Gotta finish these dang dishes," she says. That's the other thing about the Clearys. Hardly nobody cusses. It's always *dang* and *darn,* and *sugar* instead of *shit.* I offer to help dry and put away—something I'd never do at home but that I've learned any girl offers who isn't dead-assed lazy.

Mr. Cleary calls me into the living room where he's watching the news. He looks up and says, "Big bad Mary. Come hug my neck." John's body is sprawled on the pumpkin-colored shag carpet in front of the TV so I have to step over him. He's got his chin on a sofa bolster and is scribbling the last numbers on a math mimeo sheet.

He rolls over to say thanks for coming, and with that full-length gaze at him, I decide he's luminous enough in his blond body to read by in the dark.

Mr. Cleary shoos us out, and we head to the back porch, which is all screens insulated with thick plastic. So when the wind blows, it sucks the panels against the screen with a series of loud slaps. There's an old porch glider in one corner, and that's where we sit. Our feet rock us back and forth. The panels rattle in the wind to drown out the TV in the next room.

John's got his cloth binder open on his lap, and whatever help he claims to need for his essay is not much, but I coax him along. He says things, and I say things back that must sound marginally right. But the words and sentences are just background to the stomach-dropping drama of sitting by him. Mostly I breathe the oxides he gives off and study him. I watch his thick-fingered hand holding the blue Bic move across the blue-lined page. He inscribes each letter at such a far forward pitch that you half expect the words themselves to fall over on their faces and pour off the margin. John's face bent over his work in the lamplight is for an instant so serious inside his freckles that I could almost cry. Time this close to him is so magnified that you can practically hear the grandfather clock seize up between ticks.

The essay gets written and is pretty good, but I'm rocked clear out of that evening and place. I half believe that the stars outside have frozen into their sockets. The moon has stopped its circuit. John bends over his page in the lamplight. He puts the last period in place and says he'll copy it over neat while he watches the game, and do I want to stay.

In the living room, John stretches out to recopy his paper, and I remember all the stuff LaFaree says I need for my spell and head for the bathroom.

Sure enough, in the black brush on the pink-tiled counter there are dense squiggles of blond hair around the bristles, some short enough to be John's. But no way can I know which of these hairs grew from John's actual scalp. If I cast a spell on the wrong Cleary, his goat-footed big brother (a phrase I stole from the poet I loved and had for years repeated in schoolyard cuss fights like I owned it) would come lumbering after me all heated up.

I open the medicine cabinet as if the answer's in there. And, Lord is it neat, a testament to the housekeeping tips the ladies clip from the

Leechfield Gazette and leave clothespinned to each other's mailboxes. Open our bathroom cupboard, and there are prescriptions three deep. There are bottles with necks so crusty you'd need a pair of pliers to crack them open. And no other storage compartment in our house gets any better. The floor of every closet is a swamp of blouses and slacks slipped loose from their wire hangers with unpaired shoes scattered around. The clothes drawers are all jammed shut tight. And if you open the refrigerator looking for an orange, you're as apt to find a pair of dice Daddy left there last night when he came in late, or a book of paper matches announcing that you could write children's stories at home for cash.

But the Clearys' cabinet holds the bare minimum, with no repeats—grown-up aspirin and band-aids, a tiny bottle of orange methiolade, whose clean black cap comes with a little glass stick in the middle to dab that stinging stuff on your bo-bos. Even their toothpaste rolls up from the bottom, neat around the end crimp. The top's screwed on tight, and not one widget of paste squeezes out the sides like clay.

Only the cough syrup is prescription. I study the label. It's for Mr. Cleary from just last March, the bottle not one bit sticky. Somebody sponged off any drips before setting it back there, so the bottle's just slick as my ass. I unscrew the top and give it a sniff—grape it's meant to be. Then I slug down a swallow for good measure, as I've seen Mother do, to calm my racing nerves.

I get the fine-tooth comb and pick every hair out of the brush and twist-tie them into the sandwich bag I jab back down in my pocket, figuring I can burn them all in a pile, and let all the Clearys will be nuts about me, John included.

Before I leave, I notice a small ashtray with what looks like nail clippings in it, little half moons scattered. But before I pick them up, I get hit by an odd feeling. Suddenly I can picture Daddy saying, "Ain't you got a case of the sweet ass!" And I get an odd surge in my chest—something like dignity keeps me from picking up any toenails to take home. You got to draw that line somewhere, I figure.

Back in the living room, the Dallas Cowboys run around on TV. Mr. Cleary's watching it like it's the apocalypse while Mrs. Cleary crochets some bootie in a color I think of as baby-boy blue. John is bickering at his sister, Jana, who sits cross-legged with her skirt draped over her crossed knees and a physiology book in her lap. John is saying, "I'll do you. Come on. My legs are killing me." She says no, she's gotta learn all these muscles for the quiz. "Mr. Lyons always gives a quiz on Friday," she says.

And John shoots back that she was a cheerleader at our school. "It's doing something for the team," he says.

"Ask Mary to do it," Mr. Cleary says. He spits tobacco in his Folgers can, a gesture that makes Mrs. Cleary wince. Her crochet hook stops looping a second before it resumes.

I am still hanging in what I think of as the balance. John cranes around at me and says, "Would you?"

"He wants somebody to rub his legs," Mrs. Cleary says.

Mr. Cleary kicks in, "That idiot coach doesn't stretch them out right."

"Lecia ran track so I did this with her," I claim. That's how I come to be kneeling over John's brown legs with the glinting pale hair. I take one hard calf in my hands, and my heart leaps up. I mash a little on it then stop. "You can do harder than that," he says. I knead in the middle of the calf a minute till the flesh starts to loosen under my fingers' workings. Jana pipes in that I'm doing his gastroc now. Mr. Cleary, who's coached just about every sport you can think of, says I need to lengthen the muscle. So I start at the heel end and run my fingers up around the heart-shaped calf muscle. This makes John groan and say that feels good. One of the Cowboys is hauling butt between goalposts. John Cleary's whole glorious body is laid out before me, and I am saying to myself, *John Cleary under my hands.*

"That other muscle's his soleus muscle," Jana says. I say where, hoping it's up higher, but she says, "Down there, by the Achilles tendon." It's a smaller muscle, and he complains I'm pinching him, so I go back to trying to lengthen the calves out.

I could do this all day and not mind, I think. Some liquid has begun to spill and spread throughout my middle, which makes it hard to keep breathing regular. I look at the screen long enough to make some dim comment about the score. John bends his neck forward and mumbles something into the sofa bolster. I say what.

"The backs of my thighs," he says. "They're killing me."

Mrs. Cleary gets up and says she's heading off to bed. "Y'all don't be up all night if it goes to overtime." She kisses everybody and plants one on top of my head, saying it's nice having another girl around. Which causes me to feel double guilty that I'll soon be casting a spell to woo her unsuspecting boy.

I am waiting for somebody to get back to John's thighs so I don't look overeager rubbing them. But there's a penalty call everybody has to mullygrub about. Statistics go back and forth.

It's halftime when Mr. Cleary says *Goddamn,* and Jana says *Daddy.* Then Mr. Cleary with no prompting from me or anybody says, "Mary, you oughta work on his hamstrings. They stay drawn up that tight it'll send his back out."

I move up his leg, and as I do that, my whole body starts humming inside itself, like some locust singing inside its husk. I am scared to look at anybody for fear that this trembling in me shows through. One hand settles on the back of John's knee, and the two tendons are tight as bowstrings.

"You can sit there," John says. "Just sit on my calves," he says to the TV. "You can reach better with two hands."

When I was little, for a while I had a horse that carried me across meadows where long grass and purple loosestrife grew up to the stirrups. He'd stretch out long to gallop so my hair flew back and the mountains alongside me smeared against the orange sky. One day, he came to a ravine or dry creekbed I didn't see coming, and even though he wasn't much of a jumper, he had the sense to bound over it. It was a leap I didn't expect, and in my center everything fell away for an instant. I flew through blue air so long I later believed he'd briefly grown wings on his feet and some invisible sail had lifted us.

I straddle John's calves, and something of that animal comes back to me, and I can almost feel the stalks of loosestrife flower against my calves again. My thumb settles on the inner thigh muscle, which Jana names. I bear down with light pressure and start to run that thumb up the long muscle, what would be in the inseam of jeans if John had jeans on. But this is flesh, and it yields to me.

All at once I believe John feels something too. His skin quickens to my touch. He's gone super still, and the blond hairs on his thighs have come to attention. My thumb slides further up, and I feel some deeper part of him under me. It twists my very center, some knot going tight with pleasure. I slide my thumb up John's thigh to where his cutoffs end. And then I go back down to the knee, start over, stroke the muscle slow and deep its length. I think again of that horse, nudged by my heels into a gallop. How of his own volition, he could break into a full lope so the blossoms we passed close to were stripped almost bare.

When the game's over, John leaps up and runs to his room to get ready for bed, and I am down the steps and out into the dark before I know it. Mr. Cleary follows me out. He lights a smoke and stands on the sidewalk, watching me run home, waiting till I wave on the porch to go back in.

That night may be the first time I'm grateful Lecia's gone. I reach for the damp between my legs and find my panties soaked through. There are so many gross jokes you hear about stuff coming out of you down there. ("After a date, throw your panties against the wall, and if they stick, you had a good time," Darlene Smith once said.) I push these out of my head and close my eyes, for under my hand there's a fire burning cool as menthol. For some reason, I don't conjure John's body stretched over mine, or under it, or even the long muscles of his thighs hard under my hands. The fact of that body is too carnal for this sharp luminosity in me. Instead I picture John leading me under the spangled light of this mirrored ball for a slow dance. How he wheels me past those too stunned by our beauty to dance themselves. And suddenly John is there, holding me lightly in his arms and breathing his Juicy Fruit breath into my mouth. Then the horse leaps between my legs, and that soaring fall enters me, and everything dissolves.

I remember the next morning, or think I do, lolling in bed like my own bride. Maybe it was some other morning, but I remember it nonetheless. Some dense little sun glowed in my solar plexus. I'd wallowed my whole sleep away in it.

Only when I came across the baggie in my pocket did my face heat up. Touching myself didn't seem so bad. Mother said everybody did that, even people who swore to God and stick-a-needle that they didn't. What shamed me was the plastic bag, that an ardor so pure as mine for John Cleary could involve such deceit. I took the baggie outside in heavy rain and shook the squiggles of hair out into a sewer ditch of rushing rainwater, tossing the empty plastic after it.

Chapter Seven

Sometime during eighth grade, Clarice decides I'm not her best friend anymore. If she'd said this outright, I would have nattered and mullygrubbed at her. Instead, she just stops coming over. No fight, no nothing. One Sunday evening after we'd been playing dominoes all afternoon, she just strolls down to her house and doesn't come back. Not that I didn't ask her to.

I did ask, and ask, and ask again nice. The more I ask, the more broke-dick her excuses get. She'll say she has to help her mother at the doughnut shop one day. The next it's yardwork, or cleaning the house. Or her cousins are spending the night, and she has to shampoo and set the little girls' hair for mass the next day. My offers to pitch in and help just make her squirm and tack some bull dookey onto her story. Like she'll say it turns out her grandma is maybe coming from Louisiana, and her mother wants just family. Or she's being punished for not doing the yardwork and can't have company.

Lecia tells me when I complain about it to take the hint. But Lecia seldom spends a whole Saturday by herself reading two books in a row. Mother's always off at the library, and Daddy's wherever he goes. It's just me thumbing encyclopedias with Sally the Siamese or sleek black Roy laying around till Lecia's date brings her home.

That's why I won't just blindly take Clarice's dropping out of my traffic patterns without an explanation. Also I pretty much can't stand anybody my own age and it's mostly mutual. I call Clarice every Saturday till one morning her little brother Jeff picks up the phone.

"She ain't here," he mumbles.

"Jeffrey?" There's a little pause. I can hear the Road Runner on TV go *beep-beep*, then make a dashing-off whiz sound. Clearly Jeff's attention has gone back to old Wile E., who winds up—gauging from the explosion I hear—biting down on a dynamite sandwich and lying in the desert with a crown of orbiting stars and his eyes all bugged out. "Jeff, listen up!" I finally say.

"What!"

"Are you telling the truth?" I said. "About your sister?"

"She ain't here. I swear. She ain't nowheres around," he says. I hear what must be an anvil from the Acme Anvil Factory crate fall whistling from the cliff edge.

"Jeff, why do I get the sense that you're lying to me?"

"I'm not. Cross my heart!" Now the vaudeville closing music plays on their TV, and I decide that I can now weasel something out of Jeffrey.

"Have you made first communion yet?" I ask him, which is a curveball question.

"I just took it Easter!" he says. Clarice and I had grilled him on the catechism questions that still spooled through my head some nights: "Who made the world?" "God made the world."

"Now Jeff, you know, and I know, and God almighty sure as hell knows that you're lying like a rug right now. They wouldn't leave you stranded there by yourself at barely first communion age, and I just saw your momma glazing a tray of crullers down at the doughnut shop." This last part's a lie, but how would he know.

His hand smothers the receiver while he mumbles something to someone who barks something back. I can picture his little hand—the nails with half moons of black dirt, knuckles scabby.

When he comes back on, you can hear the ad for the Easy-Bake oven in the background. Jeff says, "Clarice's gone to the hospital." His voice has the hard newsbreaking timbre of a revival tent preacher.

"Jeff, if you make up that people are sick in the hospital, God hears you, and he'll think you're praying and then strike that person with something awful so they wind up sicker even than you made up—"

"She *is* at the hospital, I swear to God, Mary Karr! Stevie took her in Peggy's car right after *Queen for a Day*," he said.

"God hates a liar, Jeffrey." I hear his breath speed up and rasp out. "And unless you get your little sinning ass to confession and tell Father about this venal mortal sin, you'll wind up in a big ditch in hell where liars get thrown all festering, and they itch like crazy and rake the skin on their arms and shins the way you'd scale a carp—"

"She's gone to work there, but she doesn't like you anymore anyway." And at that his wheezing starts full bore, and his daddy snatches the phone and asks who is it, and I hang up.

Later that evening, I walk to Clarice's house and peer in the side window for some sign of her. Which there just isn't any.

Maybe she went down to help her mother close up the doughnut shop. I slouch down in the ditch by the driveway to wait so my lurking won't be over obvious to anybody driving by. During a storm, the water pours through this culvert like Niagara Falls, all the way to the big sewer ditch. I stick my head in the culvert pipe and see nothing in there but a one-legged baby doll. Then I just slump and wait. The sun's slid down, so the sky's gone all colors. You can see the red bleep of the radio tower a few blocks off.

After a while, Mrs. Fontenot's Buick comes surging up the drive, headlights swiping just above my head level in the ditch.

But when Mrs. Fontenot gets out, the yellow dome light shows a wide prairie of blue plastic upholstery totally unoccupied by Clarice.

This throws me a loop, for Clarice's daddy wouldn't let her roam around after dark by herself.

Mrs. Fontenot walks in with the white pastry box she always brings home. It's dark so she doesn't see me at all crouched nearby. A handful of mosquitoes comes to hang suspended in front of my eyes. I swipe my hand and they go away, only to reappear a heartbeat later, as if they've been lowered there by puppet strings. Sometimes I feel like I'm dangling loose from such strings of sheer fishing line, my head like a block and my feet big wooden clod-hoppers. Lying in the spiky ditch grass, I try hard to figure where exactly Clarice could be this late.

I run home for a stack of comic books and some kind of flashlight to read by while I wait. But the flashlight's dead, so I unhook the hurricane lamp from the nail in the washhouse to read by. Usually, Daddy only lights it when a storm knocks the power out, or if you're camping. It also lets me play at living back in the olden days with Abe Lincoln, scratching my sums on a shovel blade in the firelight and so forth.

Back inside, Lecia's hair's all wet, and she's toting the dresser drawer where she keeps all her curlers out in front of her like a cigarette tray from an old movie. I can smell the pink Dep hair gel she gunks up her damp hair with before she sets it. She's wearing underpants and a T-shirt she made in art class with "Brain Child" written on it above a knobby-headed creature with a low-slung belly button. She takes one look at that hurricane lamp and says, "You running off to Africa again?"

Before I can tell her to kiss my rosy red one, Mother wanders out with the *New York Times* Sunday crossword, her reading glasses balanced on the end of her nose.

"An eight-letter word for *potentate*," Mother says.

"Monarch?" Lecia says. With her rat-tail brush, she sections off a parcel of hair on her crown and slaps some more Dep on it before wrapping the ends around a brush roller.

"That's seven letters, numb nuts," I say.

When I open the end table drawer for matches, the sight of all those match packs from a hundred different places sends the hurt I feel over missing Clarice through me like a spear. We used to play this game where we'd take turns closing our eyes to draw out a pack. Whatever was written there foretold some future with a little interpretive leeway, for most matches advertise jobs you can get making hundreds of dollars a month if only you'll send one dollar to some training school for beauticians or drill-press operators.

I could make bad news out of any such message tonight, and the pack I grab up only says Mobil, like the gas station. There's that horse from my mythology book painted red and with wings on his hooves to fly him across the blank background. I worry a second it's Mobile, Alabama, but then I decide the word augurs well. *Mobile,* I think to myself. *I will be mobile. So be it.*

Mother uses her glasses to shove her hair back and peers at the lamp I'm holding. "That was my mother's," she says.

Lecia says, "She's an oddball, is little Mary Marlene." I let that slide, but she's on a roll. "I've tried," she says, and her face goes all hangdog. "Lord knows, I've tried." She stretches a hank of hair up in the air while she fumbles around for a brush roller big enough. I've been reading this long crazy poem all summer where in the best part a lady stretches out her hair in violin strings, and that's what scoots through my head watching Lecia's hair strung out.

"Every day in every way, I've tried to guide her, to make her a better person. But no. She's way too smart for old Lecia . . ."

Mother turns back to the lantern hanging heavy by my side. "What do you want with that?"

"To read outside."

"For what?"

Then Lecia kicks in again. "Oh woman of mystery," Lecia says, "searching Garfield Road for an honest man."

Mother tells me not to break her mother's antique lamp then wanders out. I tell Lecia right before I leave that she might as well slap wallpaper paste on her head as that crap. The pink rat-tail brush she's holding is so light that when she heaves it against the door I'm slamming behind me, it hardly makes a tick.

At Clarice's, I settle back down in the backyard to wait in her brother's old pigeon cage. He built it from scrap lumber and number-two chicken wire, and after the birds all died or flew off, there it sits.

I light the lantern's wick and put the glass back on, the chimney blackening as the flame laps up. In my *Wonder Woman* comic book, the first great wonder is not how she flings that rope and shinnies up the side of a building and so on, but how she keeps her D-cup boobs from flopping out of the red strapless bra-top she's got on.

Headlights swing across the lawns. The chicken wire's honeycomb lays across my face a second, then peels off. The beams plow into Mary Ferrell's driveway. Mrs. Ferrell opens the car door and stands up wearing her registered nurse uniform. Next to her, the long-limbed Mary Ferrell, who's been riding shotgun, unfolds herself out like a delicate crane. Then from the back, Clarice hops out. And she's saying see you tomorrow and thanks for the ride.

I wait till the Ferrells have gone in the house and Clarice's shoes have hit her daddy's oyster shell drive before I say hey.

"Hey back," she hollers out. She bends over and peers toward the lamplight while I edge out of the pigeon cage. "What're you doing in there?" She crosses the wet lawn right off. "What're you doing with that old-timey lamp?" she wants to know, and in the shadow of her face a smile gets cut like a slivered moon. And because her voice sounds the same as ever, I think I've been wrong all along about her not calling me back on purpose.

"I'm detecting you," I say. Then, "I like your hair." It's cropped short at the neck and jacked up and sprayed into a ball.

"I have to wear a barrette to keep the bangs from falling in my eyes. But it's what all the cheerleaders have."

"Mrs. Torvino do it?" I ask, for Torvino's Castle of Beauty is the only place I know in the county to get a haircut not from a barber.

"Mary Ferrell's mother," she says. I lift up my lamp and say again it looks nice even though I'm thinking to myself, *Mary Ferrell's mother's ass.* For to have Clarice sneak down to the Ferrells' house and let scissors lop off the short flip we both wore all summer is a betrayal of the worst sort.

So I think what a best-friend hogging slut Mary Ferrell has turned into, and the lamp in my hand weighs heavier. But to set it down would somehow leave me feeling even more unarmed. Some fight between Clarice and me has been going on and I've been taking invisible hits. The lantern's heft somehow anchors me to the instant.

Under Clarice's rain slicker she's got a name tag pinned on. And under the name tag is a by-God candy striper's uniform—the red-and-white getup worn by hospital volunteers. "Did you get drafted or something?" I say, for Clarice's becoming a candy striper is a stunner I have no idea how to handle. The lostness of my not even knowing about it freezes me where I stand. The night's cooling off. From the Gulf, I hear a far-off rumble of thunder—the devil's bowling pins, some people say. Clarice and I stand in the smell of rain coming like a pair of gunfighters.

Finally she pulls her raincoat across her front to cover her uniform and name tag all up. "I knew you'd be this way about it."

"Which way?"

"The way you're being!" She makes a little snort. "The way you just *are.* You're that way about everything."

Right away I start scrambling around my skull to defend the way I'm being. Which I don't even know how it is. I say, "Everybody is the way they are. About everything. That isn't breaking any law."

"You act like you're smarter than everybody. Like you're so smart and everything anybody likes is stupid."

I can't quite root out the truth in this, but I sense some ghost of it hovering. "Like what? Come up with one for instance," I say.

She shifts from foot to foot. "I gotta go," she says.

"C'mon," I say, in what I hope sounds upbeat. "What way am I being?" I set down the hurricane lamp and rub at my fingers where the wire handle cut into it. "I really want to know. If you can't tell me, who can?"

"You make fun of everything," she says.

"Oh and you don't," I say. I sound sarcastic, but my throat's actually tightening up. She looks back at her house like why doesn't somebody come out and rescue her from this talk.

"Not like you," she says. She chews her lower lip a minute. "You make fun of church," she finally says.

"When did I make fun of church?"

"You said the pope dresses like a girl. Plus you said kneeling in mass means that I worship dolls."

"I said Carol Sharp said her daddy said that. And it wasn't dolls. It was graven idols." I can feel my voice get loud. Still, my voice just foghorns out of me all loud, "Kneel. Don't kneel. Hell it's a free country. Suit your own damn self." The silence I'd been yelling into seems made of tin. The air keeps ringing when I quit. "And the pope does dress like a girl," I add.

"And when I want to play secretary you say—" She shakes her hand in the air as if at some unseen creature she could gin up and wave away at once. It hits me that she's been chewing on this cud a for some time. Worse, she's even been something like scared to bring it up.

"I played secretary the last time you came over chrissakes!"

"Will you just shut up and listen."

"I liked playing secretary—!" Actually, I didn't like it. But I memorized the typewriter keyboard because I figured it might help me if I couldn't be a poet and had to be a newspaper woman. "—Didn't I learn to write my name in shorthand?"

"Shut up!" she hollers, then cranes around to look at the house, but they must have the air conditioners cranked on high. I pick up the lantern which sends up corkscrewing smoke.

"Okay," I say. The word tastes like something scorched in my mouth. "All right," I say.

She cocks her hip, then bends back her index finger in an arc to make a point. "You know I'm in the secretary program at school but you say, you say"—(she bends her index finger back); "'I want to be a poet'"—(fuck-you finger back); "or 'I want to run a newspaper.'" (ring finger back)—"or 'Who wants to bow and scrape to some ignorant suit-wearing sonofabitch?'"—(pinkie finger so far it seems fixing to snap off).

Suddenly I see her like she's at the wrong end of a tunnel. She's all small and worried, standing in her side yard between the abandoned pigeon cage and empty dog run. Her candy-striped uniform is secondhand from somebody who quit, and she probably spent thirty minutes starch-ironing it. Now all the times I've urged her to go to college or leave this one-horse town—advice that heretofore always seemed good—now such words have a new tilt, for someone's urge to alter you will never feel kindly. There was never any care in my trying to steer her, just mockery of who she was, of what she'll grow up into.

I know for a stone truth that I'm the one who really needs overhauling. If I ever said out loud stuff I think about parallel sentence structure or using a semicolon, everybody would instantly place another demerit in my column.

Now Clarice is fixing to cry herself. Her round brown eyes in the lamplight seem to hold in their lower lids little low-slung half moons of mercury.

Her voice when it next comes at me seems to fly unwatched from some wide, cold Arctic place inside her. "What's so ding-dang wrong with getting your boss coffee?" she wants to know. "It's nice. Or wanting to type fast? It's that or being a nurse, which Moselle Ferrell says is hard on your feet, and we've got terrible feet, in my family." I dimly recall a discussion with her grandfather about something called "hammer toes" and being terrified that after supper he'd take off his shoes to reveal a row of tiny hammers on the ends of his feet.

From nowhere the tears that had been stacking up inside me spill out and run down both cheeks. And when I go to talk, there's a choke in my voice I can't hardly get by. "I was gonna join the junior secretary club next week," I say. Which is a lie. Mother says I want to have a secretary, not be one.

"Join whatever you want. You can't be different than how you are, Mary." Her tears seem to have sucked right back in her head soon as she spotted me crying. She reaches out for my arm, and I jerk it away. The lantern bangs my shin and I say *shit,* and she glances back at the house and shushes me. I dab under my eyelids with the heel of my hand, but my face is streaming like some spigot inside me has opened up full blast. "And you'd hate candy-striping. And I like it. Really. You get to tote flowers to people who're glad to see you, and you can take pulses and temperatures."

"I'm just afraid you'll—" I want to shore up my trying to get her to go to college instead of secretarial school. "I'm afraid you'll grow up all, all—all limited." I settle on this word as the most washed-out one I can find for what I mean, so as not to piss her off. Instead the word seems to fall on her like a high-fired arrow.

"Limited! Limited! Jenny Raines is right. You really do think you're smarter than everybody else."

That my being smarter than everybody would have fallen into dispute is a shock that shuts off my tears. I feel deep conviction that I *am,* in fact, smarter than everybody—an opinion both my parents have hammered into me my whole life.

"My daddy's calling me home," she says and turns on her heel.

I just stand there mute as a stump. I should say something. *I'm sorry* even flits through my head, though I'd never say it. Clarice hauls open the side door and disappears.

I don't feel like crying when I walk home. Somehow all the crying has been sucked out of me. The lamp at my side releases black soot from its round chimney as if from some hole in the earth. I think hell's caverns must have that kerosene smell.

Back home, there's only the kitchen light on and the dull hum of TV in my parents' room. I get into bed without brushing my teeth or washing the creosote off my feet. For a few minutes, I try crying, but nothing comes out.

PART **THREE** * **Limbo**

When the mind swings by a grass-blade
an ant's forefoot shall save you.

—Ezra Pound *Canto LXXXIII*

Chapter Eight

ONLY WHEN YOU READ A STORY in your eighth-grade English book about a minister who insists on watching the world through a black veil do you realize that a vague exhaust has come to cast a pall over everything you see.

Your limbs might be filled with sand or lead pellets. You are heavy, heavy, though you rarely eat. Lecia calls you the original buttless female. Mother says she wishes she could give you ten pounds. Daddy just stands each night holding out your steamy supper plate with its three neat compartments so the liquor from the greens doesn't invade the black-eyed peas and soak into the cornbread, saying Chrissake eat.

At night you lie on your stomach in bed copying poems in script so elaborate the words can actually vanish to let the shapes of letters take over. They become stick-figured birds perched on a blue wire, or a ballet troupe at the barre. Part of you longs for such orders. Another part feels your every move's already been plotted out, and you're only bumbling along like a chess piece.

You're not crazy exactly. No bugaboos or bogeymen appear unbidden. Nonetheless, your thinking is muddy. You feel some key moment went past that you're now powerless to recover.

Maybe it started when you saw John Cleary stepping down from the county fair carousel holding hands with a buxom black-haired girl. You thought, she's probably got the face of an ape. But when he tucked her hair behind her ear, it showed the blue-eyed countenance of young Liz Taylor in *National Velvet.* Lord, she wins by a country mile, you thought.

Not that you dwell on it. You've mostly blotted from thought the old dream of John Cleary and also Clarice's absence. Your family's remoteness likewise is pro forma, each of them a far-off blur.

But the simplest letdown can leave your normally disaffected face scorched by tears. In eighth grade it's a stupid athletic prize you met the criteria for but failed to receive in schoolwide assembly. Your striving for that—weeks of arduous wind sprints that left you limping—is your only real effort that year. The prize means nothing, really, but it's not that easy to win, though Lecia took it in seventh grade easy—a fact she'll remind you and anyone else of with no prompting.

Thus junior high seems a series of mishaps that vault you involuntarily from one mudhole to another—each time landing deeper, more remote.

Suddenly it's ninth grade. You're standing before Lead Head Briggs inside the closed door of his office, remembering you'd learned to spell the word principal from a book that said, The principal is your *pal.* Briggs has gone through the formality of opening his mail while you wait. He performs this same drill for anyone sent to his office more than once—slitting the sides of envelopes with a silver letter opener, blowing inside to make it easy to draw out the pages. He hopes the interval will unnerve you, as if he could punk you any worse. You're standing there waiting to be expelled for questioning the validity of studying algebra one more year.

Now he's taking his Ben Franklin glasses from the edge of his nose. Under his gray crew cut above one ear, you can see the old scar where they put the plate in his head. He's telling you that you'll need math more than you know.

Actually, you say, I intend to be a poet, sir.

A what? he says.

A poet, you say. Down the hall, an electric typewriter start its machine gun then halts. He seems to wait till the carriage zings its return and the hammering starts up again.

Then he says, How's that exactly?

Somebody who writes poems.

Well I know that, but how do you plan to get folks to pay you for it?

This stumps you a minute. Finally, you say, I'll sell my books. Before him on the wide desk there's a gold football mounted, gold pens at a slant in a granite holder. Behind his bristly head are the framed pictures of football teams past.

How much you think that'll make you? he says.

Come again, sir?

Let me put it to you another way, he finally says. How many books of poetry do you think the average American buys?

You see where he's going, and you jack up the number you give him. In my house? Maybe thirty or forty, you say.

And your house is usual, he says.

There's the low simmer of worry now, for no one would call your house usual. When you eke out your *yes,* your throat tightens on the word.

I don't think your house is usual, Miss Karr. (He hisses the Miss.) Maybe there's one book of poems inside every two houses, he says. Or to be generous, let's go on and say a book of poems in every house.

You're speechless a second. You want to say he's being unfair. But you can't quite locate the unfairness of it. He knows you can't outright say that people in Leechfield are boneheads and don't really constitute your audience (something that you'll grow up to believe untrue). That would implicate him and constitute insult. You peel the bottom of one sweaty thigh up from where its stuck to the chair naugahyde and tug down your skirt.

He says, So, that'll be your book, then. That single book, the one every family buys. That'll be your book instead of—oh let's say, Mr. Longfellow. The sudden reference sends the opening lines of "Hiawatha" jogging through your head on its dogged, pentameter-paced horse. He's not the first person to suggest that poets don't earn much, but your parents never give that concern the slightest credence. "Shit, you can do whatever you feel like, Pokey," Daddy would say (an endorsement vague enough to have begun fading in power), while your mother would claim those idiots wouldn't know poetry from piss ants.

Briggs waves his hand saying, Let's drop the poet thing. Get back to everything that's right with math. It's true you don't need math to write poetry. But any other task you undertake will require a thorough grounding in mathematics. Especially in the space age.

This stupefies you. You aren't even being a smartass when you say, Like what?

This is the very cue he's been waiting for. He says, You'll need math to measure out your recipes. Say your husband needs you to have a dinner party. You're gonna have to double or triple what it says in your cookbook. You'll have to multiply all those parts, not just three eggs or four cups, either. Lots of halves and thirds. There's your math! (He points his index finger down at his calendar and stabs it so hard you peer over to see if there was some bug he's smashing. There isn't.)

You know better than to invite him into the various lives you've constructed for yourself—an apartment in New York, a beachcomber's hut, a Victorian mansion surrounded by a mazelike garden. Your own silence nudges you to the edge of tears. To speak would be to release them.

His final sentence to you, which he delivers in his doorway before the entire office staff, is as follows: I assure you. Without math, you'll wind up being no more than a common prostitute. (Later you'll find out this *common prostitute* line was repeated for most girls, while boys got *common criminal.*)

Or it's later that same year. You've walked home from school with Wally Ray Gans every single day this week, hoping he'll ask you to the

Demolay hayride, which he mentions is this Friday. (Demolay is the boy's branch of the Masons.) Wally Ray is a short girl's John Cleary—blond and blue-eyed—only shy, the last one to raise his hand in class, even if he has the answers first. You decide he is, in Mother's parlance, soulful. He says maybe he'll call you about the hayride, and you're convinced that you stand on the brink of your very first date.

The call comes while you're lurking on the porch in hopes Wally Ray might amble by. So Lecia, who's tethered within hovering distance of the phone by the expected calls of her own suitors, intercepts it, and quickly accepts for you in order to hustle the caller off the line. When you come in about six all sweaty and disconsolate, having given up hope of seeing Wally Ray, she says that your little boyfriend called, and he'll be here at seven.

Yet once you swing open the knocked-on door at precisely two minutes till seven, you do not find the smiling, well ordered face of Wally Ray Gans. In one of fate's crueler bait-and-switches, the porch frames none other than Mortimer G. Beauregard—a Mormon boy from Mississippi who grins so hard at the sight of you that you have to stop yourself from recoiling. Mortimer says your sister said you'd be ready and don't you clean up nice.

Mortimer is renowned for his religious zeal and the shortness of his pegged pants when droopy bell bottoms are the fashion. His socks are white, his heavy shoes spit-shined. His shirt collar is starched so stiff that his pencil neck seems to snake around inside its vast circumference.

You are driven to the hayride by Mortimer's brother, in a car with flattened cardboard boxes covering rust holes in the floor. But before you can step out of said car on Mortimer's arm, there's a stroke of luck, what you later think of as divine intervention: a thunderstorm blows in from the Gulf to blacken the sky and threaten tornadoes, thus canceling the hayride. Mortimer and his brother trot back from the lodge to the car where you've slouched low in the backseat and are clinging to the armrest. The brother says it's called off, and Mortimer slides in next to you actually saying shucks then snapping his fingers.

You perk up immensely. On the road back to your house, you feel you've been unhooked from the taut line that would have reeled you into social oblivion with Mortimer. You chatter with a level of cheer that only seems to jack up his misery.

But your relief is countered by Mortimer's disappointment. By the time you've hit the home driveway, he looks so disappointed, so blotchy skinned under the dome light of his brother's Dodge Dart—with his hair wet-combed hard to one side like a sad little rooster—that you hear yourself inviting him in for a Coke.

Thus he becomes your first date. His pants end high on his white shins, and he leans forward, talking with the earnest ardor of a desperate vacuum-cleaner salesman. For most of the evening he is bartering for the lost state of your non-Mormon soul. (You don't have the heart to tell him you've never been baptized and are, in effect, a non-Christian heathen, a wanna-be Presbyterian Buddhist.) He explains why, in his church, even heaven is segregated: because coloreds wouldn't *want* to be in our heaven—this despite the fact that he claims it's a *higher* heaven, by which he means closer to God and Jesus.

By ten o'clock, whatever pity you felt for Mortimer has drained away to blunt loathing. He stands in your doorway, making his final pitch for you to come work at the Mormon peanut butter factory next weekend. Despite the fact that no one ever asks you anywhere, and you frequently tell your sister you'd go to a dogfight to get out of the house, you say no and no and no thank you to Mortimer, all the while longing for the door to swing forever shut on him. Your final handshake is quick enough to resemble (in memory if not fact) the drawing of a pistol.

On Monday you find a copy of *The Joseph Smith Legacy* atop your locker. Underneath it, there's a carefully folded note that holds the following poem, typed and unsigned, either written for you or for some unnamed other:

I saw you on your horse today
your eyes like eggs your hair like hay.

When you enter speech class later, Mortimer's foghorn voice shouts out—with the revved-up glee of a disc jockey—what a great time he had on your date. Of course the word *date* doesn't repeat itself in the air in shimmering neon magnifying—*date Date DATE*—all the way to the green horizon. Of course the entire room doesn't wheel in unison to gape at you frozen in the doorway. You can't deny Mortimer's claim, nor explain the trickery of it without drawing even more attention to the subject. But the dry-ice chill you emanate finally reaches him, and he shrinks back into silence like a leech on whom salt has been thrown.

Then it's summer. Your mother's taken her degree with honors and has just finished teaching art in a local junior high. Summer should bring her relief, time to knock off a few art history classes toward the Ph.D. she's angling for. But she slides into it edgy. The phonograph endlessly seems to spin the dog-whipped blues of Big Brother and the Holding Company. While Lecia cleans the house for the brief entry and exit of her next suitor, whom Mother will invariably mock for his simplemindedness, the young Janis Joplin, who's from nearby Port Arthur, rasps out:

> *I'm just like a turtle, baby,*
> *Hiding underneath my horny shell. . . .*

One weekend your daddy takes off on a fishing trip, and it's that night Mother chooses to vanish again. No note rests on the plywood table. No single one of her teacher or college friends—at least among those whose phone numbers you can drum up—seems to have crossed her path. So the evening unfolds in a series of internal cliff faces you suddenly plunge over.

No matter how often she takes off like this, you never get used to it. One minute, you're settling before the TV eating pears from a can and watching *Laugh-In;* in the next instant, the fact of her absence releases a blast of flame inside you, leaving the TV characters mouthing their lines without sound. You give up and turn off the set, sit in worry until Lecia comes home from her date.

She mocks your anxiety, but while both of you sit by the phone, cross-legged and reading, she chews her already gnawed-at cuticles down to the bloody quick. At midnight, you both set out in Daddy's green truck on the asphalt roads that meander through the county, Lecia navigating past every gin mill or liquor store in dim hope of sighting your mother's car.

Back home, the two of you sit out under the dripping chinaberry in webbed lounge chairs for the better part of the night. You're waiting for the phone to ring or Mother's car to rumble up. Because your mind has looped through the gamut of minor disasters that might befall your mother, and because all that's left are tragedies that involve swirling police lights, you bicker.

The subject is whose misbehavior might have run Mother off this time. Lecia claims your sullen misery would, in her parlance, drive Jesus Christ to drink soapy water. You maintain that Lecia's illiterate boyfriend worried Mother about her prospects as a grandmother—specifically whether such children might be born with fully opposable thumbs or not. You trade shots like this back and forth. Every now and then a car's rushing proximity will silence you, then slide away, dragging that same silence behind it.

The next morning at dawn, Lecia snaps up the blaring phone midring. Turns out Mother's at the Holiday Inn with a hangover so severe she can't drive, so can Lecia pick her up in the truck Daddy left behind and hell with it we'll get the car later. Whether Mother specifically suggests that you be left behind or Lecia decides it, when the truck backs out, you suddenly feel like a kid looking up a treehouse rope as it gets drawn inside a plywood door.

Into this garage the truck eventually appears huffing. Lecia runs around to heave open the door on Mother's side. It's rusty enough to give a deep sea-monster sort of moan. Then Mother is spilling out of it, weak-legged as a colt, and Lecia is there to catch her.

Mother lies in bed weeping silently. Every now and then some wave inside her surges up, and she'll escalate to hacking sobs. Meanwhile, Lecia bustles around with the crisp certainty of a field nurse. How does she know what remedies to dispense? A dish towel of ice for Mother's forehead. A glass of tepid ginger ale for her stomach. A pillowcase warm from the dryer. Such gifts never occur to you. You watch Lecia minister till Mother finally sleeps, coiled on her side in that massive bed like a fossil you'd find hardened in a dry riverbed.

Lecia says only that the hotel room was a mess. Over the course of hours, she details that—Mother had thrown up down the hall and on the bathroom floor and along the side of the car. She'd lost her credit card somewhere, and Lecia had to pay for the room with her own money plus change she scrounged from the bottom of Mother's purse and the floor of the car.

It's dusk when Mother's eyes open. Her hands tremble for a cigarette you help her light. She says the cigarette is lifesaving. She says yes to Lecia's offer of chicken soup.

But before the can opener has hummed around the can's circumference while you watch, Mother has bolted to the bathroom. Lecia tests the knob to find it locked. Only after a long string of silence does Mother answer. She claims to have your daddy's Colt .45, with which she plans to kill herself.

And that's the tableau you're held in while the sun falls: Lecia in the hall, her spine stiff as a drill sergeant's though her voice speaking to the closed door is reasonable and plaintive at once. She cajoles Mother while you stay shushed into silence. But you scribble notes to your sister—perhaps your first ever true action in the face of Mother's locking herself away. *Let's call the law!* Or *Let's go around the house and bust out the window!* Lecia waves these away. Every now and then the conversation stalls. Then the stillness emanating from the locked door becomes massive. It can set the air in the linoleum hallway aripple.

By the time the moon has risen halfway up the sky, the injustice of the whole situation suddenly strikes you. Before you know it, you're shouting down the hall at the locked door where Lecia stands as if to block your words—*Go on and do it, goddamn it. I'm sick of waiting. Just shoot yourself then if you've got the guts—*

Lecia tries to shush you and wave you back. Finally she shoves you down the hall, saying just go somewhere else if you can't handle it. Once the cruelty of what you've shouted floods you with its countercurrent, you run to your room and fling your body down on the bed, pull the pillow over your humming head, and wait for the gunshot that doesn't come and doesn't come. Then you're crying hard, not for your mother or Lecia or your poor daddy, who's probably half-drunk and innocently frying bass under the stars with his pals. No you're crying for yourself. This eventually plunges you into the stonelike sleep born of unrelieved self-pity.

Just before dawn, you hear a pinging, chipping noise—stone against stone, maybe, or metal against stone. It's rhythmic, too slow to sound purposeful, but loud enough and near enough to wake you through the low, dinosaur-like drone of the air conditioner.

On the back porch, your bare feet are cold. Lecia sits on the top step with her back to you. She's wearing somebody's overgrown football jersey. She bends over so far her chin rests nearly on her knee.

You finally ask what's this dogshit racket out here.

Just jick-jacking around, Lecia says. When you lean over her shoulder, you can see she's holding a ballpeen hammer, chopping the edges off the step bricks with it.

Daddy sees this, he's gonna tear you a new asshole, you say. Lecia doesn't even register this, just finds another sharp edge of brick to start shearing off. The air is still. The fog in the yard seems to muffle all sound, but for Lecia's sharp *chick* (pause) *chink chink*. In the washhouse, the dryer is tumbling its racket. You tell her she's gone stark staring nuts. He's gonna know she did this. And what good's it do, just piss him off is all, after Mother getting all drunkedy-ass?

I don't give a shit what he thinks, Lecia says.

In the yard next door, somebody is heaving sacks of something heavy in Mr. Lawrence's truck bed, powdered concrete maybe, or sand or lime. If it's Aaron—the black carpenter—and if Daddy were here, they'd soon meet out back by the garbage cans to pass a pint bottle back and forth across chain link.

Lecia glances at you full face a minute. She must have rubbed her eyes in her sleep, for last night's mascara makes dark rings around each one. She says, These people don't have any sense, Mary. Hasn't that dawned on you? Not the sense God gave a goat.

What are you talking about? you ask.

Already it's hot. You watch the Siamese roll on the warm patio bricks.

Lecia turns back to you, borderline rankled. She says, It hasn't even dawned on you yet, has it? In that instant, your colossal sister looks so small—her brown body bent in on itself that way—you almost believe you could gather her whole in your arms like a puppy. But she's brushed you aside every way she knows.

You mean Mother and Daddy? you finally say. In the chinaberry tree, a bird whistles a two-syllable tune that sounds like a question, *Bob White? Bob White?*

Lecia says, Neither one of them has a lick of sense. Sooner you figure that out, the better off you'll be. I don't listen to shit from either one.

Then it's later that same summer. No long episodes from that dull time exist. There are no lost plots, or tangled dramas. There are only brief snippets of memory, outtakes, captured instants where your sagging performance becomes plain. You remember the last report card you got saying you'd missed forty-seven days of school. Another where you got a D in art. You remember lying stretched out in a green canvas hammock, rocking yourself with a broom handle on a blistering day with the distant noise of kids splashing at the town pool and a ragged paperback of *Great Expectations* open to the same page all afternoon. You have no attention for novels or even stories anymore, just poems.

Oh you are manufacturing an arena of darkness in your sullen self. Poems that romance suicide are accruing in your head like so much trial evidence. Maybe it was the Keats—"Darkling, I listen, for a long while/ I have been half in love with easeful death . . ."—that got you first. You memorize it, along with Hamlet's hand-wringing suicide speech and more than a few nasty bits by Sylvia Plath. You read Camus's play *Caligula* where the mad emperor so torments his senators that they wind up stabbing him in the face while he screams, "I'm still alive." On the unused black upright, you teach yourself to read music—one note at a time—solely in order to play the same morbid Chopin prelude over and over till everyone in the house threatens to move out unless you stop.

You are waving hope off like a stinging wasp.

You sit on your bedroom floor and unshelf another well-thumbed novel. A brilliant girl your age in a mental institution invents a magical world of gods and monsters. Then she keeps opening her veins the long way. You know you could never cut yourself. You can't even stick your finger with a pin, much less take up a razor. Still there's some seduction to the idea, a silky feel that it draws over you.

You spend a whole night writing an elaborate suicide note, in which you list every minor gripe and oversight. Lecia, you shouldn't have hit me over that chicken pot pie. Clarice, I was a good pal to you, and you were a turd. John Cleary, no grinning and large-breasted pompom shaker could reveal the high-minded wisdoms I truck in. And the givers of athletic prizes. And the designers of children's shoes. Before long, you've worked up to your parents, who are blind to the spit you feel yourself to be writhing on. Just thinking how bad they'll feel reading this note makes you cry, but you keep writing, letting big tears splash the page so they'll know how bad you felt.

Anacin from a brand new bottle get counted out till you reach one hundred—"one hundred bitter wishes," the poet Craig Raine will write someday of another girl.

Thus readied, you step into this puddle of dress—the closet's only black one—and pull it over your legs and up waist high. It's satin-back crepe and slides over your skin like water, but too small so you have to struggle to get the zipper up. It's short enough to pass for a shirt, and your hands hang down too long from the sleeves like a chimp's.

You wash the pills down three and four at a time, but only get as far as ten or twelve before the melted pill taste is too bitter to stand. So you mash some with the spoon back, mix the powder in orange juice, hold your nose. Still the bitterness starts a gag. And since discomfort is not now (nor ever will be) your long suit (and since it's less death than family attention you crave), you decide you've swallowed enough, skinny as you are.

Having cried yourself quiet, you now lie down in the bed and cross hands over your chest and arrange the skirt so your underpants aren't gaping out at everybody. In this pose, you wait to die.

Then comes the first sliver of fear, a sharp and shining itch of it from the prospect of snuffing out. If you don't exist, who will impart your tremendous insights, write the great poems you design in your head that never see paper? You lie there and listen to the neighbor dog yip-yipping, cars idling by.

Mr. Lawrence is digging in the side yard. He shouts to his wife, *This deep enough?* And she says deeper, it's rose bushes. The blade crunches through the wet ground, and the spadeful of dirt and rocks hits the wheelbarrow. You want to fling open your window and shout, Show some respect! I'm killing myself here. But they keep remarking on color and fullness of bloom.

Socrates never had this kind of insignificant crap to listen to after he took the hemlock. Somehow when he described the cold inching up his shins, it was sadder. But then Socrates had Crito leaning over him weeping, saying, *Don't you have something more to tell us?* Good old Crito. Where is he when you need him? You have only the disinterested gaze of that cross-eyed Siamese and the nerve-wracking chatter of morons. You're nowhere near dead—just wicked queasy, like that time deep sea fishing—when the sprinkler gets turned on so fake rain slaps your window at stunned intervals.

You pad through the house looking for an audience. Then it's through blazing heat to the studio where—peering in the window—you see that Mother's constructed a huge giraffe of papier-mâché for some play at her school. How can that garish yellow contraption find a home in this pit when you can't? It's an indignity even to look at.

By the time your mother walks in less than an hour later, you're kneeling on the cold floor tiles emptying the emptiness from your stomach into the small white emptiness of the wastebasket in your room. She helps you to the bathroom, dampens a washcloth to drape around your neck. You poor little duck she says, rubbing your back. You must have eaten something bad, she says. I'm throwing that old potato salad out, she says, and those shrimp your daddy brought home.

Bent over, sick and ashamed, you feel like the worst sort of fool.

When the heaves pass, Mother takes your angular self onto her lap in the ebony rocker. Your feet hang over the arms on one side. Poor poor you, she says. Your head lolls over her shoulder, your nose near the source of the Shalimar cloud that drifts around her—a smell of rose attar in oil. She says, You're never too big to rock, but you'll appreciate it, I know, if I leave off singing to you. Once when you wake up she asks what are you doing in that old dress, and you say seeing if it fits. And she says, That would be a negatory.

Still later, she strips you out of it and jams your arms in a cotton nightgown you wriggle on. Thus sheathed you lie on the couch, your head pillowed nearby while she combs your hair with her fingers.

When Daddy comes in, he carries you to bed. Is there anything you feel like you could eat, Pokey? Anything at all?

All you can imagine putting in your mouth is a cold plum, one with really tight skin on the outside but gum-shocking sweetness inside. And he and Mother discuss where he might find some this late in the season. Mother says hell I don't know. Further north, I'd guess.

The next morning, you wake up in your bed and sit up. Mother says, Pete, I think she's up. He hollers in, You ready for breakfast, Pokey. Then he comes in grinning, still in his work clothes from the night before. He's holding a farm bushel. The plums he empties onto the bed river toward you through folds in the quilt. If you stacked them up, they'd fill the deepest bin at the Piggly Wiggly.

Damned if I didn't get the urge to drive to Arkansas last night, he says.

Your mother stands behind him saying he's pure USDA crazy.

Fort Smith, Arkansas. Found a roadside stand out there with a feller selling plums. And I says, Buddy, I got a little girl sick back in Texas. She's got a hanker for plums and ain't nothing else gonna do.

Through the window you see the Lawrences' new rosebush, its base of burlap sticking out of the fresh red dirt. Its white buds are tight-clenched knots. But it's when you sink your teeth into the plum that you make a promise. The skin is still warm from riding in the sun in Daddy's truck, and the nectar runs down your chin.

And you snap out of it. Or are snapped out of it. Never again will you lay a hand against yourself, not so long as there are plums to eat and somebody—anybody—who gives enough of a damn to haul them to you. So long as you bear the least nibblet of love for any other creature in this dark world, though in love portions are never stingy. There are no smidgens or pinches, only rolling abundance. That's how you acquire the resolution for survival that the coming years are about to demand. You don't earn it. It's given.

PART **FOUR** * **High**

"Was it you that killed me, or did I kill you?" Abel answered. "I don't remember anymore; here we are, together, like before."

"Now I know that you have truly forgiven me," Cain said, "because forgetting is forgiving. I, too, will try to forget."

—Jorge Luis Borges *Legend*
Translated by Andrew Hurley

Those who live here are chained; those who leave must return.

—Curse of the Karankawa chief on the Gulf Coast region before Jean Lafitte's invading pirates chopped off his head and flung it into the waves

Chapter Nine

IF THERE WAS ANY PLACE WORTHY of escape in the seventies, it was Leechfield with its mind-crushing atmosphere of sameness. Sitting in your room, you often felt the town spread out around you as inescapable as the stench it gave off. Sometimes you even fancied you could hear the traffic light over deserted Main Street blink. Time lagged mule-like in muddy traces. You had to beat it and cajole it before it plodded forward even a few steps and the earth swung you back to another tarnished sunrise.

With drugs you could endure it. Question mark. Maybe. *Better living through chemistry* was one pervasive (if unintentionally ironic) company slogan. That first year of high school would be your last as a pharmaceutical virgin.

Sure you were told that drugs cut a coiled and downward swerving path to degradation if not death. That was part of their allure. In the fifties, teenagers had fought the boredom of this place with games of chicken in souped-up cars. Your sister's first steady had been an older hood with a sinister slouch who liked to face off against other drivers

Saturday nights, revving up and peeling out toward a head-on crash till the other driver (he always claimed it was the other guy) lost nerve and swerved. The daredevilry of your generation's chemical adventures differed from this not one whit. The only trick was to cut your wheel at the right instant. To ride as far out as you could before being forced out of the game. Sure one alternative was your skull flying through a windshield like a battering ram. That was part of the thrill.

So for your first week of high school, a drug film is scheduled, and you file down the auditorium slope with this new herd hoping solely to blend in. And you do, sort of. The white daisies on your dress are not incongruous with the sea of floral patterns bobbing around you, though its black background makes it one of the darker frocks amid the sizzling oranges and Day-Glo pinks. While you've hemmed this dress exactly three inches above your knobby knee—dress-code perfect—the white threads of that quick basting will draw comment all day from home-economics masters (whom you secretly call the home-ickies).

The drug film seems pointless in a school so stalled in the 1950s. You don't even know anybody who smokes pot, doubt it even exists in this county. The film says marijuana resembles dried oregano and smells like burning garbage, though you're fairly sure the garbage part was just made up to shoo kids off it. School films are always doing that, saying beer tasted like cow urine, or boys you sleep with won't call again. (In fact, the opposite proves true: the girls who put out—scags and skanks in local parlance—are swarmed on.)

The girl in green paisley next to you is—with regard to pot—a tight-lipped Baptist-type. She announces with loud authority that everybody's brother in Vietnam smokes marijuana. She heard it from Walter Cronkite.

Some cowgirl behind her says, Bullshit, my brother didn't. She's one of those low to the ground, hillbilly-looking girls who never says much, but who manages to convey the physical seriousness of people who do field work and therefore aren't worth messing with.

Green Paisley says, There was a TV news thing last Sunday that said—

Hillbilly says, TV's big hairy ass. My brother died a Christian, you sack of steaming horseshit.

You list forward and away from the squabble. Part of you wants to scream at both girls it's not heroin, for chrissake, my own mother smoked it in a big-deal jazz club in New York and didn't wind up robbing liquor stores at gunpoint for it. The rest of you wonders who else's mother in this auditorium would brag about getting high in such a kittenish tone. Or ask if you knew where she might get any. Maybe Jane Maculroy's mother. But she also screws a red lightbulb out front of their trailer on Saturday night and is said to have accepted from one trucker for her favors a pallet of canned hams.

The film ends by telling you about LSD and the schizophrenia it induces. On the screen, a cartoon beatnik is balanced on the ledge of a high-rise for a suicide dive. This makes you think, hell we don't even have a building tall enough to jump off—somebody's ranch house or carport wouldn't sprain an ankle, much less kill you. Maybe a little brother's tree fort would work. The beatnik is holding his face in a scream while the zipping cars below him mutate into scorpions and spiders and all variety of insect. They don't show the splat at the bottom, of course. Which is typical. Only the cartoon smoke of sudden falling suggests he'd been there at all.

That was one message—Drugs will kill you. On the other hand, lots of parents stayed medicated out of their gourds on perfectly legal substances. Maybe the county's few martini mixers and country-club pill heads could blame stock prices or work stress. But such luxurious complaints were denied the average refinery worker, who also couldn't let slip the soul-nagging brutalities he brought back from World War II or Korea. Nor did these guys often bitch about the innate hideousness of their jobs—waiting at the massive gate in a long line of more or less identically chugging trucks to reach the time clock's vacant face—punch in, punch out. It was a life of meat sandwiches, and the shift whistle screamed to end it.

The long repetitive hours were punctuated by panicked frenzies of back-wrenching labor that could turn lethal. There was a famous anecdote about a pit of waste chemicals somebody forgot to fence off and into which a new guy fell, only to be fished out a skeleton. Maybe true, maybe not. Still, somebody's dad or uncle or cousin was always falling off a tower or getting scalded by pressurized steam. Most people had a grisly story about visiting a neighbor or relative in Galveston's famous burn unit. Or every few years, some guy would wrench open the wrong valve and blammo. Vapor. Him and everybody in the vicinity. The paper once ran a photo of a metal ladder that had been welded to a tank that blew. On rungs going down, at exact intervals, four pairs of steel-toed work shoes were melted in place. These facts told a man exactly what his life was worth.

Such earnings were sufficiently high to make a man of your dad's generation and social stripe talk big in a bar. His father had been a logger who trucked very little in hard currency, with earnings that mostly vanished into script at the company store. Other locals were born to hardscrabble sharecroppers or shrimpers or seamen. A union salary paid a mortgage and doctored the kids and kept two cars mostly running. If you chipped in with buddies, you could buy a place down on Village Creek, or a fishing trailer, or a bass boat with an Evinrude motor. For your dad's generation, these undreamed of luxuries doomed them to don hard hats. Day in, day out, as your daddy used to say. No time off for good behavior. (His gold retirement pin would document forty-two years' service: four diamond chips and two ruby—none bigger than a roach's eye.)

Result? Step into the VFW at eight in the morning, and there on the red diner stools were dads stopping off after graveyard to throw back a quick bourbon. Or two or four. (Not all of them, of course. It was a dry county, and there were loads of teetotalers.) Drinking a few bumps could ease a fellow to sleep even with the goddamn ingrate kids slamming doors and blaring the TV to bust your ears.

Plus the average home medicine cabinet held a virtual army of pills, a wanna-be drug addict's cornucopia. Valium was common, at least one type of sleeping pill. (Your mother had two or three varieties and in variable strengths.) Diet pills could perk up the basic hungover or low-level-miserable housewife, then power her through the daylight jitters till she could mix a blender drink at five. Speed didn't hurt a guy pulling a double shift either. The milder doses of Ritalin snitched from various hyperactive little brothers were the first tablets you saw crushed up with a hammer and snorted.

If your dad had a bad back or your brother played football, faux opiates could be pilfered—the fat white pills with numbers carved in the chalky surface—one through four. Refills aplenty.

Small irony that many of your friends' names would someday be carved in almost the same blocky typeface on a whole scattered flock of tombstones in Greenlawn Cemetery. But all that came later.

That fall, you enter the glossy halls of high school unsullied by any chemical other than the fluoride everybody guzzled with the drinking water. You're not yet looking to drugs for rescue. You're still expecting to transform magically into one of those chipper, well dressed girls whose name-box on student ballots is automatically checked, to open the yearbook and find your tiara-wearing self in full-page color next to John Cleary. But the instructions for such exalted status are vague and seem only to drift to you in negative form—things NOT to do. Some linger in fragments for years. DON'T:

* Wise off bad enough to get sent to the principal or swear in public (girls only).

* Give any evidence of knowledge concerning bodily functions or fluids (includes everything from the obvious ejaculate down to nose-blowing during a head cold).

* Collapse in tears in a public place even if your dog's been run over, or you got your period on the back of your dress and everybody says well gee, who wouldn't cry, it's okay, let it out.

* Hit anybody unless you can fake it's accidental (i.e. kidney-kicking somebody in a pushball pileup).

* Linger too long saying hi to somebody who might be overencouraged by your lingering to buddy-up to you. (Remember Mortimer G. Beauregard.)

* Wear two kinds of plaid, red on Thursday (means you're queer), anything you can't feature a cheerleader wearing. Wear the same thing twice in one week (stockings excepted).

But first and foremost you have to restrain yourself from displaying the reckless ardor of the unloved toward those strongly disinclined to love you back. These standards seem virtually ingrained into the exalted few, but demand conscious effort and attention from your ilk.

Basically, you're hoping to manufacture a whole new bearing or being, some method of maneuvering along the hallways that will result in less vigorous psycho-social butt-whippings than those endured in junior high.

Every morning, the rubber-edged bus doors slap together in a kind of hermetic seal that undoes itself at school, unveiling without ceremony whatever persona you've cobbled together for the moment (or day, or week—some lasted longer than others). One day you wear burgundy velvet, try a stripe of liner along your lids, and seek to project the deeply tranquilized mystery of *Vogue* models. Their disaffection seems the ultimate armor for their frail, praying-mantis bodies. Another day, you try to master the head-ducking shyness of those clean-faced, freckle-spattered blonds in the Clearasil ads, those whom boys patiently leave messages for or wait for answers from. (At college you actually meet one of these models, who suffers a psychotic break sophomore year, thus proving to you the strain of bearing such scrubbed innocence through the world each day.) People who knew you translated this pose as sulled up or pouting rather than shy.

Still, a few triumphs start to ease you into social slots that just didn't exist in junior high. You win a district journalism prize for a piece in the school paper. You run track, albeit too slowly for varsity, but you're coming along.

That spring, you "try out" for—and win a slot in—the exclusive drill team famous for high kicks, a tight clique few sophomores (especially from your neighborhood) ever "made" and whose membership could have hoisted your narrow-assed self high up in the football-crazed hierarchy of that school. Clarice, who was a better dancer and a higher kicker, never got in but had tears of something like victory in her eyes when she congratulated you as if you'd done it for the whole block. (At some point, the two of you got friendly again without actually hanging out. You still seemed to occupy different realms.)

You manage to doubt you'd won the drill-team spot justly. In a bizarre twist, Lecia, who was a senior, had made away with the ex-boyfriend of the gym teacher supervising the drill team. This former Miss Texas contender was rightly known for sweetness and integrity, and you always sensed she picked you so she wouldn't seem indirectly spiteful toward Lecia.

So these minor victories left a sour aftertaste. They'd come too late or been too hard won. Once you'd made your way inside the circle of weeping drill team members, who swayed side to side with arms around each other's waists to sing their theme song ("My Best to You"), you felt like a fool. You'd spent so much time telling yourself how false such circles were in junior high, to keep the acid drip of disappointment from eating out your liver, that the music was now far too sweet. When the girls sang those cornball lyrics in harmony ("May your dreams come true/ May old Father Time/ Never be unkind . . ."), some snide falsetto repeating the words in your head kept you from feeling particularly tearful. The other girls, so moist-eyed and sweet-faced, belonged here. But you had to disguise your own sense of irony inside these ranks. Already you were scanning for an orange exit sign.

After school every day, sapped by the strain of these various phony performances, you lie on the floor tranquilized by reruns of 1950s sitcoms. How was school today, dear? the ear-bob-wearing mom says over the cookie dough, her hair coiffed into its stiff bubble, her dark lipstick unfeathered into any lip lines, though her chicken-lipped face doesn't offer much surface area for lipstick at all. By contrast, your mother drags home from teaching eighth-grade art—the big reward for her years of study—strips off her clothes and climbs in bed, saying, Don't talk to me, Mary, not yet. I'm on my last nerve.

Chapter Ten

As a public school teacher, your mother espouses dosing the water supply with birth control, or that's how she justifies putting you on the pill before your fifteenth birthday. Even the mention of birth control would send most mothers into a frenzy of either tent-revival hollering or else candle-lighting and novena-saying. But your mother holds loudly forth on any and all pussy-related subjects, with nothing falling too far off limits. You'll be sitting at the kitchen bar wolfing cereal, and she'll say out of the blue, Do you know what a blow job is, honey? Or: I hope you feel comfortable touching yourself down there. It makes you want to bury your head under a pillow for the remainder of any meal.

You go along with the birth control idea because you read somewhere estrogen makes tits bigger and might kick start a girl's period. Your mother books a gynecologist appointment in another city—"so you won't be embarrassed, I could give a shit—." She yanks you out of school and calls in sick to keep you company, which rattles you slightly, like she thinks you're drill team sisters or something.

You've got your learner's permit, and standing in the garage, you lobby to take the wheel. But it's still spitting rain, she says, and after all the water last night those roads are slick as glass. And it's close to Houston so there might be traffic.

While you don't belabor the point, you wonder how Lecia managed to drive alone at thirteen, but road conditions never seem quite right for you so far as your mother is concerned. It's also a damn strange thing that she can look at you and think "too little to drive" and "birth control pills" simultaneously.

Once the yellow wagon pulls onto blacktop, you point out that even though the rain's not that hard anymore, all the other drivers have their lights and wipers on.

Oh baby, she says, I can see through those little dots of rain better than through that whapping blade, and hell, I navigate best by instinct anyway. She's got her window cracked a few inches and is trying to wave the smoke from her Kool out the slot, but it manages to whoosh back in and dive-bomb straight to your eyes with its stinging menthol.

You're slouched down reading and minding your own business when she kicks in the talk you know she's been burning to have and that you'd rather dip snuff than hear. Straight out of the blue.

She says, I've seen too many girls turn up pregnant, Mary. Too many bumpy-headed toddlers come staggering through after school on leash-and-harness deals their mothers hang on the ends of. I swear. Little girls who never got out of junior high, no business making babies.

Mother I can't get pregnant when nobody even asks me out. Not more than that once anyway. I mean—

It only takes once, honey, she says. She's still talking when you start to read signs and notch off the yardage between telephone poles. Live Bait. Boudain! Fat Boys Sausage. Then long stretches of grassland. At a four-way stop on a farm road, you lock eyes with a crusty-looking old pearl-colored bull and are tempted to roll down your window to shout what are you staring at.

You look back at Mother after a long silence, and she says, with no segue whatsoever, If you want to have sex, so be it. Just don't get pregnant.

Mother! you say with all the virginal outrage you can marshal given the amount of time you spend reading Henry Miller in the bathroom. You've never had a steady boyfriend. Nobody's ever even tried to feel you up. Some girl on your volleyball team who talked about making "dry love" with her boyfriend gave the closest firsthand reportage you've received on actual boning. Even Clarice, who's been going steady for more than a year, doesn't do more than French kiss and dole out the occasional hickey her boyfriend can hide with a band-aid at home and wear like a badge with his buddies.

Mother says, And abortions can be got, Mary. Believe me, even in Jefferson County, and by real doctors. I know some people from when I worked at the paper.

Mother, you've got me splayed out and knocked up like a tube top ho'—

Some of those tube tops are cute, she says.

—and I don't even have a boyfriend.

That nice little Demolay hayride boy seemed nuts about you—

Mother, I swear to God if you mention Mortimer G. Beauregard again like he's my last, best hope, I'll—(You sputter at this point, for it's hard to find something that would really set Mother free other than becoming a Republican, which Lecia is leaning into.)

You'll what? she says.

I'll start wearing blue eye shadow.

Oh, Mary, you're so damn funny.

Why aren't you driving old moose boobs to do this?

Your sister? I don't worry about her.

Well she's got tits out to here and boys swarming six deep, if I were a betting woman, I'd be doing the birth-control expedition with her.

Even while you're saying this, you intuitively know that, despite all those suitors, Lecia will wind up being the oldest living virgin in the state of Texas. She knows that pussy is a high-ticket item right up until and during the night you relinquish it. Then it becomes a commodity and you along with it—with no more value-added than frozen OJ or pork belly. Of course the instant you take the pussy back, you return to former glory. (In years to come anytime one of you suffers a breakup, the other will say, by way of reassurance, Remember the pussy goes with you.)

At the gynecologist's office, the doctor ushers your mother into the hall from the examining room, for which you're grateful, for you never know what she's gonna say during such a deal. But once he has you alone, door closed, laid back on the paper scroll on the table, the cold rod of each metal stirrup pressed into each foot arch, his fingers inside you, he says he expects that his own college-age daughter will remain—in his word—"intact" until marriage. And weren't you ashamed at your age? And didn't your church teach you better?

(As a grown-up, you'll consider dropping a note to this green-coated worm of a physician. Tell him how bare you felt inside that paper nightgown. Ask him who died and made him God. Remind him of that oath doctors are meant to take: *First do no harm.*)

The pill's manufactured hormones do seem to work some magic. By spring of your sophomore year, Mother says your skin looks radiant. Plus your heretofore nonexistent tits have swollen to fit a C-cup. Even Lecia is forced to stop calling you titless, and Clarice (whose novena-induced D-cup has finally come in—and it's worth mention that no other women in her family are so well endowed) asks whether you started praying too.

After a dance one night, you sit on the porch with John Cleary, who counts on you to relay and decode some of what girls whisper about him in dance floor circles. Against the black northern sky, the refinery towers burn aquarium blue. It's spring—warm enough to go barefoot, but you have to pull a red sweatshirt over your pajamas, bury your hands in the front pocket to stay warm. Moths the color of ash flutter around the yellow porch globe.

At this particular dance John was triumphantly crowned with his brand-new cheerleader girlfriend (for your money, a particularly offensive little troll) something like Most Adorable Humans in the Universe.

This honor was expected by everyone but him. His blond head bows shyly, almost inadvertently, at your congratulations. At some point, he tells you that you're "actually getting sort of cute."

"Wasn't I cute before?" you ask, feeling toward him with invisible antennae for some tremble of a desire that might match the ancient intensity of your own.

"Not overmuch," he says. Then the instant passes, and he's crossing the wet lawns home.

You test the power of your new body by asking out a popular Cajun boy during Sadie Hawkins week, and he surprises you by saying yes with considerable force. You double-date with another couple to the drive-in, taking the front seat in the boy's car. He's someone with whom you'd barely exchanged even a few words, but what begins as a mild kiss—almost a joke in the context of the other couple's sudden entwinement—becomes elaborate before the screen's dancing popcorn boxes and long-faced corn dogs have faded to whatever unwatched movie.

The boy's full mouth works some spell on you to obliterate most every other aspect of the night. It banishes from your knowing the far screen squirming with shapes, and the rows of crouched cars hitched to speaker poles, and the other couple listing in the backseat. Even some learned stigma about being "easy" vanishes, not that the boy ever put an impolite hand on you. In that sense, your kisses are innocent. You don't even have a full-fledged crush on this boy, asked him out on a whim, to see if he'd go. But you can't seem to withdraw your mouth from his, though you feel you've edged past the lighthearted flirting that should mark a first date. Some unnamed luster has rushed into your pelvis with whole swirling star colonies and nebulae, and to withdraw your mouth from his would extinguish that glitter and leave you shivering cold.

In bed that night, your hands are gently busy on your body. You don't yet think in specifics like "cock" or "mouth on my breast." Such language and imagery are somehow the property of boys. You can only relive the luxury of those silent kisses until some ocean rushes through you and you wake hanging off your edge of the bed with a pillow hugged to your middle.

But morning brings a schism. In the bathroom, the face staring back at you from the swung-out mirror is out of kilter with the altered image of yourself from the date. The edges don't align—what happened to you? Your real face looks too plain for the wild luxury of those kisses. And in that chasm of self—between what you thought you were and what you are—comes a tight, internal cringe. What was wrong with you last night kissing that boy for those lost hours, hardly saying a word?

(Undercurrent: a boy in the dark bucking over your seven-year-old body. Later on the side of the house, your thighs sticky. Water gushing warm from a spigot. Was it the blood of a lost cherry you washed off? Had you brought this on, exuded some whiff of innate longing to be taken like this. Or had you merely been taken to ride like an animal?)

When Lecia jokes that you still smell of the boy's hair oil, the truth of that so repulses you that his failure to call is good news.

Monday on the school patio at lunch, he saunters into view with a pal, and not since ancient games of catch-and-kiss has the urge to flee powered you so fast. There's a door frame you duck into, standing straight and slim, crushing your Algebra II book and the bag of half-eaten Cheetos against your chest. But once his profile slides into view—the black waves of his oiled hair—you know you'll have to keep moving. The patio suddenly transforms into a complex course of clear sight lines and obstacles to dodge behind. A circle of Pentecostal girls with high-coiled bouffants briefly blocks you till you run-walk up the steps and past a scolding teacher to the library.

There the factoring of polynomials becomes somehow cleansing, a ritual of baptism. (Abstraction in huge doses can starve off yearning.) There's sunlight on the tilted windows. Cars scoot up the street. You can nearly forget that on Friday night your solar plexus had lurched and careened from that boy's tender mouth. Away from him, you're briefly safe from your own ardors.

Chapter Eleven

A DANCE PLACE OPENS UP in a deserted warehouse that sits on the edge of Leechfield sloping toward the swamp. It's the only gathering spot in the tricounty area for bored and listless teenagers, among whom surely you might find (please God) at least one heart's companion. The Towne House, they call it—the little "e" being tacked on to supply class to that place formerly known for cheap auto parts, and whose busted up parking lot holds so many dandelion tufts shoved through holes in the concrete that from the far road it resembles an open field.

For you, the Towne House is nothing less than a stage set with a whole new audience, one more willing to accept at face value your sudden renovations in clothing and demeanor. At school, any deviation from the norm or one's past draws scorn. Behavior outside the bell curve is adjudged a pomposity, any full-fledged difference a frontal attack on the reigning order. *Uppity* was something no one wanted to be accused of. *Who do you think you are?* is the militant sentence of the threatened Leechfield citizen. (Translate: who do you think I am?)

A kid who let his hair grow over his shirt collar in the summer didn't always get sent home for a haircut, because boys in the parking lot might kick his ass for that personal daring before the kid even got through the school door. Nor were girls treated with any delicacy. Once in the hall, you overheard someone saying: "Becky, you were ugly enough yesterday without wearing that hat." So your tentative experiments with, say, going to school dressed in black crepe invariably caused some kid from the neighborhood to say, Who died, Morticia? The African dashiki you talked your mother into buying at a street bazaar in Houston had people calling you (alternately) Jigaboo or Sheena the Jungle Bunny—that kind of thing.

A few times you try to explain to certain people—Clarice, for instance—that your Old Self had been falsified, a mere mask tacked over this Real Self, which you only now have guts to reveal. You remind her of that light-skinned black girl you met at the track meet who faked she was white till her sister's car rumbled up. For her—and formerly for you—chasm stretched between the Real Self and the facade. Such gaps make self-denial akin to suicide.

In response to this spiel, Clarice looks at you quizzically, saying something like, I love you no matter what you wear, but everybody thinks you act weird.

You know that on this broad planet sympathetic others exist, at least a few beings somewhere who might feel alien as you. Books prove it—characters like old Holden Caulfield wandering among the "phonies" at his prep school. The words and sentences you take into your body from books are no less sacred and healing than communion. Surely at least one such person lives in your zip code.

You used to look out the window of your daddy's truck riding to the Towne House and imagine that somewhere from one of these tract houses amid the razor grass and the industrial-maze skyline of contorted steel, a boy riding to the dance might also be pretending that he was being ferried over snowy fields in a Russian sledge. Or perhaps in another truck cab, a girl your age was rethumbing *Catcher in the Rye* and halfway believing that in the Towne House Holden Caulfield would be waiting under the exit sign in all his wounded, cynical splendor. And that very evening conversation would be struck like a flint, and endless isolate dark illuminated.

But how would such a person find you unless you hung it all out there?

While other girls are zipping themselves into pale blue church dresses or pastel linen, you go out on a fashion limb by slithering into a brown leather dress with square buttons. Your daddy dropping you off looks down at the floor of his truck and says that the yellow Mary Janes with boxy toes you have on look a helluva lot like clown shoes.

A few acts that'll later garner fame come to the Towne House at regular intervals—ZZ Top and Jerry Lee Lewis, a psychedelic band called the Fever Tree. When Johnny and Edgar Winter visit nearby Beaumont, where they grew up, they also kick in. Admission: one buck—double a movie ticket. You get a tribal hand stamp that glows under black light and won't wash off for days.

Inside, the band (the Top, as you've come to call them) is at first dwarfed by the throbbing light show on the back wall—multicolored amoebae made from clear glass plates sandwiching together an eerie elixir of salad oil and food coloring. The colored squiggles get thrown on the wall by an overhead projector with a Leechfield Library tag. Weird.

Plus this band differs from any you've seen, for they wear no powder-blue suits or ruffled prom shirts like the Boogie Kings. They lack the polished and pointy-toed shoes James Brown and the Famous Flames had on the time your daddy took you to a college concert, and you felt for the first time your unalloyed whiteness amid rows of black faces.

The Top wear jeans, torn and patched. Leather cowboy vests over T-shirts. Billy Gibbons's beard evokes an old gold-miner's. He and Dusty Hill seem to ride the great bucking rhythms of guitar and bass (respectively) with the stoical stares you've seen on prison rodeo bronco busters. You don't yet recognize their riffs as deriving from Mr. John Lee Hooker. But the beat pounding from those black speakers finds some natural home in your pelvis. It hooks right into the dance moves you picked up either from Lecia (who goes across the river to Louisiana roadhouses like Lou Ann's or the Big Oaks) or from your slavish devotion to *Soul Train.* Even kids who start out doing go-go-boot stuff from *American Bandstand* or *Hullabaloo*—waving their arms and ponying around like fools—eventually ask you to break down the Cold Sweat or Harlem Shuffle. The music just gets some swivel working in a person.

On stage, a Day-Glo skeleton holds a foreboding sign that says *Speed Kills.* No one in the band explains that speed refers to methedrine. That even hippies are getting strung out on it. Eating it in pill form, snorting it, or shooting it, forgoing food for weeks on end until they pare themselves down to skeletal form, and having full-tilt heart attacks before the age of twenty on it. (What did you know of velocity then, of weeks eaten by your brain's own skitter—drops of water on a hot iron skillet? The trick in that town was getting through a night at all without stalling in the sludge of your own thoughts.)

Suddenly, and without instruction, even the farm girls in their corny, matching dresses with different color polka dots are talking about speed with the feigned insouciance of old heads, as if some invisible lightning bolt has shot through every teenage brain in the county searing in this common language. Actual drug use of any kind still seems farther away than Vietnam. But (like Vietnam) some of its lingo seems to infect common parlance in a collective instant. Maybe you'd all brought home the same *Weekly Reader* from school or watched the same TV drug-addict movie. Maybe the hard-driven bass line of the Top just wordlessly hammers all that drug lore into everybody's skull.

The leather dress you wear is an airless sheath, and every week you soak in your own sweat but can find no other garb appropriate to who you're trying to become. At one point, you find your body rocking in the arms of a boy from Houston whose iron surfer's cross clicks against the square dress buttons.

Clarice once told you that tickling a boy's neck just under his collar would drive him to a sexual frenzy that tethered him to you like a dog. You at first hesitate trying this on the surfer boy, because while you want the power such a response would accord, you don't want to look like a skank. With all the tentativeness of a cat testing water, you touch his neck lightly then draw back, half expecting he'll mistake your fingers for a junebug that needs swatting. But sure enough, the minuscule gesture from you signals him. He draws you closer. You try it again, and his breath quickens. By the end of the song you're tracing your initials lightly on his neck as if to brand him your own.

Later you sit in the folding church chairs at the hall's perimeter. His arm slings over your shoulder so his hand hovers inches above your breast without even once grazing it—no small feat. (What did you talk about? Was talking permitted, or was it all you could both do in the rushing terror of letting your bodies touch to endure it?) You ask him—more trying to make conversation than from any true curiosity—about that burnt peanut smell in his clothes, and he tells you he smoked a joint with his sister between sets.

You don't blink in the face of this fact. Yet he suddenly seems wholly alien to you. Though you've been languidly hanging in his arms all night waiting for a kiss, you're subsequently glad it happens only once, during the last song. His mouth is arid and sour. At the hesitant touch of his tongue, your body seizes up with a fear that masks itself as arousal, even conjuring for a fleet second that night with John Cleary. For years, you'll confuse terror and sexual heat this way. Whether it's your peculiar mistake, or the curse of anyone new to bodily discernments, you'll never figure. But the feelings do favor each other, i.e. sweat rolls down the ribs; breathlessness kicks in; the skin surface become hyperalert. It's baffling that you feel phosphorescence gather in your body—as you had with your Sadie Hawkins date—given your slight revulsion at the boy's heavy body and sour kiss.

You draw back from his embrace and pretend to see your daddy's truck through the far window. Outside, you sneak glimpses of the boy shooting pool in the game room. And when he calls the next day to firm up plans for a beach trip, you won't come to the phone.

Maybe a friend of high caliber can only arrive after several months of parched loneliness, or after a string of psychic outlays such as you endured those years in junior high, because only the erasure of beloveds can force you to reveal your need for a friend to a stranger.

For the first months of high school, your lack of friends isn't a worry. You're too busy trying to absorb the shock waves of your own new strangeness. Occasionally loneliness manifests as a specific longing—harsh as thirst—for Clarice or John Cleary. But a new awkwardness infuses your dealings with them.

Clarice has hooked up with a traditional Cajun boyfriend from the cross-town rival high school. He keeps a close watch on her and has a whole list of stuff she's not supposed to do, like cussing or going out at night without him. She lands a job at the Chicken Shack, and despite the boyfriend's rules, she still manages to flummox customers by chirping things like, "Fuck you and come back," but so fast the words are nearly (just barely) unintelligible. Some nights, you sit out under the stars about the time John pulls in from a date, and he trots over smelling of shaving lotion to scratch the cat under its chin, but there's a void between you now.

One source of succor is the drama teacher. Maybe you migrate to her for help in playacting your new self into existence. But drama teachers in that town also have a special role for readers—they're the only school-based source of contemporary plays and poems. Otherwise, the school curriculum keeps you lashed to the mast of previous centuries—*Ivanhoe* and Tennyson and Dickens out the wazoo. You even manage to resent Melville till you actually read him.

But the twentieth-century works Miss Baird favors for interpretation have an antique flavor and could easily be culled from the past. She adores patriotic and religious sounding stuff, or work with homespun characters—corncob-smoking uncles and head-rag-wearing "mammies." Edgar Lee Masters's *Spoon-River Anthology,* so despised by you, is oft-quoted by her. For district poetry competition, you propose Edward Arlington Robinson's "Richard Cory," whose title character in the final line "went home and put a bullet through his head." Soon as you say it, Miss Baird cringes deeply over her desktop. She hurries to the podium, waving her freckled hands at you as if the offending image hung in the air and could be dispersed like so much chalk dust.

Whatever her literary proclivities, she's obliged to haul you to speech and drama tournaments. And just as the Towne House dances broaden the territory in your search for like-minded souls, so do these trips. Kids from other towns and schools pour off yellow buses, and always you look among the books they carry for one subversive enough to recommend its reader as a friend.

It's after school, and Miss Baird stands a stubby five-foot-one before the Drama Club, her flaming orange hair sprayed into a man's stiff pompadour. She reads in clipped syllables the muster of contestants picked to compete at the University of Houston that weekend. (Miss Baird made you do tongue exercises, saying phrases like *cutta-butta* and *toy boat* over and over.) The school dress code forces her to wear skirts, but she always strides and stands with her legs so far apart that if you sit on the front row, you can see the side seams strain against their stitching.

For the premeet pep talk, she continues to pace before you all, taking the slow, swinging steps that would suit somebody with a peg leg. (Later, you'll never think of Miss Baird without imagining a riding crop in hand to slap her jodhpured calf with.) "There's someone who's worked extra *hard* for this meet, someone who deserves *special* praise. *Special* consideration." On the stressed words, Miss Baird tends to lapse into an English accent, so *hard* becomes *hah-ed.*

Usually this fake accent would rankle you. But at the very word *special,* a dim hope ignites. You fix a rigid half-grin on your face until you note that Mortimer G. Beauregard's face has welded itself into the same rictus.

Miss Baird whirls in the opposite direction. "Rarely do I call attention to a *single* person's work. We're a *team* after all. We *rise* as a team—" (she raises her hand like a choir conductor calling up all the altos' power)—"We *fall* as a team." The same hand dive bombs downward. "But *this* young lady has been so *tireless, brilliant.* Her *talent* borders on *genius* . . ."

With your hand over your mouth, you try to adjust your expression to an indifferent vapidity that opposes Mortimer's death smirk, while your fellow students glance around the room for someone deserving of this praise.

"I'm absolutely *heartbroken* she can't be here this afternoon, for she's *new* to our school. I'm *speaking,* por supuesto—which means *of course* in Spanish—of none other than *Meredith Bright,* who's just *joined* us from the *noble* state of Mississippi." Miss Baird stops mid-room, removes her glasses, and pinches at the bridge of her nose as if in great pain. "*Meredith* certainly deserves the full *Indian war whoop* welcome. Let's show her some *school spirit* on the bus Saturday. Shall we *give* it a *go?*"

At this Miss Baird starts whooping—slapping her fingers over her O-shaped mouth with its faded stain of tangerine-colored lipstick. The other students kick in so the sound rises from the chairs around you. Usually a war whoop leaves you feeling stranded inside some gorilla gang. But in this instance, it's the only way to hide the sneer your upper lip is drawing itself into.

Lying in bed that night, you decide that Meredith will doubtless resemble one of those prissy, stringy-haired girls from the Honor Society, who view their ugliness as a kind of modesty, something to be pious about. (Inducted into the Honor Society, you're kicked out within a year, by which time, you'll have grown into enough of a wiseass to say to the principal, "Aw dang, do I have to give my pin back?")

The Saturday of the meet, your mother says of Meredith Bright, prophetically enough, "Maybe you'll like her." She's fresh from the shower and whapping talcum powder on her back at the time, each touch leaving a frosty chrysanthemum on the pale skin. Her injunction on competing with other girls is a challenge, a gauntlet thrown down: "You just have to be smarter than the ones who are prettier and prettier than the ones who are smarter."

Your first sight of Meredith is on the bus amid the dreaded war whoop welcome. She holds a beige folder with a casually posed self-possession. Also, she looks totally unlike anyone you're ever seen. For one thing, she's done her honey-colored hair in the corkscrew curls of a young Shirley Temple. This is the era of straight hair. White girls often buy the same chemicals black people use to "conk" or scorch waves from their hair.

Meredith is also stout—not fat-girl stout, but well padded around her big-boned frame. This makes everything about her round—her face is round and shiny pink; her mint-colored eyes are round and heavy-lidded. Using your mother's gauge for female success, she seems prettier than the smart girls, and smarter than the pretty ones. She also wears slung around her neck a leather thong bearing an orange clay disk slightly smaller than a saucer in circumference. It bears the word POT floating dead center in avocado-colored print. In the midst of the war whoops (which you refuse to actually whoop for) she carries herself—grinning, but with disaffected stateliness—to the very back corner of the bus. And there you leave her unmolested, though you spend some intervals picturing her tied to the center of a straw-filled bull's-eye propped at a slant while you draw an arrow from your quiver.

She crops up in the auditorium during your recitation of "In Flanders Field":

We are the dead. Short days ago we lived,
We lived, felt dawn, saw sunset glow,
Loved and were loved, and now we lie
In Flanders Field . . .

Miss Baird has charged you with several rather sweeping hand gestures. Your stiff arms wheel to indicate a flying lark; later, the arms spread low with palms up in a pose you think of as Christ-like. You intone the words "We are the dead" in a sort of cotton-mouthed manner stolen from Boris Karloff. (Years later, you'll see these replicated on an airport tarmac: a man in a beige jumpsuit using two flashlights to wave a plane into place will send *In Flanders Field the poppies grow* tumbling through your head.)

Meredith slips out before some kid can perform his hysterical rendition of "The Charge of the Light Brigade," which involves a lot of head-whipping back and forth, his neck wiggly as a goose while he refrains: "Cannons to the right of me/Cannons to the left of me. . . ." At the awards assembly, you pick up a red ribbon. The only blue ribbon from your school goes (small wonder) to Meredith, who wins for some Shirley Jackson short story.

On the trip home, the students on the bus belt out songs that combine aboriginal hand clapping and foot stomping with tireless repetitions. Still, Meredith sits serene in back, her great, leonine head of curls tilted above Dostoevsky's *Idiot,* a rarity since books by Russians can make teachers question you over vigorously about Communism. To see her reading a book by a foreigner emboldens you.

Anybody sitting here? you ask, holding onto the curved metal seat backs as you jostle.

No, she says. She's almost got a grin on her face, but somehow seems far away, as if internally afloat in some glassy lake.

Her silence is formidable. You figure out after a few minutes that she'll sit there sphinxlike until you prompt her again. You drum up a more provocative opener. I hear you're a genius, you finally say.

You wait for her to deny this with a demure shake of her curly head, which denial you could then judge for its falsity. Instead, she gives a nod that strikes you as sage. This is true, she finally says.

You're edged off balance by such certainty. She is, after all, the new girl, somewhat chubby and very oddly dressed. She should be beholden to any local who might deign to speak to her. Rather than solicitous gratitude, you've been faced with what you'll come to call her Chinese empress pose.

I'm really smart too, you say. (The audacity of this forces you to shrug, as if shedding the great mantle of smartness you're forced to bear.) You probably heard that already.

No, she says. I hadn't.

Well, anyways, you say. We should be friends. These other people are idiots.

She nods again, saying, This is also true.

You ask her what religion she is, and when she says Baptist, you tell her she's too smart to be Baptist. She should be Buddhist like you and your mom. She snickers at this, saying, I'll look into it.

The bus bobs along, and your mind lurches back to her not having heard you were smart.

You say, You didn't hear I published a book of poems in fourth grade?

No, she says. She considers this for a few heartbeats. Finally she says, Fourth grade's pretty young.

You sense some scant disapproval in her tone. Here you'd always figured that youth made your talent both more rare and your long-term prospects more certain. You'd collected stories about young writers from which to sip encouragement. You recount for her how Arthur Rimbaud at fourteen published some big deal poems.

Wasn't he dead by twenty? Meredith says. Gangrene of the leg or something. In Africa.

Yeah, I remember that now, you say. (You never knew it.)

Meredith says, Milton thought he had to read everything before he was educated enough to write poems.

You scramble to think what you know about this name, Milton, which you skimmed past in your mother's poetry anthology. You don't even know if Milton's his first or last name. You messed up that way once with Dante, which was one poet's last name and another one's first. You've lately stopped reading anybody who wrote earlier than Elvis because a distant idiom is harder to steal from.

Is he the dwarf, Milton? you finally say.

No that's Pope. Milton's the blind guy. *Paradise Lost.* His daughters had to write stuff down for him.

Well, anyway, you say. You look out the window at a field of rice, its sheaves of green leaning. Watching them, you remember a poem that you're fairly sure she won't know. You learned it off some standardized test, but they didn't have poets' names for fear that would lend test takers some clue:

. . . Coming home at noon,
I saw storm windows lying on the ground,

Frame-full of rain; through the water and glass
I saw the crushed grass, how it seemed to stream
Away in lines like seaweed on the tide
Or blades of wheat leaning under the wind.

You pause and scramble through your head for the next lines. You relocate yourself in the cafeteria where the test took place, how you stopped penciling in the empty bubbles, entirely stopped the test to memorize the lines—a contemporary poem was that rare a thing. Even in the relatively quiet test-taking room, you'd had to plug your ears, for even the heel clicks of the overseeing teacher were an intrusion.

Once again, you plug your ears—this time against the bus racket, as if to re-create the seashell roar from the moment you found the poem. Inside this roar, Meredith tugs your sleeve. You unplug your ears to the loud world, and she says:

The ripple and splash of rain on blurred glass
Seemed that it briefly said, as I walked by,
Something I should have liked to say to you,
Something . . . the dry grass bent under the pane
. . . something of . . .

Now Meredith stalls, and after a brief inward drifting, you find the final lines:

A swaying clarity which blindly echoes
This lonely afternoon of memories
And missed desires, while the wintry rain
(Unspeakable the distance of the mind!)
Runs on the standing windows and away.

The bus rocks you both over the gritty roads of east Texas. Yet some immutable shift has altered the air around your bodies. Glib chatter is no longer possible. Your own need for braggadocio has been washed away in that moment of reciting together. Meredith's round eyes seem to have grown even rounder.

Nemerov, she says. Howard Nemerov.

That's who wrote it? you ask. This is data of the rarest kind. With a name you can ask your mother to find his poems in the college library.

(Which your mother does. Once you discover that he teaches at Washington University in St. Louis, you draft an obsequious fan letter over the next few weeks, asking Meredith to correct various versions. Eventually Nemerov writes back a typed letter of thanks and encouragement. And nearly ten years later, he'll be lecturing in Boston, and you'll introduce yourself, and he'll shake your hand and stare with wonder and say, My God. You're that little girl from Texas.)

Meredith continues to nod slowly at you, and you at her. You're lost in some capsule of wonder that will sustain you both in years to come beyond anything you could hope for. When a smile breaks large across her moon face, something worthwhile has been granted.

Chapter Twelve

While boys are cruising roads in search of liquor or pussy or fistfights that can prove their adolescent prowess and vent their spleens, you and Meredith forge a friendship based almost entirely on indolence, a monastic passion for doing virtually nothing. A camera trailing you would find neither plot nor action—two girls laze around on sofas in various stages of torpor reading or talking about what they will read or have read or plan to write or make or do in some vaporous future. Or dead silent in mutual paralysis, the two girls stare at a ceiling for hours, just watching idle thoughts drift by.

You languish on her mother's sofa, Thomas Pynchon's *V.* open on your chest. Meredith claims it's the greatest book ever. You can't get through the first chapter. Tedious as all get-out. Some sailor singing doodley-do sea chanteys and whatnot. In the Russian books at least if you write down the different names and nicknames, you can get a dim idea of who's doing what to whom, and who the good guys are.

What we need's a fainting couch, you say. Something in red velvet.

It's the longest string of words you've uttered in what seems like hours. You've been listening to the air conditioner's roar.

Victorian? Meredith asks. She seems to have names for distinctions you haven't yet begun to make.

And of what does that consist?

'Of what? Of what?' The wild beast has some syntax.

I mean it. Edify me.

I think all those curvy frou-frouy couches are Victorian. You know, like they have at Snooper's Paradise. A slopey thing. With fringe.

I also wouldn't mind a barge, like Cleopatra. I could really go for a barge, with some Nubian slave boys to fan me with palm fronds. Gliding under leaves of . . .

Meredith looks up to say, Elephantine leaves.

Dripping elephantine leaves, you say. Then, This book is all turkey gobble. Tell me again what's so great about it.

Language, mostly. It's a world created rather than a world described.

Come again.

He's not trying to copy anything that's real.

So he's just making shit up?

Yep.

And that's an upside thing?

Don't read it if you don't like it. I loved it.

You saying I'm not smart enough to read this. I'm just your noble savage friend.

More savage than noble, she says. I personally think you're adorable. Extremely cute.

Cute is for poodles. I want to be dark and enigmatic.

You're absolutely dark and cutely enigmatic. One of the untapped mines of literary genius.

This kind of banter is part of an unspoken contract whereby Meredith will pat you on the head a few times before she actually undertakes explaining whatever book has stumped you. The charade somehow dilutes the fact that the most meritory opinions invariably stem from Meredith. Without this oblique shoring up, the friendship would consist of her lecturing while you take notes.

Meredith finally says, Like the whole V thing. It keeps coming back up and back up—geese flying in a V, somebody's shirt open to show their chest, the triangle of pubic hair. It accrues power, meaning. It becomes something.

And what exactly is the V thing?

Well, it's a lot of stuff. It's death, I guess, the arrowhead we're all flying in . . .

From obscurity to oblivion. From this fucking suckhole to anywhere else on the goddamn planet. Tell me why if you don't believe in God, how come you refuse to cuss?

Because I'm pure, untainted. My lips unsullied by obscenity.

And I'm the fucking whore of Babylon.

Cuss your brains out. It doesn't bother me a bit.

Say fuck, c'mon.

I don't want to.

What if you were in a play by T. S. Eliot, and a character had to say *fuck*, would you just not do it? Up and walk offstage? Leave your fellow thespians sputtering?

That's not Eliot's vocabulary.

But what if? Okay, who *would* say fuck? Other than me, of course, in my little foulmouthed self?

I don't know. Maybe Beckett. Not Oscar Wilde or Eugene O'Neill—

These are people I don't know.

Remember that two-person scene that Stephen kid from Beaumont did? Endless. Him and this other guy swishing around? Tugging off each other's cowboy boots and putting them back on?

Waiting for Lefty?

For Godot. *Waiting for Godot.* That's Beckett.

That didn't make any fucking sense either. And I don't remember anybody saying fuck. C'mon now, say it just the once.

In such ways do your days unwind in a haze of aimless blabbing with Meredith's literary opinions introducing intervals of quality.

Every now and then someone tries to spur you both into a project. Mrs. Bright will ask why you don't go play putt-putt in the scalding heat, or your own mother will suggest drawing. To such ideas, you'll both jovially claim to be "depressed out of our minds." But depression as you bear it is less pathology than a kind of cerebral accessory.

Long, long are the hours of each leaden day for girls who've sworn to devote their entire beings to what they call "the life of the mind," but who find themselves unfairly stranded in a town where the proudest sign in the library is one proclaiming every extant issue of *Popular Mechanics.*

The art forms or projects you occasionally rally to are markedly static and wholly conceptual, demanding nothing more than talk. After Meredith's brother Michael brings home an underground comic called *Despair,* you spend hours concocting static theatrical tableaux that you've no real plans to perform, staged and epigrammatic scenes each a minute or so long.

Let's say the curtain opens on a man and woman. She looks outside an upstage window, and both his hands clench the overstuffed chair arms. (*Both* hands: this is high drama.) There are small empty cans that once held Vienna sausage all over the coffee table and two plastic forks. She says, Harry, where's Asia? He says, I don't know. Let's find it on the globe. She says, Where's the globe? He says, It was burnt with all the other things. The curtain closes.

You spend hours generating titles and names for books or bands you'll never even start. Meredith's autobiography will be called *Ennui on Me.* Yours is *Hooves Over Texas—a lusty brawling tale set under the savage Texas sky.* You will form a soul group called the Chicken Supremes. These projects never endure the failures inherent to execution. They let you luxuriate in possibility.

The summer you and Meredith reread *Franny and Zooey* together, you evolve in a mystical direction, combing libraries and religious bookstores all over the county for a copy of the medieval Christian tome called *The Pilgrim's Way.* It describes the Jesus prayer ("Lord Jesus Christ, have mercy on me") that Franny chants mantralike during her unbelievably attractive nervous breakdown, the repetition being meant to burn the prayer into your very breath and heartbeat resulting in all kinds of tranquillity and saintliness.

When your mother fails to find the book in several Houston bookstores, you give that up and found a yoga club. (Hatha Yoga at the time being about as common as speaking Urdu.) You aim to achieve Nirvana itself. Hopefully before school starts.

But you're no more smoothed down by yoga with Meredith than when your mother offered it as a way of calming your nerves before junior high. If you can't pull off a pose the first few tries, you click on the TV and topple onto the sofa, watching a rerun of *Father Knows Best* and mocking it while you long to enter those well-mopped rooms where you're certain the candy in the milk-glass dish hasn't been soldered by humidity into sticky, inedible concrete.

Meanwhile, Meredith actually slides into poses. She also reads the yoga book that for years you've just studied the pictures of. There she finds various directions for cleansing—fasting, drinking buckets of lemon extract and room-temperature green tea. In one case, you're meant to cleanse your sinuses by snorting up warm salt water that floods through your nasal passages and comes out your open mouth: a kind of hosing out of one's sinus that Meredith masters right off. But your effort leaves your skull pounding as it does when you eat a snow cone too fast.

Later, Meredith constructs a meditation mat from a great rectangular piece of foam rubber as you watch. She covers it in a cotton madras the colors of grass and apricot culled from the cheapo remnant section of the fabric store. On the same trip, she picks up a bolt of black flowered cotton to sew you a floor-length monk's robe with a hood. (You figure on being dressed right for transcendence once it hits.)

The next morning, you leave the house for Meredith's wearing the monk's robe and what you call Lecia's slave-girl-of-Caesar sandals, with leather thongs that wrap around your calves. But unless they're tied so tightly that your circulation's cut off, they tend to slop down around your ankles. Halfway to Meredith's, you untie them and sling them over your shoulder like a string of fish.

Thus monastically clad and unshod, you walk the tar-sticky roads holding your mother's orange-and-black yoga book. About halfway there, a roaring truck draws up on the rough shoulder holding a whole crowd of bikini-clad girls and boys in cutoffs in back, including the luminous John Cleary sitting high on the side, a blue towel around his neck. Some girl asks real loud, where's the Halloween party, while everybody else breaks in half laughing. Somebody (you want to think it's John) says, C'mon you guys, and the truck roars off, leaving a wake of titters that you halfway believe visible—little clicking black birds swarming from the silver truck to where you stand, eyes welling up.

At the threshold of Meredith's icily air-conditioned house afterward, she says, Well, hey. Don't you look all Buddha'd up.

You shove past her, saying, Lemme in fast. I'm baking alive in this thing. You dive the length of the sofa, letting your hair shield your face since crying ruined this morning's Egyptian eye makeup.

Unzip me, you say. I feel like a pork sausage in this thing.

Just a minute, she says, and tugs at the zipper behind you trying to manipulate it back into action.

You're choking me to death there, you say. Your fingers claw toward the zipper tongue you can't quite reach.

This is one of those old brass-looking zippers, she says.

It's an old broke-dick zipper, is what it is, you say.

Another tug from behind, and the neckline chokes you. It yanks tight against your throat as if you're being hauled up by some tether you've dared to lunge against.

Meredith says, You have to soap one sometimes to loosen it up.

You're struggling to twist free when another choking tug comes, and in that instant, all the indignity from the truckload of kids seems to break into a thousand wide-flying shards.

I've almost got it, she says.

Well goddamn get it or get the fuck out the way.

Meredith lets go the fabric. She retreats in a movement both liquidy and sudden. Her shadow slides off you.

Drawing the robe over your head, you manage to yank it off and emerge blinking as from a tunnel. A handful of hair caught in the open zipper tore out several strands and left the back of your skull stinging. You're standing there in cotton underpants and Penney's bra feeling impossibly bare. Across the room, Meredith's blank look says you've offended her.

She seems so colossally untouchable that you're almost shocked she could be wounded. But her carriage is caved in slightly, like someone who's received a hard blow but hasn't yet decided to fall down. You'd like to take it all back, but the word *sorry* hasn't yet entered your vocabulary. All you know how to do when faced with conflict lately is leave.

Maybe I should go home, you say.

Maybe you should, she says. She's using the polite tone she saves for teachers and movie tellers. When you snatch up the monk's robe, you don't even know what fury it is that you're so devoted to sustaining, just that you have to storm out. (Friendships often seize up at such an instant—the standoff in which two people either deepen to each other or part company. For decades you'll tend to be counted among the parting variety.)

But you're trying to work the zipper's brass tongue, and it will not budge past the torn-out hair. And you can somehow feel Meredith looking at you. Her eyes have settled on your face as palpably as a shone light. Without moving an inch, she's reached out some tendril.

She says, You need help. (It's not a question.) She takes the robe and fools with the zipper, looking down while she asks, Were you crying when you got here?

In that moment, extremely athletic sobs burst from you. There's great heaving rigor and an extreme runniness of nose. You feel like a fool and say so. Crying in your underpants. God. And when you tell her about the truck and the mockery, it seems like nothing really, the kind of thing that happens every day in Leechfield. So why can't you even catch your breath in the gale force of it? You weep a while before you can say much.

And Meredith listens. Finally, she says, Those people are just jerks. You can't explain to her the ways they're not, how John Cleary is really a glorious being even though he plays football and baseball—for to tell her that would betray some pact, leave her stranded in this strange world you're fabricating together.

Later, Meredith works to change the zipper in the monk's robe. You're in her pink chenille wrapper watching. It's a complex task that requires a wicked hook you'd expect a dentist to wield. Meredith handles it deftly, undoing the seams often without even tearing a thread. Bent to the work, she resembles some old fashioned girl from a calendar, her wild mass of hair electrified by the pale blue light through the curtains.

So she's a little heavy, you think, what your mother would call Rubenesque. That shouldn't blind everyone to her beauty. It does, of course. No one in that truck would invite her to go swimming or to a sleepover, though she has enormous entertainment value and a great heart. (Also in all your life, you would never see her commit an overtly cruel or vindictive act.) Somebody might invite you, and if you brought Meredith along, no one would be rude to her, for she had a bearing that usually thwarted such treatment. But no one would talk to her much or ask her back.

Suddenly you say, You look really pretty doing that.

Thanks, she says, and her face lights up with what you call her Rockette grin. Plus I'm a demon with a needle.

This is true, you say. Then you tell her how everybody in your family is hotheaded. The least little thing, and you blow. That's the closest you can come to an apology.

Lots of native peoples are like that, she says. She takes up a tiny pair of scissors to snip a thread you would have torn with your teeth. Meredith's civilized that way. (Soon she'll speak excellent French.) She hands you the old zipper, saying, Here study this. There'll be a quiz. Then she bends back to the task of pinning the new zipper in.

You say, It's a big old geyser of my tresses caught in a broke-dick zipper.

And Meredith says that reminds her of a Camus novel, the one about the plague, and she tells the story of it, the tale holding you in thrall, and she ends her version with a line you'll write down in your notebook, the place where the atheist doctor hollers at a priest: All your certainties aren't worth one strand of a woman's hair.

Chapter Thirteen

KIDS IN DISTRESSED FAMILIES ARE GREAT repositories of silence and carry in their bodies whole arctic wastelands of words not to be uttered, stories not to be told. Or to be told in sketchiest form—merely brushed by. It's an irony that airing these dramas is often a family's chief taboo. Yet the bristling agony secrecy causes can only be relieved by talk—hours and hours of unmuzzled talk, the recounting of stories. Who listens is almost beside the point, so long as the watching eyes remain lit, and the head tilts at the angle indicating attention and care.

Without such talk by the kids of these families, there's usually a grave sense of personal fault, of failing to rescue those beloveds lost or doomed. That silence ticks out inside its bearer the constant small sting of indictment—*what if, what if, what if; why didn't I, why didn't I, why didn't I . . .*

It's the gravity of such silence that you detect in Meredith. At some point, she levels her sea green eyes on you and says: I can tell that you've suffered. Which observation takes your breath away in its simple nobility.

I have, you say, nodding in acknowledgment. I have suffered.

You've known real despair, she said. I can see that.

Me too, you say, I can see that about you too. Then you dare a question that airs your own ignorance: What is it about suffering that makes people like us so different?

And Meredith says, It teaches you about the human heart. Suffering and despair force you to plumb the depths of the human heart in a way normal life can't. It makes us wise beyond our years. Most people just go along.

Just one cylinder firing upstairs, you say.

If that, she says. Unless you've suffered.

No one has placed any sword to your shoulder to appoint you to a legion of honor—Those Who've Suffered. Yet the notion lends you a new kind of dignity. It also permits you both to air family dramas abstractly, as evidence of the world's inordinate suffering, without exactly betraying the tribal silence you've both forsworn.

The sources of Meredith's own suffering never fully register on you as dire at the time because she reveals them so matter-of-factly, as if recounting episodes from a soap opera. She stays so cordoned off from showing the grief one might expect with her life's events that you buy her act. Partly you credit her with massive courage (true enough); partly you're grateful to ignore some of the awfulness of her past (which was a betrayal of epic proportions).

The obvious distress is the Brights' being poorly off. Their house was the only rental you knew, a tiny shotgun structure—meaning if you fired a gun through the front door in the living room, the shot would fly clean through and out the back kitchen door. It was square and plain, painted the stark white of a boiled egg, and it rose on short stilts that made it seem ready to run—like a cartoon house—out of the oyster-shell drive it was doomed to perch in. (There was no real yard.) It never did run off, of course, just hunkered there, as sterile and ornament-free as a doctor's office. Which, in fact, it used to be.

Dr. Boudreaux ran his old office there when you were a kid, and Meredith found this a pleasant coincidence, almost a foreshadowing of her arrival there and your taking up with her. You explained the house's oddities—a massive hole in the bedroom wall plaster once held the x-ray machine. How at the kitchen table, your chair leg tended to edge into one of the four scooped-out places where the examining table had been bolted. (As a five-year-old facing a booster shot, you'd leapt from that examining table to that very linoleum floor and led three adults—the doctor, his nurse, Mother—on a chase beneath it and around it and eventually over the counters.) Because you were so often carried through that door wrapped in a quilt, your mind swimming with fever, the house kept an otherworldly air, spooky in its familiarity, yet wrong in detail—with doily-covered armchairs and polished upright piano where straight chairs and metal tables once stood.

Meredith never complained about the house or not having money, and she always insisted on paying her own way.

Nor did she talk about her dad running off except to mention it in passing, as if giving the formal précis of a novel. One Saturday shortly after they got to Leechfield, while her mom worked at the cleaners, he secretly cleaned out the bank account, loaded up their only car, and whisked away the house's portable TV under a blanket. But in his hurry to get away, he accidentally slammed the car door on the extended antenna, so Meredith saw it sticking out and puzzled over its presence there as he backed from the drive.

He left no forwarding address, just vanished, fell off the earth. Years later he'd turn up in San Antonio, delivering pizzas while shacked up with a woman whom Meredith and her brother referred to as Ralph. Meredith recounts all this with enviable calm. You never remember her even saying she missed her dad, a fact that flummoxed you because when your parents split up back in fourth grade, you pitched a series of black-eyed fits (a seminal one involving a BB gun).

Sometimes Meredith might make a cavalier literary remark about her dad, like quoting *The Glass Menagerie*'s line about a lost father—"He was a telephone man who fell in love with long distance."

Who could blame him for leaving this shithole, your mother always said.

In response to her husband's flight, Mrs. Bright, a Mississippi lady who'd seem at home under a silk parasol, set out cheerfully to support her family (including Meredith and her brother Michael, just out of high school, her oldest brother Ray having stayed in Greenville), on the $120 per month she could rake in working for Aunt Willy and Uncle Jack, who owned the cleaners.

So picture this woman of about forty—Mrs. Bright—who's blessed with good looks, a slightly genteel manner, and more than her fair share of IQ points (way more by local standards). Now picture her standing on her feet all day amid industrial irons and whole football fields of wrinkled, spilled-on fabric. Even visiting the cleaners depresses you no end, though you sometimes go to ask Mrs. Bright's permission for something or other (a gratuitous visit, since the answer's always yes).

On one such day, you're greeted at the back door by her coworker Drusilla, a wizened old black woman about a thousand years old. When you sidle up, she's sitting on a cinder-block perch smoking a hand-rolled stogie. Steam and cleaning solvents billowing from the door wrap her in a hazy cocoon. She stands saying hey and wiping tobacco crumbs off her skirt.

The cave-mouthed grin she breaks into is itself hard to take, since the loss of many untended teeth causes her cheeks to collapse inward. So it always seems to you that her very skull is edging forward through the flesh. She's holding the screen open, asking are you girls being good? studying? getting educated so you won't have to work like she and Francine (Mrs. Bright) in a sweat shop?

The noise inside the cleaners overpowers thought itself. Some unseen machine is banging out blind, inanimate blows in the gloom. Metal against metal. Ratchets struggle to catch after the effortful turning of interlocking cogs. And always there's the hiss of steam you'd associate with a nest of vipers.

Meredith disappears to find her mother, heads off behind a rack of dresses draped in glistening plastic, and Drusilla takes your arm saying she's got something to show you.

She often does this, and every time your initial urge is to wrest free, for her hand is like some sandpapery crow's claw, and what few teeth she has are so loose in her head you can't look her full in the face without fixing wide-eyed on that mouth's odd mobility. But you go along. Her being black so absolutely trumps most other forms of suffering that you feel proud to be treated as an ally.

On this day, she beckons you deeper into the thumping bowels of the machinery. She reaches under the counter for an oxblood-colored purse, leather peeling, from which comes a plastic accordion of school pictures.

You can never look at photos of little kids without wondering why they get their adult teeth so long before their faces grow to fit them. A girl with a blue bow on her short braids grins out at you.

Thas Elinor, Drusilla says, my youngest girl's baby. She helps with the other grandbabies and gets straight A's. She comes home every day with that dress clean as a whistle—never spills a drop from her thermos.

You ask automatically after the girl's mother, but Drusilla shakes her head. *She sorry,* she says. Then as if in dismissal of that sorriness, she slides her thumbnail down to the next bend in the plastic, the next picture. Joe in an outsized Easter suit has a missing daddy who, according to Drusilla, *isn't worth killing,* and each plastic window holds the shining countenance of some kid Drusilla's charged with because of the inscrutable moral emptiness of one or both parents—*sorry* being the catch-all term, shorthand for failings that range between dull laziness and assault with an ax handle.

You bend over Drusilla's accordion wallet, straining to disguise the knee-jerk piety that comes at such moments from being white, which affords so much unspoken social ease. Surely you'll never be indentured to some packet of grandbabies staring out of yellowed plastic windows. Surely the world will land you in some more elegant circumstance, one that pays you extravagantly for your opinions and brilliant insights into the human condition. One of your favorite fantasies places you in the well of a plush theater during a rehearsal, while actors holding scripts you wrote await instruction.

Before you leave, Drusilla issues a dire warning about the evils of fornication with men, all of whom, she says, are dogs. She lowers the great metal plate to the presser fitted with a man's gray dress slacks so steam engulfs her small flowered form. She then peels the pants off and carries them smoking to where you stand, to show you how white men leave "love juice" stains around their flies.

At the back door, Meredith seems to puzzle over a sheaf of papers in her hand while her mom squints over her shoulder. Mrs. Bright is saying, I'm going slab dab out of my mind what with this percent of that and who's a deduction. Your daddy used to handle that—

Meredith uh-huhs. Mrs. Bright has the skin of a cover girl and keeps her hair coiffed just so even without beauty shop. She asks, Do you think you can help me out with it? I don't want to take away from your schoolwork, . . .

Meredith says, I'll look at it before you get home. That's all I can do.

You note how blank Meredith's face is becoming, just yielding up every line of animate expression. But slowly. It's like watching a flower close.

Mrs. Bright looks back and forth from the papers to Meredith, finally saying, Does it make any sense at all to you?

It's not very straightforward, she says. I mean. They could make it easier. Meredith's still unreadable as stone. But you catch a glimmer of Mrs. Bright's burdens—their gravity. Tiny worry lines are growing around her eyes, yet she also seems to cringe while asking Meredith's help on these minuscule chores. Can she set the hamburger out to thaw? Then maybe check and see if the bread's got spots on it, and if it does, call back so Mrs. Bright can walk to the store after work for another loaf. She might need to come home and take the bottles back for money before she can manage it. She'll have to check her change purse.

You're already edging toward the street when she calls out, Little Mary, do you have to help your mother this way? And you say, Oh, yes ma'am. Which is a flat-footed lie. Really you're dimly annoyed that Meredith has to worry with these nit-size tasks. They always interfere with your program of unalloyed indolence. In truth, you can't face these small frets from Mrs. Bright, for they thinly mask a circumstance too bleak for you to absorb, one that might send the average woman screaming down the street.

Is it that day or some other that you excuse yourself, leave Meredith with her mother? You race off to Hanson's Jewelry to stand for a long time, just letting your eye rove over the ordered display—cases of cool diamonds and sapphires, the occasional square-cut emerald, the gumdrop-colored birthstone rings and necklaces. You'll later wonder why this instant stays with you so long—your warped face reflected in the filigree of a silver serving tray.

Chapter Fourteen

You can't evoke the first joint you took a hit of. Or the second or third, for that matter. Nor even the first tab of acid. (Old hippie dictum: if you remember Woodstock, you weren't there.) Other equally key moments have likewise dispersed into the ether. Which isn't necessarily the fault of those chemicals. ("Coincidence does not imply causality," you wrote in a journal back then, not bothering to note the source.) You could as easily blame your lack of recall on the sexual wonder that left you stunned and staring.

Still, the three things came almost at once—the vagueness of mind, the boys, the drugs. Which one prompted the other you'll never quite discern. It's as if that sweet smoke you inhaled blew from your lungs in a burgeoning vapor that ultimately draped over the world's objects like so much cotton batting. So one minute, you were toking on a joint, the next you woke bare-legged between sheets with some guy staring at you all google-eyed.

Actually, you never much liked pot, never smoked scads of it. You found the wordless, laconic stupor it left you in so disorienting that smoking it was (at first anyway) mere social formality. Grown-ups always imagine that denizens of the underworld lure naifs like you down into drugged squalor, but you went out looking for a ritual of transformation—anything to spirit you from the doldrums into those airy districts traveled by smart boys who study Nietzsche and practice Japanese calligraphy on rice paper. Pharmaceutical and libidinal relief turned out to be all anybody was selling.

Some boys from that time stand out. You fall in love with one met in 1970, spring of your sophomore year. High school's first annum. What the poet Dylan Thomas might have called your fourteenth-fifteenth year to heaven. At some forgotten occasion, you smoke your first joint with him.

Let's call him Phil. He's tall with a great bushy head of ash blond hair, and he projects a seriousness you always think of as French. He's three years older (in Lecia's graduating class) and from another town, but a small role you capture in the spring play brings you near enough for him to acquire you—a task no harder than plucking fruit from a tree, for you'd been looking for him. Within a few weeks his senior ring on a thin chain around your neck thumps your clavicle any time you hit a volley ball.

Phil that year was undergoing his own stark transmutation. Not long before, he'd spoken at tent revivals as a child evangelist. In a Holy Roller church he'd thundered out the scorching rhetoric you'd later associate with the Puritan Jonathan Edwards—sinners thrown like spiders into the coals by the hands of an angry God. But somehow he had, in his mother's words, strayed. He'd begun smoking pot and protesting the war and generally pissing off his parents and the school authorities, who nonetheless had to let him get his picture taken with all the smart kids of Lecia's graduating class because he'd discovered a new way to calculate something. (Plus everybody knew he had a big scholarship to a fancy-schmancy school, and you couldn't exactly blow him off because he started acting pissy. Christ, look at his GPA.)

In the spring play, Phil stars as God, and it's Meredith who points out that he never once laughs at the casting. This complaint partly estranges you from her for the better part of that spring and summer. Till Phil takes off for college come fall, there's just suddenly less Meredith. You can recall no quarrel. She still holds best-friend rank (who else would have you), and if Phil's busy at lunch, you share chips from the same bag. But some tacit vote was taken, and with Phil's arrival she drifts away. (Later, you'll discover this happens a lot with early romances, which can be encompassing enough to nudge out other intimacies. Yet the quickly dropped friend often knows you better and endures longer.)

The drama is Archibald MacLeish's *JB,* a takeoff on the Book of Job—the blasphemous irony of which escapes the audience, who might otherwise have tarred and feathered Miss Lanson—your adorable new drama teacher and blessed antidote to Miss Baird.

After rehearsal, you often drive in Phil's two-tone Ford to the home of his friend Hal, who'd somehow been voted ruler of the student council just before his big brothers returned from Mexico, their duffel bags stuffed with enough pot to transform their baby brother—who has an official-looking gavel for chairing council meetings—into the school's first and foremost head (translation circa 1970: ingester of illegal substances, point man for the counterculture).

It's the bohemian company of which fifteen-year-olds' dreams are made. Hal's bedroom is painted black, its ceiling abillow with parachute silk, and its walls hold a sound system that blares "Yellow Submarine" (about acid) or "Crystal Ship" (about heroin) or "Let It Bleed" (about whipping it out) at volumes that desiccate talk. Pot's a hallucinogen that can also flatten you (not unlike a ballpeen hammer to the cortex), and this effect suits your vapid silence, for you feel dwarfed by the boys' seniority and still untried enough in your new self to know what to say. The two of them lie in bed exhaling vast volumes of pot smoke while you sit cross-legged on the floor by the Lava Lamp, surveying their thin, stoned bodies as a wolverine might a pair of pork chops.

You're transfixed partly by the urges their nearness ignites, by the head-numbing buzz of secondhand marijuana smoke, but also by your crush on Phil.

Phil's more or less steady role in your life solves so much that it's hard to take your eyes from him. Lecia finds the whole romance nauseating. Your mother's tickled by it, while your daddy says of him he seems like a nice enough little boy, but isn't his hair awful bushy. But Phil has dimmed the power of their opinions, somehow reduced them, which bolsters your fledgling sense of independence. He also has a car—a fact made no less thrilling because there's nowhere to go. Even a nonparental ride to what your daddy still calls the picture show has a heady feel.

Beyond this, he provides escort, his gaze on you certifying your romantic and sexual worth (the only value girls seem to have in that time and place) as surely as the blue USDA stamp proves a T-bone's tender. It seems most girls don't wander far unescorted. They stay home alone, or in twos and threes, waiting for boys to fetch them and jump-start some adventure. Showing up alone at certain places can make you look either desperate or like you're asking for it. (Rules for this seem delicate as clockworks, and you may well have read them wrong, for Lord knows misreading signs will—with chemical help—become your métier.)

Still, it seems to you that no girl in drill team ever goes to the beach alone, the way a boy would just to surf. Nor do most "make the drag" alone (drive up and down Gulfway in a Sisyphean oval while watching other teens drive up and down, etc.) without appearing either to be chasing some lost boyfriend or trolling for a new one. But she can stop by Dairy Queen solo as long as she quickly buys her dip cone then leaves. This mobility Phil lends you feels like a great triumph over everything stifling and dull.

He also defies the school's dominant rule, opposing in word, thought, and deed the cruel social pyramid you've mostly failed to scale. By mocking most conventions, he becomes your longed-for defender, some knight busily slaying the old monsters of orthodoxy, while praising in you what others have heretofore damned. When some Holy Roller relative of his questioned your pagan status and morals, he said, She's a better woman than you. And he got smacked with the flat blade of a butcher knife for his trouble.

In public, he tends to draw sharp glances (if not vague slurs) from burly rednecks. It's his weirdo clothes, his hair curling over his collar.

Quite simply, Phil is cool, a state to which you aspire. (If only you'd had the edict a punk pal would give you in 1976: Anybody who spends more than half an hour per day being cool isn't.) You hope to mirror his pose of cynical defiance. Your very survival seems to depend on it.

Most of all, though, you need his attention—to be gazed at, admired, to have your face tenderly held.

Time will never again stretch to the silky lengths it reaches that spring when you and Phil first sit entangled in his car, the odor of narcissus and jasmine and crab-apple blossoms blowing through the open windows on black wind. Nor will kisses ever again evolve into such baroque forms, delicate as origami in their folds and bendings. Because the nights don't have sex as an end (for you anyway, though doubtless your eighteen-year-old partner trembles in hope), the kisses are themselves an end. And in that, they become endless. (There's a line in Hopkins you copy: "O the mind, mind has mountains, cliffs of fall . . .") You float in some watery demimonde where normal laws of physical gravity and identity boundaries vanish. You find yourself looking at your own hand, thinking, Well there's my hand. Or touching the hard shell of his kneecap through blue jeans with awe, unable to name it.

You often go meandering inside his breath until you feel yourself vanish into the plush warmth of his tongue, each movement of which is a word or piece of punctuation in a conversation so intricate, all your diligence is required to keep up. He runs his tongue along your lower lip like a question, and you return the inquiry. Then in unison your tongues meet all soft on that same territory and glide together the small distance. Touch and withdraw, taste and test. All the light of your being seems to pour into him at such moments, and his into you. His tongue barely spirits along a closed eyelid leaving a light stripe of cool damp. For the whirled cartilage of your ear, it's cyclonic. Or he can hypnotize you by lightly tracing a finger along your jawline as if he were drawing you into being. (Maybe as you recalled your mother once doing.)

And you have the same power to fascinate him, something a girl's not supposed to acknowledge, for this particular expression of power makes her, in popular parlance, a prick tease (the moral equivalent of, say, scab labor). But being able to capture his focus so completely works on you like a drug, and you're blighted by the power of it. You can hold his entire being rapt for as long as you care to. You can feel his eyes on you, almost feeding off your form and movements. Even stepping from his car for a movie, you catch him staring at the curve of your calf. Or in the deep cauldron of the theater, he pinches your small wrist as if measuring it, turning it in his hands in a kind of wonder till you feel airy-boned as a bird.

Shooting pool with him once, you bend the length of the table to sink a far ball, your brown legs in shorts in the wide-straddled stance you'd learned as a kid would lend a long shot stability. After the shot, you turn and catch on his face a longing akin to thirst, fierce enough to be contagious, heat rising in you like mercury in one of those cartoon thermometers. It's a va-va-voom moment, and you're drunk on being both source and recipient of that desire. After the vast years of solitude, his aqua eyes somehow carve you into the air. Incarnate you. Your fleshly image of yourself is deriving from what he sees. (You're also giving up very cheaply the freedom to be unself-conscious about how you move, for never again can you lean over a pool table without being at least cryptically conscious of how it appears to any man standing behind you.)

What power each gives to the other, with just a look, just a kiss, for you can't recall him so much as cupping a breast. (Though time doubtless erodes certain facts like acid till only the so-called mythical truths remain.)

It's either spectacularly sad or spectacularly innocent that while your solar plexus churns and all your body rushes with desire, you don't long to unzip Phil's pants or otherwise dismantle his clothing, nor do you even get so far in fantasy to actually envision sex, the brute carnality and mechanics of which would ruin all the verdant, soft-focus power of his kisses. It would slip you both from eternal time into the time of furrow and field, entering and leaving, start and (no please God) finish.

It's also, in retrospect, tragic that however bound you are to Phil in this passion, his dream of sexual paradiso seems to differ quite strongly at eighteen from yours at fifteen. He is, in effect, hardwired to procreate, to get the deed done, so the kisses you find so luscious in their endlessness must translate into painful yearning in him. He tells you this, as politely as one can say such a thing. But you also sense it—this enormous biological pressure bearing down on you, even when he is (from love or terror or the new wisdom of a young seducer) doing everything in his power to court you by reining it in. You get the feeling that, unleashed, this tender boy would throw you to the earth and boff you into guacamole. (In the words of a latter day friend, the guy has a boner he can breathe through.)

Still, this schism ultimately rings the romance's death knell. When you won't "go further," he takes back his ring, escorting a more popular senior girl to some dance. He doesn't put it this way, exactly, just talks about your ages. He's going on nineteen, en route to college, has a car (and needs to get laid). You're fifteen; shipwrecked in this suckhole; and, for reasons neither moral nor religious, you're a putative virgin—though your ancient worries on that count have been tidily banished from conscious thought.

After a single day of your misery, Lecia appears in your doorway like a teased and lacquered rescuing angel. She's holding a damp washcloth, saying, "Get your skinny ass up and double-dog fuck him. Who'll he find smarter than you?" And it's true that one coy rival for his affections—a senior beauty queen who once intimidated you—proves her limited intellect in the talent portion of a town pageant, the story of which you never tire of retelling. First, she listed sewing and poetry for her talent entries. Then onstage, she slipped behind a folding screen to change into various outfits she'd sewed at home, and all the while she was reciting verses to the audience:

Tonight at eight
I have a date
With that very special guy.
My evening skirt and bolero
Will surely catch his eye.

Hearing these lines over lunch trays for the first time, Meredith reminds you of your brief exchange with Julia Osborne in the lunch line at the start of the year.

Tell me again, I don't remember, you say. Your knife-taps on the burrito are audible.

Meredith says, I think they're cardboard.

Get on with it, you say. I have a spiritual need to hear what an idiot she is. Then you fall to sawing at the burrito with yeoman-like vigor.

Don't you remember? Old Julia was saying Colleen Stanley is so dumb, and you said, Talk about the pot calling the kettle black. And this made Julia have to think for a minute.

I remember that, her thinking. You could smell the wood burn.

And she finally says—with the meanest face I've ever seen on a twirler—*That's right!*

Meredith has floated back into your life while remaining detached from the whole drama of Phil, as if it's some dalliance you'll any day now snap out of. You eat lunch together every day, but afterward, when you go outside to socialize, she always seems to ease away from whatever circle of boys Lecia is steering you into. (Or do you ease away from her? Maybe you've forgotten—in the self-absorption of the age—some spring project of hers or series of labs she went off to.)

Lecia has undertaken a campaign to rally whole swarms of boys to your side whether you like them or not, if only to piss Phil off for breaking up with you, which somehow served as a personal affront she's intent on correcting.

Not that Lecia approves much of the new bell-bottomed you. She seems evolved from a 1950s ethos and has a friend who actually asks you why hippies don't take baths. But Lecia also tries to endure your eccentricities while coaching you on how to handle the boys who see her approach and automatically start digging in their pockets for money to buy her a Coke, for you still seem to require much adjustment and correction. Your natural enthusiasm often outstrips social propriety.

One day, you start off to tease this guy with the child's prank of pointing to a shirt button till he looks down, then raising your finger up to hit his nose as a joke. But you manage to hit him with such force that blood gushes, and while you grab napkins, Lecia quietly points out that busting his face in public before the first date might sour him on the deal. You feel safe moving in her shadow and with her instruction, mimicking her flip carriage, as if you'd shed not one tear over your ex-sweetheart.

But despite her efforts to shore you up, Phil still exerts enormous pull on your heart. When you try to picture the boys who do ask you out, they're absolutely featureless, like old carvings eroded by centuries of rain and wind. You're sitting on one side of a tire-size pizza, staring out the window because some car the same shade as Phil's has blurred past, and when you look back, you actually jump—the person across the table is that great a shock. You announce to these guys when they pick you up that you don't kiss on the mouth, which strangely enough seems both to arouse them and to fence them off.

(You eventually ask one persistent guy why he keeps buying meals and movie tickets without a single kiss to egg him on, and he says he figured you must be really good at it. Plus he thought eventually he'd wear you down.)

At the oddest moments, missing Phil flares up and threatens to leave your whole charade of indifference in ashes. The odor of camphor from his mothbally old grandpa jackets as he whisks by you in the hall trailing a brief hello prompts stinging regret. He knew all the words to Dylan. He found your swearing cute. He used to buy you cigars to smoke out by the seawall while he and Hal blew pot (that they were filthy drugstore stogies pungent as buffalo dung was slid over in these moments of reverie). Lecia says, for God's sake, zip it. She eventually bans radio play in the car because all the stupid pop tunes (stuff by the Archies for God's sake) start your grousing.

So you ride home most days in the silence of one who's lost an irreplaceable soul mate. You fail to account for the fact that your body's glands have (coincidentally) begun to dose your brain's pleasure centers with a substance more powerful than opium. Phil's face and smell alone stimulate this fierce response, so the deliriously pleasure-soaked brain attributes all this body-juicing desire solely to him. (Again, you've forgotten that the pussy goes with you.)

Only pissing off school authorities seems to distract from your heartbreak. The habit comes almost inadvertently since your public alliance with Phil branded you subversive and landed your name on whatever list they keep in the main office. You actually cherish this identity and seek to cultivate an aura of careless desperado.

Lecia's reputation also helps. She's been skipping school at will for years, using excuses penned in her own hand so often that Mother's real writing prompts both scrutiny and a phone call from the long-suffering attendance clerk. Mother will swear to be the author of virtually any note, no matter how outrageous. Hence:

> *Lecia Karr's leprosy kicked in, and I had*
> *to wrap her limbs in balm and hyssop.*
> *Please excuse her.*
> *As ever, Charlie Marie Karr*

Or:

> *Lecia Karr's malaria caused her fever to spike to 105°*
> *last week, and while her delirium had abated this*
> *morning, her blurry vision made driving, in my view,*
> *a danger. Please excuse her.*
> *Your pal, Charlie Karr*

The only time the assistant principal and neo-fascist truancy cop you and Meredith dub Godney LeBump dares to call your mother in for a midday consult about Lecia's absences, it backfires. Your mother explains to LeBump that the less time her children spend in his tutelage, the smarter she figures they will be. The episode ends with her shouting in the attendance office—loudly enough to carry down the echoing hallway where the cheerleaders are hanging posters and thus can memorize and repeat her words the next day—Go ahead and hit me, you pious sonofabitch. Nothing would make me happier than to get your ass canned!

For the last month or so of school, Lecia barely shows up unless there's a test; otherwise, she's out in the woods on endless squirrel- or dove-hunting expeditions with her ex-marine boyfriend, whom you've dubbed Grizzly Adams. Or she vanishes into his aunt's house, where she's mastering a gumbo roux few can equal in its blackness without burning the flour and leaving a bitter mud no decent soup will grow from. But your tenth-grade attendance record gets good—partly because you want to catch every glimpse of Phil you can; partly because you relish being the administration's poster child for dress-code infractions, the girl of whom an example will be made.

Little does LeBump know that a summons to his office not only holds no sting, you actually glory in it, for it permits you the fine-tuning of your wiseass persona. The conversations go something like this: Miss Karr (pregnant pause), I'm sure you realized when you got dressed this morning that your skirt is way shorter than three inches above your knee.

I'm a growing girl, sir, you say, smiling the false smile you copped from Meredith and favoring the southern drawl of Ellie Mae Clampitt on *The Beverly Hillbillies.* My mama and daddy can't hardly keep me in clothes. LeBump scribbles in your folder, and it's hard for you to ignore how thick said folder's become by just sophomore year. (How, a tiny part of you wonders, will you ever get into college from this place? The distance from here to there seems oceanic.)

The third or fourth time you get suspended, the school year's almost out, and the heat in the boxed-up classroom you're slouched in would peel house paint. It's Algebra II, and the single floor fan is whirring on the far side of the room when an office helper appears at the glass side of the door waving a slip. But before your teacher—one stern but fair Miss Gacy—even reads the slip or beckons you, you've grabbed your notebook and begun to disengage yourself from the cage-like desk of curved metal and plastic laminate.

Miss Gacy follows you through the doorway, saying, Just a minute. She pulls the door shut after, so the two of you stand alone in the shadowed cool of the glazed hallway. You arrange your face into the snide untouchable expression of one about to receive another in a long series of metaphorical ass-whippings.

She says, I just want you to know, they're doing this on purpose, with a goal in mind, and I think it's unfair.

The obliquity of her wording doesn't escape you. She's saying that Mr. LeBump has fixed you in his sights and will pull the trigger anytime he gets a clear shot. They want you out, not suspended but expelled, and for good.

The enormity of Miss Gacy's generosity in letting you in on this, however indirectly, is hard to convey. The action has the political resonance of a narcotics cop taking a drug dealer aside mid-bust to say her civil rights are being violated.

And Miss Gacy is your least expected champion, being about a million years old, cursed with a thin comb-over hairdo and the bad breath that seems to plague any teacher who winds up bending over close to help. You suck at math and suspect they only keep you in the advanced class so it won't be all boys and Ruth Gallagher. You should be grateful for Miss Gacy's shocking confidence. Instead, it upends the entire cosmos and the frailty of your constructed self which relies wholly on stereotypes, black-and-white judgments.

You tell Miss Gacy it's okay. Then you give her the ancient lie of adolescents everywhere (which she can't possibly, after her years of teaching, still swallow): That you don't care.

But you should care, she says. And as you stare flatly at her, she lays a palsied hand on your forearm. The humanity of this touch shoots along your arm like thin lightning. She says, You're not a bad girl.

This gentleness shapes a compact knot in your throat, and your eyes start to well the hallway blurry, for nothing is more shocking in that environment than unbidden care.

You turn your back to her and head toward the office in what you hope appears a casual amble. Soon as you round the corner from her sight, you duck into the smoky girls' room, lock yourself in the first stall and bend over, fighting sobs, and what is wrong with you, snap out of it, for God's sake.

Later at the sink, washing your face in cool water, you glance up at the shrunken image staring quizzically back from the industrial mirror. How little you've actually changed since junior high.

Miss Gacy's insight also sets your scalp aprickle. For the first time this year (perhaps ever), you fear for your prospects. Before, you assumed you'd skate through high school like Lecia—the underachiever who won't play the game but still pulls off A's, her flippance endured for the sake of the shimmering promise she embodies. But flippance in one so unaccomplished grates, and promise loses its sheen if it goes undelivered long enough.

Plus the pharmaceuticals just trickling into some student bodies will hit flood capacity by fall, and this will strike such horror in administrators who've only toyed with suspending you so far that their tactics for suspected druggies will get more radical and involve civil authorities.

But even this fleeting shiver of helplessness won't edge you one millimeter from your plotted course with LeBump.

Outside his office, the line of chairs holds the usual boys who list and study their feet—one saying *Hey,* another *You again.* My peer group, you think, with no small parcel of chagrin. Two of these are large boys with mysterious scars and inked icons on their forearms, boys you and Lecia used to swim and steal watermelons with in the summers. Within the week, they'll be arrested for robbing liquor stores with sawed off shotguns, the paper claiming they called themselves Butch Cassidy and the Sundance Kid. First felony arrest. State pen. Double-digit sentence.

In LeBump's office, he says, Miss Karr, you've failed to come equipped with the proper undergarments.

You ask him, sir, to repeat the charge. You're secretly picturing the college you'll soon vanish into—some leafy place with broad playing fields and girls in plaid skirts and cheerful Irish groundsmen cheerfully snipping at hedges saying, top of the morning to you, little miss.

You're distracting the boys, Miss Karr. Proper undergarments are required.

You inventory yourself for what you've done wrong. Skirt and Capricorn T-shirt and sandals that neither flip nor flop.

I'm sorry, sir, I'm not following.

He leaves his desk and comes back with Miss Smith from the guidance office across the hall. Mr. LeBump closes the door. He says, You tell her, then starts staring out the window like some jail guard turning the volume down on the torture session before it kicks in.

A brassiere, Mary, she says. You have to come to school wearing a proper bra.

It's distracting the boys, he says.

You ponder what can be said that's enough of a fuck you. (The problem with fuck you's in this sort of place is that you habituate them; they lose their potency, and ergo must increase in outrageousness.) Finally you say, What makes you think I'm not wearing a bra, Mr. LeBump?

In algebra next day, Miss Gacy sits gray-faced behind her steel desk. She doesn't look up from the quizzes she's sorting when you pass by, nor when you wedge yourself noisily into the desk, drop your book a little too hard on the floor. Dale Badgett pokes you with a pencil, saying, Got the proper underwear on today, Miss Karr?

You've always had a weird little crush on him. You turn around to mouth *asshole* just as Miss Gacy floats by, laying the previous day's test on his desk with its typical 100 percent, on which you draw a smiley face. He suddenly reaches up across his desk to grab your bra strap through your blouse, draw it back, and let it pop between your shoulder blades. Just checking, he whispers over your shoulder. The urge to swing around with your arm outstretched like a sideways piling is barely quelled.

Suddenly you realize Miss Gacy's returning yesterday's major section test, 20 percent of the final grade, the one you got suspended from taking. The one you missed just for having tits, you think. And no makeups allowed for dress-code convicts.

She starts around the room a second time, handing out a dittoed worksheet, its odor of fresh-baked rolls and solvent wafting toward you while you study her face for some hint of the humanity she showed yesterday. But she won't even meet your eyes when she lays the still damp worksheet on your desk. Well fuck her. Fuck polynomials and factoring and college altogether. Your bitterness is a numbing iceberg you plan to cling to.

Imagine the letdown when you find paper-clipped to the worksheet your own blank copy of yesterday's test, the one you should've gotten a zero on. It's another blind act of kindness that denies you the martyr status you long for. You could have whined about that zero for a week. Instead, Miss Gacy's meticulously printed *Do in class* in the high right corner.

Chapter Fifteen

By summer you're back in Phil's two-tone Ford, parked at the seawall with the black satin sky and its myriad pinpricks glued across all the car windows. He's repledged his love and recanted the previously unspoken fuck-or-walk ultimatum that broke you up in the first place.

You'd decided in advance of this particular night to up the ante on rolling around by taking your shirt off, yet you have to get drunk on cheap apple wine to justify doing so. You have to sneak Phil into your parents' dozing house and light a listing candle in a Chianti jug before you start to peel yourself bare. It's a sad perversion that you only know how to display your own desire by evoking his. (Only years hence do you guess that his desire was so great he was doomed not to express it.) In fact, you possess neither the sexual generosity nor the unbridled instinct to unbutton his shirt or to search his body for the nether-pale square inches neither you nor sunlight has ever touched. You determine to raise up your shirt and set out doing so with a heretofore unknown modesty, an awkward shyness the night seems steeped in.

Which also highlights the so-called respect Phil shows by not rushing to fumble under your shirt.

Phil waits on the sofa with openly beguiled attention, and you kneel beside him to lift your T-shirt slow as a rising curtain to show him your new breasts. His hands tremble to cup first one, then the other, and you feel the new expanse of your nipples contract in that touch. (A phrase overheard somewhere: nipples like pencil erasers.)

He doesn't even dare lower his mouth to a breast, nor do you think to ask for such a thing. There is no asking yet for you, and there's a loneliness in the warped truth that though you hold a cyclone of desire in your body, you abandon it by pandering to his wants.

On another such evening, you unbuckle his belt and the one silver button atop his jeans and don't unzip him or reach deep but only let your fingers slip just into the elastic of his jockey shorts to touch the head of his rigid cock, and when it leaps at your light touch, it seems more intelligent and less bluntly dumb than you'd expected and the fluid that issues from the tip is so much like what you feel soaking your panties that the gesture furthers the myth of how similar you two are, how ideally matched. What rare luck to have found each other so young when the whole carpet of your lives stretches before you.

You tell Meredith about this adventure in some detail, and she acknowledges how serious this is without the characteristic bemusement she usually brings to your Phil-based confidences. Her earnest tone is the first blessing she's bestowed on your union, though she still lapses into teasing. When you explain how his dick leapt at your touch like a living thing, she accuses you of being an animist.

Meaning what, o Merlin. Dictionary me.

You know. In animism they think if it moves it's alive, has intelligence. Like the trees are alive, rivers and clouds. Meredith picks at the crew collar of her T-shirt. Because she's heavy, she suffers in the heat.

Like gimme a for instance, you say.

Like if you lived in Bali, you might leave some mangoes or rice at the temple of the penis god. So it'd jump at your whim. That kind of deal.

How do you know this kind of obscure shit?

Innate genius.

No I mean it, you say. Everything I read falls right out of my head. Mind like a sieve.

You've got yards of poetry up there.

Yeah and I don't know what half of it means. I'm like one of those ponies they train at the fair. Pound the ground with my hoof to count. But how'd you know that about the penis god?

I made up the penis-god part. So you'd get the parallel.

Okay then, about clouds moving and all that?

I can't remember. Michael was real into Tarzan in junior high. I seem to remember he had a lot of pygmy books. Or Ray took an anthro course.

See, Mother took a course like that, and all I remember about the pygmies is how the guys tied their dicks up around their waists, so it looked like they had hard-ons when they went into battle. And how the women's breasts got all long and tubular.

Pendulous, she says.

I guess I've heard about animus before—

Mist. Ani-mist. Like you spray from a can. Animus is ill-will. Meanwhile, you think his penis actually has big ideas?

Say dick, just say it one time. Or boner at least. Say, big old hard-on.

My mouth is pure. I'll say, *le serpent.*

You could French-fry a dirty joke.

Phil and Meredith have entered the détente stage of their relationship, each still giving the other wide berth as if suspicious, or as if protecting you somehow by keeping distance from the other (though maybe that's untrue, and only reflects your narcissistic desire to serve as locus for all thought and action). Phil relishes the role of seductive older man that's worn very lightly by truly seductive older men and not at all well by the average teenager. That he's smarter than everybody also makes him arrogant in a way Meredith likes to deflate.

Somewhere in the course of several weeks before he leaves for college, you decide, in a phrase, to give it up to Phil—pussy being the only wolf bane you can imagine draping over him to ward off the smart college coeds he'll doubtless bump into. You book your official deflowering for a Friday night at Meredith's house, when Mrs. Bright's working overtime or at Aunt Willy's using the good sewing machine to jazz up Meredith's wardrobe.

Meredith has invited your new friend Stacy to play chess with her in the living room while you and Phil "do the deed." (She'd lived invisibly in your midst for years till Meredith discovered she knew more about T. S. Eliot than either of you.) Stacy's a terrific poet, a budding photographer, and a strapping state champion volleyballer (whose announcement in college that she's a lesbian will only prompt a *no kidding* from everybody). Before going back to Michael's white bed, you and Phil stand in the living room with your arms around each other's waists as Meredith and Stacy align chess figures, and suddenly you can just as easily imagine not being defiled this particular night, just saying to hell with it and piling in Phil's car to go out for chocolate dip cones at the soft-serve joint. But the girls are assembled here as for a fiesta, and through the fabric of Phil's T-shirt, you can feel his rib cage tremble from internal percussion.

Once the last black rook is in place on its board square, everyone seems to wait edgily for you to do something. Here I go, you finally say without moving.

You've done this before, right? Meredith asks Phil through a maternal grin.

Not as much as I'd like, but enough. (Something he later tells you is a lie, and then after that says is true, so you in fact never know if you jumped over that broom alone or not.)

I wish I brought my camera, Stacy says. This seems like a moment for the family album.

Maybe a before-and-after shot, Meredith says. Flowered and deflowered.

What would the caption be? you say, only halfway kidding, because you're looking for some tag line to label the event with.

How about, something from Eliot: *I should be glad of another death,* Stacy says.

We use Thomas Stearnes for everything, Meredith says.

Well, if it ain't broke, don't fix it, you say.

Which seems to set everybody gawking at his or her own individual piece of floorboard. Nobody says a word. You wish there was a mantle clock to tick loudly. Or that Meredith was absentmindedly playing that ravishing Chopin prelude you learned back in junior high. The stepping-stone melody would make a funereal deflowering march to carry you back to the bedroom. Or you wish some military attaché would enter bearing the license that sanctioned this. There should be more ceremony, you think. You want momentum.

Stacy is starting to pick at the sofa nap, and you can feel Phil staring down at the top of your head from his gentle height.

Here I go, you say again, and as he steers you off, Meredith says *bon voyage* at your backs.

Of the actual episode, only the oddest details will remain. He's under the sheet with the entire expanse of his nakedness while you undress matter-of-factly, explaining all the while that the hole in the wall plaster is where Dr. Boudreaux's x-ray machine used to fit. You're not scared of the physical act, for Phil has been kind. But you have one raging horror of looking like you don't know what to do (you don't), and another horror of looking like a slut, and so don't tell him that you're on the pill, hoping the rubber he winds up using will numb his smart dick from knowing that some brute stole your cherry. (How odd, you'll later think, that you embarked on your first love affair—meant as an intimacy—with such a large sexual secret in tow.)

The lustrous warmth of him along your body is like taking a long drink of something you've wanted all your life. But his kisses seem to come from some boy you never knew. He's trying to be slow, to wait for your okay, but this urgency emanates from him. In your eagerness to please, you stand aside for his passion, let it dwarf your small wants till you feel somewhat beside the point. You've brought a whole bunch of towels from home to lay under you, and you keep spreading their edges so the sheets won't mess up. Also, Phil read somewhere that a pillow under the woman's hips puts her at a helpful angle, and there are towels over two of those until you feel raised up on some pyramid of wadded towel and pillow like a Mayan sacrifice.

Afterward, you feel somewhat deflated and can't wait to get up and dress. This urgency to re-create your public self after a private dismantling must be innate to your age and expectation, but it's disappointing somehow. In truth, you'd hoped this physical act would magically yield up emotional intimacy. (But for a long time sex would merely replace the closeness you longed for, almost usurp it.)

You bust out the door in your underpants and announce to Meredith and Stacy that you had an orgasm (astonishing lie). Meredith says that must be from all the practice alone at home you do. Then on the porch Phil declares his undying love and handles you with immense tenderness, but you feel remote. The myth of absolute like-mindedness, cathexis, soul-deep entwinement that you cooked up inside those infinite kisses has been banished. You could have wallowed forever in the silky infinity of those nights, whereas for him, those wordless conversations were doubtless arrows aimed at this night, precursors to it, erotic cheese and crackers.

Henceforth, your power over him seems increased. But you feel exiled from the sexual pleasure he seems to drown in. That's how trying to open the door to libidinal adventure closes it, and how trying to seal your closeness to Phil makes you eager to get away, to run.

Chapter Sixteen

BY FALL, YOU ARRIVE AT SCHOOL A WHOLE NEW CREATURE.

The drill team, for one thing. Your desire to stand on the football field and kick over your head with a line of other girls also wearing outfits (or getups, as your daddy would call them) covered in what can best be described as a kind of matted silver fur—this once-desperate desire has evaporated like so much flash paper.

Back in August, when other drill team members were lowering their hot roller sets into various train cases for sleep-away camp, you'd (a) stopped shaving your legs and armpits, (b) learned how to clean pot and roll a joint, (c) made a trip to Austin, Texas on the very day 40,000 screaming hippies protesting the Kent State murders would be tear-gassed by National Guardsmen (one of whom would, in a few years, become your brother-in-law, the Rice Baron), (d) been sleeping with Phil.

As a result of all these events, you've (e) stopped going to drill team practice unless you come stoned out of your gourd. While the other girls wear their beaded headbands underneath their teased flips so the band is just a stripe across their foreheads (a kind of cerebral band-aid, you often joke to Meredith), yours is tied over your long straight hair like a hippie trying to keep her head (so called) together.

So while the boys you fancy leave for their various far-flung colleges, you wow them with the dramatic move of quitting drill team at the start of your junior year. Which fires up a minor scandal. No one's ever quit before, Miss Stanley says in her office, without being in a family way. Either she has a bad cold that day, or she actually tears up once you've told her. Are you expecting? she asks, and when you say no, the answer seems to flummox her. Like she'd had a whole speech ready, and you left her sliding her thumb down this year's roll book looking for the last time you'd said *regular* to announce your period during roll call.

In LeBump's office, he eyes you wearing the expression animals get smelling something. But by then you're unflappable. Without flap, whatever that means. Scenes like this have begun to unfold with an air of unreality. You can't help thinking as he pontificates and gets up and paces behind his football-field-size desk like a coach in a locker room pep talk that he resembles those square-headed cops from *Big Ass Comix*.

He says, It's clear to me, Miss Karr, that somebody once told you that you were clever. Well clever doesn't compensate for bad citizenship. Not here. You've thrown aside great opportunities, honors other girls would have killed to enjoy, but you have chosen to slam shut those doors. You've bolted and latched them. Those paths are not for you. And we get the message in this office. It's been delivered loud and clear. Be forewarned that henceforth these walls have eyes, and you will be under scrutiny, Miss Karr. And we'll not put up with one inappropriate action.

At this, he walks around the front of his desk to sit atop it and peer down at you to deliver this insult: Neither are we a home for unwed mothers, he says.

This is particularly comical because if they were to expel every girl with a so-called bun in the oven, a good chunk of the senior class would just vanish.

I'm not pregnant, sir, you say.

Are you positive?

Not unless it's the immaculate conception, sir. (Lord but the lies come easy).

He pulls off the glasses he's been peering down through. He reaches behind himself on the desk and grabs your folder to consult for some pertinent detail, then stares back at you with dark eyes. It does give you a twinge of fear to be flat-faced stared at with such fury. You automatically look down, then hate yourself for giving him that triumphant point.

Finally, he says, Were you aware I'm a practicing Catholic?

No, sir.

Don't get a smart mouth on me, he said.

No, sir, you say.

Because I won't tolerate it. Not for a Yankee minute.

No, sir.

He glances down at the folder through his specs, then looks back up at you with a glare that must have been searing when it came framed within his football helmet's grate. He says, It might surprise you that I have taken personal interest in locker number 481.

Why, sir?

Let's just leave it at that.

The prospect of a locker search actually fills you with juvenile glee, for number 481 swung open would reveal an ancient, unlaundered gym shirt the color of cat piss; a graveyard of old papers; some novels by Salinger and Bellow and Hemingway; and a sack holding an orange so lustrous with green and white mould and caved in on one side that you might well pawn it off as a bio experiment.

We've also made some changes in your schedule, Miss Karr.

This is a slyly palmed trump card he's playing. You've heard rumors about a few criminal-type detentions they set up for incorrigible guys who'd punched a teacher or blown something up. The offending party would get isolated from general population, left to sit all year in a steamy, padlocked storage room behind the field house—the only contact being some tobacco-spitting coach who came in periodically to collect homework, or the lines the boy had to write repeatedly, stuff like "I will not sass." It was said that one guy had been forgotten entirely over some summer, was found in fall either swollen and crawling with maggots or else shriveled like a mummy, his Venus pencil clutched in his finger bones.

Like what changes? you say.

Sir, he says. What changes, *sir*. He must see the fear spark in you, for he seems invigorated—a predator who's caught the whiff of a wound. You don't say anything, just slouch a notch lower in the hard chair.

We've taken you from Miss Park's English class and Mrs. Theriot's history, and put you in Mrs. Wylie's English and Coach Kryshak's history that same period..

Don't they do, like, remedial classes, or something? (Long pause) Sir.

It's true that we've taken you out of AP English and history.

For what reason, sir? I've stayed on the honor roll. I believe I have A's in both subjects.

There are issues of maturity and citizenship—

What!

—that we feel could affect the learning environment.

He hands you a pink hall pass. End of interview.

You plod from the office trying for the first time in a while not to cry, for you've been cast into the academic equivalent of a dungeon. It's only a few weeks before the kind-eyed Mrs. Wylie insists to the head office that you move up from both classes into AP—a feat that must've cost her considerable ill will from LeBump.

Meanwhile you spend two weeks in Kryshak's class, where it turns out he passes whole class periods reading aloud from the textbook, often until he himself corks off, dozing in the valley of the pages while hell breaks loose in the room. On Moratorium Day, when Meredith stitches black armbands for you both to wear in protest of Vietnam—her one act of civil disobedience—he catches her alone and shoves her against a locker, saying, Take it off or I'll take it off for you. Her hands tremble all the way home.

Before Thanksgiving, you travel to Phil's college for a plotted weekend escape of illicit sex and drugs. You find yourself stepping down from the metal Greyhound steps like a bride with the Samsonite suitcase that you borrowed from Clarice despite its hideous salmon color. As soon as you see Phil leaning in jeans against the wall in a pose worthy of the young James Dean, he somehow seems unbelievably goofy-looking and beside the point.

How did this happen? For weeks, you've carried a snapshot of him in a pair of overalls the way Catholic girls carry mass cards of their name saints. Nights, you'd stood at various 7-Eleven pay phones, risking arrest and jail to use a fake credit-card number, just to hear for three minutes (before they could trace the card and discover it was fake and call the cops) his voice—the low pitch of which could mesmerize you with desire.

But in the steamy, diesel-soaked air of the bus terminal, he looks all wrong. He's bought a wide-brimmed felt hat of the kind Western farmers wore in cowboy movies. (His American Gothic hat, you call it, after that Grant Wood painting.) On the way, the two-tone Ford he drives—the same one you'd kissed in all the previous summer—chugs like an Okie tar-kill. His fingers entwined with yours are damp with sweat.

Once you get to his dorm room, you find the odor of old pizza unfathomably discouraging. The same holds for his agenda of things he wants to show you. The worst of these is a record of two guys having a fart contest, which ends when one actually batches his pants.

(Twenty years later, this notion and its attendant memory will strike you as wicked funny. Also you could then recall the boy's tender, odd ministrations with the fondness they warranted.)

Phil seems to know you and yet does not in any way know you. After some awkward introduction and small talk, his nerd-ball roommate is conveniently dispatched with sleeping bag to some other where. At that instant, Phil adopts the sheepish sidewise look of the amorous cartoon skunk called Pepe LePew, whose cookie-cutter heart beat through his furry chest whenever he saw his sweetheart.

Suddenly you feel too much like a child in Phil's hands. When he pulls your T-shirt over your head, it tangles in your hair for a blind minute and you feel choked and push him off.

He says, Hey slow down—we've got all night. But in saying this his face warps, his teeth suddenly looking bucked as any mule's (which they weren't). In that hallucinatory instant, Phil somehow embodies everything in your life you want to get loose from. In this way, your soul mate on the slopes of Parnassus (translate: college dorm room) thus becomes a kind of Gomer fawning over you in a cold cinder-block purgatory.

He's all kinds of sweet. He holds you a long time, fighting to breathe while touching your rib cage with shy fingers. His neck smells of patchouli oil and his mouth of cumin from the Mexican food you had earlier. You want to take a shower and brush your teeth, but being concerned with hygiene at such an instant would sound so uncool. Also, you aren't sure that cleaning up would help. It's the whole blunt corporeal exchange that's eating away at you.

Soon after you make love, you curl in the fetal posture in the narrow bed and fake sleep for hours, staring at the luminous dial of the roommate's clock face. Once you think Phil's breathing deep and slow enough, you slink into the bathroom downstairs—on the girls' floor—with your ragged copy of *Anna Karenina.* You sit on the cold tiles in your sweatshirt and shorts and have just begun to ponder the lunkheadedness of the cuckolded husband when Phil appears in the doorway. He looks tousled and fond. He wants to make love again, and you swear to yourself that on future nights you'll lie still till dawn rather than risk these additional ministrations.

Once you're home, Phil sends flowers—a box of peach-colored gladioli. The florist's card with its calligraphy birthday wish contains a vow from him to love you forever. Your mother grinds up aspirin with a spoon back to mix in the water, to keep the blooms fresh. But the phone rings, so she forgets, and you just wipe the powder off the countertop with a sour sponge.

Chapter Seventeen

Doonie first crawls into your life on his hands and knees like a reptile. You're spending the night with his sister Elizabeth (aka Elizabeth Louise Deets), who lies in her own twin bed in a somnolent heap with her dark hair arrayed across the pale covers, just across the leaf-shadowed room from the identical bed in which you lie staring ceilingward, your insomniac skull crawling with words like a veritable anthill.

For hours each night, you lie awake this way composing letters to woo the far-flung, cherished college boys (the Adorees, as Lecia calls them) from the tidal wave of pot-sodden pussy that—if their letters are true—seems to be crashing down on them inside their various zip codes. These correspondences are your chief modes of expression and human contact. Without them, you barely exist, and never again will you bring such lapidary fervor to the manufacture of a single paragraph, nor will language ever hold more totemic power. The wooden English essay that won some prize this week took less time to conceive of than a single supposedly clever postcard. At school you're laying low, angling for "good kid" status, part of a ploy to weasel your way sans high school diploma into some hippie college far from here. With the new dress code, thay can't even kick you out much this year.

Lying awake in Elizabeth's white bedroom that night, you're wholly absorbed in the skullwork of polishing some transition or other when the knob on the door starts to twist. First left, then right. Then the door cracks open to let an inch of hall light pour in, a knife blade's width, then more than a yard of yellow hallway light spills in. You stare transfixed at the place a face should appear—expecting some quizzical parent come to loom a few seconds en route to the can. But there's nothing. Unpunctured quiet.

Till the squeak of hands and knees on the linoleum announces someone crawling low around the end of the bed. You sit upright to watch Doonie in his pajama bottoms using his elbows to drag his skinny body forward to the side of your bed.

Then his giant sunburst of frazzled black hair pops up. He says in a whisper almost wholly starved of air, Wanna see something?

Like what? You say curious.

At which point, Elizabeth bolts up like some marionette jerked from full slumber into straight-backboned fury. (She studies ballet and has admirable posture.) She says, Get out of here, you little pervert.

Doonie says, Nobody's talking to you.

You say, It's okay. Really.

And it is okay. Though Doonie's just a piddling-ass sophomore to your exalted junior status, you're actually the same age. (You skipped a grade.) Plus his nervy entrance has piqued your interest, set you fumbling around for a sweatshirt to pull on. Whatever is he hoarding that would warrant such stealth?

Elizabeth says, He wants to show you his dick.

At which prospect you bust out laughing, and Doonie, outraged, says, That isn't it. Get your mind outa the gutter.

I swear to God, Elizabeth says. Somebody told him he had a big dick—

I never showed anybody my dick! Doonie says.

—and he tries to show it to everybody.

'Cept people who asked. He says under his breath if you ask nice, he'll show it to you.

I promise you, I don't wanna look at your dick, you say. And you can see in the moonlit room Doonie's eyes glint with the faith that someday whole herds of females will clamor to see his dick, so he can good-naturedly forgo showing it tonight because he can see that happy day approach. Besides that's the kind of pedal-to-the-metal individual he is. (This facial expression of his is so inspirational, so able to infuse hope in its absence, that it will carry you and many others through acid trips and drug deals, across various state lines, through sagas that invariably end with the sentence, And the miracle is, the cops just let us go.)

It isn't my dick I'm gonna show you, he says. I swear.

Elizabeth says, Get outa here before I call Daddy.

By then, you're really wondering what exactly Doonie might have to unveil other than his johnson that would prompt him to steal in here like a jungle operative and risk Elizabeth's hopping up and down in his ass. So you say to her, That's okay. I couldn't sleep anyway.

You get up while Elizabeth topples back down, saying, Just yell if he whips it out. Doonie, I'll call Daddy if you whip it out. I swear to God. Don't test me.

You'd barely noticed Doonie the summer before when you'd first met. It was one of those flattened-out Sundays when you'd been blowing joints with Elizabeth and the college-bound boys in a car, all of you winding up gathered per usual in the Deets's yard in the aimless loitering of the stoned and willfully unemployed. The older boys were already shining like bronze icons you'd already cast them to be in memory—Phil and Raphael, Hobbit and the blond-haired Raj. (Hal was already in Mexico.) Each exuded a sly radiance that blinded you to anyone else in the vicinity in that early dusk amid the *whisk-whisk* of sprinklers. Distant refinery flames flapped against the apricot sky.

Those boys had the allure of transience. They'd already mentally checked out, like explorers before the anchor is hoisted, or astronauts during the countdown. They were setting off on quests and would come back (question mark) to regale you with slain dragons. This charisma of departure so beguiled you that sentences were already assembling for the letters you'd write to each. So Doonie had been background noise: a scarecrow boy on a bike popping wheelies with his pal Hogan.

His greeting to you spoken while circling the whole crowd on the bike was, You gotta cute butt.

You were way too cool to respond to this acknowledgment of your ass before the Adorees. Still, you had to stifle a grin when he whizzed by on his bike close enough for Elizabeth to swat at him. Then he affected a quick stop that left a skid mark, a kind of exclamation point to the whole exchange.

Months later, you find yourself in Doonie's room, a veritable graveyard for wadded up jeans and T-shirts and one Cheerio-encrusted bowl. Surf magazines scatter glossy blue oceans across every extant surface. He opens his closet door and hauls out a garbage bag that's heavy enough to need dragging. He undoes the yellow twistie-tie with great drama, saying, You not gonna believe this. The bag yawns open, and it holds neither the Holy Grail nor pirate treasure nor bearer bonds you can cash in. No, it holds pills and capsules and powders and elixirs in every shape and size. Quite simply, it's the largest stash of pharmaceuticals you'll ever see excepting TV footage of government sting operations.

Where'd you get all this? you ask.

To which Doonie answers, with the grin of a kid who's hit a home run, Hogan hit a drug store.

At the entrance to King's Pharmacy there'd once been—for decorative purposes—this apothecary jar big around as a truck tire and aswill with pill samples. Hogan had stolen handfuls from there before, but this time he slithered down through an air vent with a garbage bag for the whole stash. But as his feet hit the floorboards, an alarm sounded, and shortly after that cops started in the back door. Since the front door was dead-bolted, Hogan had to toss a vacuum cleaner through the plate glass and dive out behind it while pedestrians gaped and screamed.

According to Hogan, he jumped and looked one way like a cartoon burglar, then jumped and looked the other before he took off, tennis shoes flapping.

He left the whole stash with Doonie for safekeeping, because Hogan knew the cops were after him. In Doonie's psychedelic hyperbole, the arrest involved SWAT teams and a hovering helicopter. Hogan walked out with hands in the air and feeling the whisper-light touch of two dozen pairs of crossed hairs fixed on his big knobby head.

So he's in jail? Your friend I met?

Aw he's all right. It's just Gatesville. He's just sixteen. Be out before he'd have to hit the big time. Want me to get him to make you a belt from in there? They nice, those prison belts. I got one. Big old buckle'll pick up your basic Cuban TV station. Get your name tooled on back.

You laugh more in Doonie's company than in anybody's since Clarice. He claims he does crappy in school (in contrast to his brilliant sisters) and wants you to tutor him in geometry. But his mind dodges around like a pinball bouncing, lighting up in places so odd you know it's driven by the torque of great smarts.

For one thing, he's isolated the tastier drugs into labeled sandwich bags. There's valium by the packet and even birth control pills in round spaceship-like compacts, which you take in hopes of saving your Catholic pals from the early pregnancies they're heading toward (two are knocked up within the year). Plus there are colored pills for any mood—methamphetamine (black mollies and white crosses), opiate derivatives like codeine, phenobarb in every dose level, nembutal (yellow jackets), seconal (red birds).

How'd you figure all this stuff out? you ask, scooping up a handful.

That's the beauty of it, Doonie says. I made Hogan go back before his trial and steal this book. Told him, hell, you going to the joint anyway. In for a penny, in for a pound.

From under his bed, Doonie hefts a giant crimson volume, just smaller than the library dictionary and with gold-embossed lettering like some alchemist's tome. It's the first Physicians' Desk Reference you've ever seen. He's marked it with flat toothpicks at dozens of places.

Don't they keep that thing chained to the counter? you ask.

Not like fence chain or anything. Just needed lightweight wire cutters like Mama totes in her glove box. Walked out the door with it tucked under his arm like that professor dog. What's his name? Mr. Peabody.

Doonie sits in the room's center cross-legged in pajama bottoms, the book open on his lap, holding up various baggies and describing their contents. It's his hobby, pharmaceuticals. The way other kids glue model airplanes together, Doonie pores over the *PDR,* thus undertaking the study of chemicals with a vigor he'll never bring to the geometry you wind up tutoring him in.

He says, Now here's something meant to be what they call soporific. You gotta love the lingo, man. Soporific. Rhymes with *so terrific.* Don't you write poetry or something? There's a poem for you. (He grins up at the ceiling.) My soporific/ Is so terrific. You like that?

Not a whole lot, you say, and it's dawning on you that you're not gonna be able to tell when Doonie's actually kidding. So when he says—Wanna eat some soporifics and get nekked?—you don't want to insult him by laughing outright at his audacity. You just say no thanks.

Before long, you and Doonie strike up a friendship without which your life in Leechfield would prove duller than a rubber knife. He belongs to the underworld of surfers and beach bums you instantly meld into. That's how you wind up traveling to the Gulf on weekends in all weathers. You pass the unspoken entrance exam to this fraternity (it was mostly guys) by displaying savvy about a wide array of chemicals, for every substance carries its own voodoo ritual or ceremony. In little over a year, you'd mastered most. You could clean bricks of pot or peyote buttons, roll a joint while driving, drive while tripping, and talk down the average acid-raging screamer. If a guy at the surf festival nodded off after smoking a tarry ball of opium, you'd walk him up and down the beach, all night if need be, pouring jugs of distilled water into his mouth and keeping him alert to stave off coma.

The exception was smack, which was both pricey and scarce in those days. (Junkies speak with nearly childlike glee about cooking stuff up in a black-bottomed spoon, tying off, etc. But the one time you blammed heroin, you puked your way into nod-off, waking up astonished that guys would steal TVs for that stuff.) So aside from Doonie's hilarity, the promise of narcotic anesthesia drew you to the shore, where it was all take a toke, sister, slap five. Plus there's a powerful romance to surfing.

A surfer catches a wave for the same reason a rodeo cowboy throws his leg over a barbarous horse: to break the wild thing for personal use, to bend the brute will, or to be carried inside that rush of blind power for a fleet instant.

That's partly why you're enticed to the beach where few girls go. Not that anybody would hassle a girl (shouting as they will a few years from now in California, *Chick in the water,* when you dare to paddle out, thus exiling you to beach-bunnyhood). Girls just don't come here unless brought by boyfriends. Eventually you'll choose or be chosen by a sweet and sinewy blond boy in his twenties back from California, and you'll go in his blue truck when the tidal charts and surf reports dictate, sleeping in the back or under the pier and waking soaked by fog for the first high tide.

Till you meet that boy, you come for a zillion reasons. Because the college Adorees have vanished. Because it's the electrified Doonie who asks. Because Meredith's ever-present new sweetheart captures all her attention with whispers and hand-holding on her mother's sofa—all of which seems to spike in you a mean-spirited jealousy. The same holds true for Elizabeth Louise Deets whose beau likewise occupies most of her free hours. You go to do drugs and to flee the doldrums of Leechfield and the airless state that composing letters alone for days can leave you in.

Plus it's about the only beauty spot within striking distance of the blighted Leechfield, and it's easy to reach. You only need drive thirty minutes past refineries and along the intercoastal canal to hit the beach road.

Start at the Breeze Inn where you used to go as a kid. Stay on that road, and your right window will show slopey barbed wire marking off oil rigs and a sparse herd of blotchy Brahma cattle somebody's trying to make a go of. On the left, a low break of grass separates you from a shallow, flat beach and waves. An hour past that first stop is a burg called (no shit, check the map) High Island. On that beach there's a bait shop (or was till summer 1998) called Meekham's on a fishing pier, the narrow slats of which offer partial shelter from rain. There the water turns jade and smoothes out to offer the cleanest break east of Galveston.

You'd learned to surf in a halfhearted way (as most boys and at least a few girls did in that region) about age thirteen. Since the choppy Texas waves lack the integrity and vehemence of California surf—only gaining truly righteous formidability during hurricane season—even candy-asses give surfing the occasional go. But that chop also makes it harder to catch a wave, much less to wring out a ride of any force. Come summer you'll body-surf with some ease. But that first winter you come to the beach with Doonie and his posse as an affable observer, one who lacks both the heart and the body fat to bear the cold wind. (Though the Gulf Stream keeps the water fairly tepid, the wind cuts straight to your bones.) The few times you borrow a wet suit from some guy, you feel straitjacketed by the black rubber, and the foam you stride into is ankle-breaking cold. It'll turn your lips popsicle blue, and set you ashiver.

So you don't go—contrary to what you tell those who bother to ask—to surf. Mostly you read on the beach bundled in sweats or wrapped in a scratchy blanket, or you gather shells. Once you find a massive clam half and spend the better part of one stoned-out day shoveling up wet sand and using sticks and yards of kelp in the assemblage of a castle-like structure that dissolves by evening when the moon's lure tugs the water over it.

In truth, you're so bored and stalled and lonely, you would have gone anywhere to escape your own house and the cramped parameters of your own skull.

You also love to watch surfing, since those who brave all waters and weathers have a conviction and zeal most blank-eyed citizens of Leechfield lack. A guy paddles out, digging hard before an oncoming swell because he has to match its speed to drop in—catch it, have it pick him up like a hitchhiker. Then he rises with some exquisite mix of wonder and tentative triumph and jags slantwise up the wave's face. In rare winds, when the swells break smooth and wide outside the far sandbar, a wave can curl over a surfer and hold him soaring inside this translucent aqua tube, making a phantom of him from the beach.

Surfers talk little enough, but for Doonie. This lets you invent wisdom to overlay that taciturnity—like your daddy, you'll think decades later, for like him their silence rarely contradicts your private fabrication of what they're thinking.

On days a tropical storm warning shuts down schools, you drive with wipers fighting rain while high-pitched winds scream through the faulty seals around the glass. The few times an actual storm hauls the waves up past the tide line and over the beach grass and dunes to swamp the road, you move the state highway patrol's sawhorses to plow through shorebreak where you can only guess the road might be, and from your tires wings of seawater flare up so the wet brakes barely catch.

Doonie likes to say that all the loose marbles roll downhill, and it's true that the beach serves as both a geographical and social low. It's a kind of hideout for the disenfranchised where questions of one's future or origins never come up. In fact, there are dozens of pier rats whose family names you'll never even learn, using just their assigned tribal monikers: Critter, Maddog, Easy, Murph the Surf, Captain Flash (aka Flash), Skeeter, Melonhead. Only Doonie's best pal, Gary, goes by his last name, Forsythe (which in the tragic future will echo *foresight*).

The beach at night with its bonfire ringed by a strung-out company of sun-weary surfers passing around a joint under far flung stars feels like the ancestral village you never had. You're all sipping V-8 juice from the same triangular hole in the same ritual can, also passing tapwater brought in washed out orange juice jugs, for the salt and wind parch you, and local water's brackish. Not that there's a house with a sink spigot into which you'd be invited. This crowd around the snapping fire substitutes, in most of your cases, for hearth and home, for actual kin.

People back in town are referred to—if at all—as straights or civilians, as if you're soldiers in some covert war. Against what enemy it's hard to say. Tedium. Life by rote. Simpleminded adherence to refinery routine. And you're also in a series of undeclared domestic wars. In retrospect, it seems that in every single home, at least one parent is flat-out drunk or pilled-up or heading that way or hungover or otherwise absent.

Beyond earshot, somebody might say, Poor Critter, his mother's such a souse. Or, Maddog's daddy beats the shit out of him when he's loaded. Or so-and-so has to sleep in the garage when his mother's boyfriends come in blasted. Odder than the taboo against discussing your liquor-related miseries is the piety with which you all return to separate homes stoned out of your minds on other substances, as if illegal chemicals constitute magisterial progress over being a drunk. As if the mind were a rabbit hole you could each vanish down into (like in the Jefferson Airplane song). As if this vanishing were progress.

That's the year Doonie somehow acquires nine ounces (oh-zees, in his parlance) of psilocybin. You help him to load gel caps in trade for the two-dollar per hit fee. While Doonie cheerfully chops mushroom powder, he chants: *Who will help the little red hen/ to cap the dope/ to stash in the pants/ to take past the pigs/ to eat on the beach/ to trip through the night*...

So spring of 1971 starts to vaporize on the beach alongside Meekham's pier with Doonie's hallucinogens. The days on the calendar lose their solid boundaries, and the nature of time alters, swinging one way then another. Sometimes whole weekends evaporate beneath your feet, but time can also need to be done, like in prison. Maybe to honor those mythic creatures like Hogan, who's graduated from kid prison to what Doonie calls the Big House, you actually etch off the days you have left till college on your bedroom doorjamb as onto a cell wall. You're just trying to get a grip.

In the stories you pass around the fire about various freaks and heads, less and less hyperbole is needed to spice up the telling. Tragedy is edging in. There are actual prison terms and car wrecks to recount, parole officers and freak outs to keep up with. Once two boys might have fought over a girl. Now so-and-so's cousin has vanished into a Mexican jail.

In one dope deal gone sour, Jerry McCoy ties your pal Skeeter to a chair in front of his girlfriend to pistol-whip him (her witnessing this being the greater insult than the subsequent broken jaw and smashed ribs). And when Jerry is later stabbed to death under the stands at a football game, Skeeter recruits Flash—who's telling the story—to travel to the cemetery blazing on LSD with a truckload of others who hold grudges against the foul-tempered, well armed, and always over-muscled McCoy. Flash even claims his mother went along. She allegedly cheered while those guys stood on the grave to empty their bladders into the fresh-dug earth.

Even this atrocity doesn't strike anyone as beyond the realm of civility. You've logged some mileage since your first hesitant sojourns into smoking pot, your legs dangling from a kid's swing in the public park while talk veered to Simone de Beauvoir or the budding ecology movement. Some unforeseen darkness has been slinking into your circle. The old flower-child pose of gentleness has decayed into cynicism. The bumper-sticker slogan *Make Love Not War* has been usurped by *Sex and Drugs and Rock and Roll.* People in your midst are changing in ways you can neither control nor predict.

It never once occurs to you that the chemicals that have so efficiently soothed and amused could—in certain quantities, over time—change a person. And not just in degrees either, not just cranking you up or down to intensify or dilute you according to the evening's whim—that was the myth. We're talking qualitative upheavals, all out mutations, the way yeast alters beer. Or the way a single grain of arsenic in one's morning coffee every day will—if unjudiciously increased—too quickly saturate one's system, until after much mouth-frothing and stomach agony, death ensues.

Who saw it coming?

You're standing around a campfire tripping your brains out on psilocybin while hoping the pipe full of hash somebody passes around will take the spangled edges off the ongoing high and permit sleep's approximation if not its actuality.

The pipe has come around again, and you ask if it's primo hash or keef, or that blond hash from Afghanistan?

Flash says, When did you get so effing persnickety about other people's hashish?

Every toke inflates some balloon in your skull another quarter inch to nudge out more racing thought. Taking any substance poses this kind of constant quest for the perfect combination, the "right" high. You think how you'd explain the variables to Miss Gacy, and suddenly there she sits in phantom form outside the circle, on the driftwood log, holding her purse in her lap as if waiting for a train. Miss Gacy, we need *x* caps of psilocybin with *y* tokes on the pipe, and if we only had *z* glasses of Boonsfarm apple wine, I'd be perfectly leveled out.

Doonie says, Wanna see something freak you out?

Somebody says, Long as it's not your dick. Which there's no real danger of Doonie actually showing. That's just a long-running joke to laugh at on cue. In the background the waves go *hush, hush* every time one collapses.

Doonie pulls a photograph from the kangaroo pocket of his hooded sweatshirt.

You say, Or a picture of your dick. So laughter surges up again.

Doonie hands you a creased snapshot he claims is Mike Hogan, but it's no Hogan you remember, though certainly this guy's the right height, and there's some snide familiarity in the badass curl of his mouth, like he's laughing at whoever holds the camera. This guy is beefed up like a Charles Atlas ad, striking a weight lifter's pose next to a bench whose barbell must hold plates in excess of three hundred pounds. This guy's lats rip out behind him like great wings he's forcing to sprout through sheer psychic will.

This is Hogan? you say, Holy shit. And you feel the picture slip from your fingers, leaving you to stare at the blank smoky place it used to be for several beats before you turn and see that Forsythe's holding it. You peer back into the chilly dark for Miss Gacy to comment on Hogan's transformation, but the log she sat on is bare, as if her train came and went the second you looked away.

Forsythe's wrapped in what looks like a horse blanket with his girlfriend, Bianca—a shy Chicana so demure and straight-looking that if you're high enough, you expect some country club patio to assemble around her. In eighth grade, you angled unsuccessfully for an invite to her slumber party. Now her genteel awkwardness in this company stirs something like a dim worry both for her comfort and for how you specifically might look to someone so (quote unquote) normal. So you find yourself smoothing her passage in this strange world when possible. This morning, she worried that eggs cooked in the skillet you'd only scrubbed with sand would give her salmonella, so you double washed it with bar soap even though you knew it'd make the eggs stick. When she borrowed some toilet paper to carry into the beach grass, you went before her with a flashlight, shouting and beating the fluent sedge with a stick to scare off any reptiles or rodents.

While Bianca's cupid's bow mouth draws on the clay pipe as if sipping from a soda straw, some neckless homunculus of Hogan shapes itself from wood smoke like a genie. His head's shaved. Six-pack abs. Biceps what you call swole up. The fire hisses and pops. An ashen log caves in on itself.

Hogan's looking a lot like Bluto, you say—mostly to hear the orienting sound of your own voice. Wind blows him away. More laughs. The hand Bianca passes the hash pipe with has an actual tennis bracelet on it.

Forsythe asks where'd he get the fucked-up looking tattoo.

That's a jailhouse tat, Doonie says. Do it yourself. Poke yourself with some pins and some hardass shit. I ask what it is, and he says it's Bazooka Joe.

There are more laughs.

I'm sure, Doonie says. Remember those smeary old tats we used to get wrapped up with that Bazooka Joe gum? That hard pink stuff? Little line down the middle like a butt crack. Nasty.

He takes his place in the shadows just on the edge of the firelight and raves out Hogan's prison exploits while the picture goes around. Hogan shoots up typewriter fluid and has to have the veins in his arms stripped out and replaced. Extended sentence. Hogan organizes the largest prison break in Texas penal history. He's first one out, third one caught.

Found him up a tree, Doonie says. Dead dogs on the ground all around him.

How'd he manage to get a gun in there? Bianca says. And again you think she should be in town folding crepe paper streamers for some dance.

That's the sick part, man. He hung them, Doonie says. Using his belt. Is that coldhearted or what? One of those baying bloodhounds leaps up, and Hogan lassos it around the neck and yanks up and snap—breaks its neck. That's why they sent him to Huntsville finally. The dogs bummed them out too bad.

Easy says, People get attached to dogs pretty good, working with them. His clear blue eyes seem to have miniature clouds drifting across the massively dilated pupils.

You think how fast Hogan transformed. The last time you saw him, he was a gangly boy on a banana-seat bike who didn't even need to shave. This guy looks like he could rip the door off a Volkswagen. With his teeth.

You ask for the picture again, stare through its window as if to peer past Hogan's armor of ripped flesh and find the stark skeleton boy who pedaled around the Deets's driveway that day. For an instant, it's like x-ray vision kicks in, and you can see him there, a thin blond boy in cutoffs, held captive inside this other massive body. Then the light shifts, and it's the big dude in the picture again, and he's laughing his ass off at you.

(Later, Hogan's metamorphosis seemed not that far from what some parents underwent when drinking—they could vanish entirely, or go roaring through their houses in the masks of monsters.)

Damn, you say and hand the picture off again. The hash is making your head feel injected with molten lead. You're fighting the urge just to nod off in the wet sand. But you know you'll wake up all crooked up and achey. You say, I gotta go somewhere and lie down.

Under the pier in your sleeping bag the waves aren't saying hush anymore, they're receding like so many sighs, some vanquished army in retreat. You marvel at how Hogan hardened up, and did he know beforehand the darkness was about to rise inside him? Could he feel that internal tideline climbing?

Suddenly you know that the boyfriend you've been longing for wouldn't solve anying. No one could stave off the bad feeling that wells up inside you lately. Something is going wrong, but you can't get any kind of bead on it, much less name it. You look at the surfboards scarred with sand and wax and tilted against the pier until they become great shields the longbowmen hauled back from some battle in the King Arthur book. The black wet suits peeled off and draped over them are the flayed skins of vanquished heroes. You're thinking it's been a while since you wanted to be Queen Guinevere, and will you ever again wait for some knight to gallop up and sweep you away? In the new fairy tale you're concocting for yourself, the armored chevalier as rescuer holds negligible value. But you'd damn sure like your own horse, some glossy animal tethered loosely to that piling over there. Anything to ride the fuck out of here.

Morning brings a gray wet you crank yourself stiffly up into. Neck crack. Shoulder shrug. Stand and stretch backward: a half-assed yogic salute to the nonexistent sun. Doonie's already in his black wet suit kneeling like a postulant to scrub wax on his board. Everybody must have tripped or snorted speed all night, for through the mist, people's movements resemble the jerky efforts of the extremely dingy. Bell's still ringing, no one's home. Critter's draped his Mayan warrior form in a chenille bathrobe the color of a honeydew melon. He's squeezing toothpaste from a single tube onto the outheld brushes of Flash and Maddog and two boys you don't recognize who must have wandered up this morning or driven out last night after you crashed.

You drape the unzipped sleeping bag around your shoulders like a sodden cape and walk down to the water's edge where Melonhead's sitting cross-legged on a self-styled throne of driftwood adorned with coiling ribbons of brown kelp. At first it seems he's wearing some peculiar Samurai helmet. But on closer inspection you can see he's scooped the tentacles and innards from a cabbage-head jellyfish and slapped the translucent casing on like a skullcap. You say, Whoa, Melonhead.

He says, Don't call me that no more.

Why not? you say.

That ain't who I am no more, he says. He stands with regal posture facing the breakers. The skeletal hull of a shrimp boat ducks and rises in the fog.

Well you sure as hell look like Melonhead to me, you say. He doesn't blink, so you push a notch further. Who are you then?

Doonie hollers over, Leave it alone.

Melonhead stares imperiously into gray mist. Turning from him, you speculate about your own unsupervised self, if you could be acting out some equivalent strangeness and be as blind to it.

Doonie's done scrubbing wax and is balancing his board carefully against a piling when you stroll over. What's Melonhead off into? you ask.

Who the hell knows? Doonie says. He wants you to call him Robert.

His name's Robert?

I don't know. Flash says that's not what teachers call him at school.

What warms your countercultural heart about this fraternity is such total lack of judgment, for you all learned at home how to ignore the blatantly peculiar. How to let it ride. In this company, any eccentricity warrants sanction. That sense you feel in town of being some freak whom passersby have secretly bought tickets to gawk at—that just doesn't bubble up here. Who cares if these surfers don't seem to read like you do? Most don't seem to read at all that you notice. Still, nobody squawks about lending you a flashlight if yours goes dead in the night, and on more than one occasion, guys you barely know have without question driven you thirty miles to buy a pen or extra paper, never asking what you're scribbling or to whom, with no mockery inherent in the not-asking either.

Bianca is picking her way barefoot across the sand, tiptoeing around razor shells. She's holding out a bag of bread and a jar of peanut butter Forsythe must have run to the store for.

Are you hungry? she says.

Flash also appears through the mist about this time, his toothbrush in his breast pocket, a clown's mouth of white foam around his lips. You marvel at the oddness of him. His strangely chinless face wears a gape of perpetual wonder, seeming almost slack-jawed, with little pegged teeth like a hamster. You decide in that instant that Flash is the quintessence of Leechfield, untranslatable away from these environs, borne of burning pot and scorched refinery air. You can take fresh bread home from the bakery and warm it, but to lift it from the wooden paddle right from the brick oven, to break it open steaming in your hands inside that hot room—that's something else entirely.

You're spreading peanut butter on white bread, having these benevolent thoughts when Flash turns his gape-mouthed face at you.

Can I fuck you? he says. Howls of laughter seem to start ashes blowing around everybody, gray moths loosed from some long-unopened armoire. The ocean roars applause.

Hell no, you say, laughing. Then you say, You're still tripping. You're on dope. Meanwhile, you keep spreading peanut butter, jar between your knees, open bag of sliced bread between your feet.

Oh come on now, Flash says, pleading. A tremor of giggles around the ragged circle.

Don't get sand in it, Critter says in reference to how you're handling the peanut butter.

It's in a jar, for fuck's sake.

I mean the bread, Critter says.

It's wrapped in plastic. What are you little Lord Fauntleroy or something?

Everybody stares blank-eyed.

Doonie fashions a translation. He says, So, Critter, you think you James Bond now instead of some raggety-ass freak? Think you got on a tuxedo? Not some funky-assed shirt from Penney's you had on for two days?

Well look, she's got sand on her arms there. Critter's pointing at you.

You pass the jar and loaf off to Maddog, saying, Critter, anything you eat on a beach is gonna have sand in it. Grind your teeth. It's the Sa-fucking-hara.

Maddog passes the bread along with his pinkies held out, saying to Doonie in a prissy voice, Don't get sand in it.

Then Flash pops out with, Can I fuck you when you dead?

You choke on a wad of sandwich, and a few guys howl out second dibs or third dibs. But that's pro forma, meant to make you feel, let's say, attractive. (Though in fact, none here will ever broach courtesy by laying an unwanted hand on you.)

Great guffaws are dispersing when you notice that Bianca's stood up, one hand clamped across her mouth as if forcibly containing a cry. Forsythe's whispering to her intensely as she jerks away and heads down to his car, from which she won't emerge the rest of the day but to pee.

You have this urge to run after her, to explain how this brute crack—seemingly designed to offend—is actually a testament to the grim loneliness Flash suffers for being so mutt ugly. A brave public admission of it. He meant somehow to charm the two girls into feeling easy about his presence when he's so malformed.

Doonie says to him, See what you did now, motherfucker?

Which causes Flash to cock his noggin in this bewildered angle, like a chickadee. How about, he asks of Doonie, Can I fuck *you* when you dead?

Doonie hikes his board under his arm, saying to Flash, You a sickity-ass motherfucker.

Flash keeps after it, saying, Come on now. Let's go on down to Motor Vehicles. Have them put it on your license. Get two witnesses to sign off. Your money goes to you mama and your kidneys and all that shit can go to science. But Flash gets to fuck you.

You wave both hands to stop him, coughing lungfuls of sea air out across your hash-scorched throat. You're not even eighteen months into high school.

Who saw it all coming?

It's only later that you'll marvel at how fast things changed since you strode with forced boldness into the high school auditorium wearing that daisy-spattered dress, scanning for the right place to sit. That poise was empty, of course. But the shrill hilarity that underlies this beach gathering is also built on restlessness. A swart and skittering wind cuts under the glib surface. The changes are coming fast and blind now, and in your skull sits an hourglass with a grainsize hole through which numb seconds are sliding.

Chapter Eighteen

In the first blurry TV shot longhaired boys trudge down a brick corridor. In the next, they edge into a paddy wagon. A few pull shirts up to hide their faces so their bare chests show. But the picture is nearly indecipherable, rolling and etched over with static, since the rabbit ears were broken off long ago in a foiled attempt to refine the bastard reception—the worst part being that no one could recall whose fit of anger did it. So at moments like this, there's no culprit to curse. You stand in the living room wearing only your plum-colored Dewey Webber Pig Board T-shirt and underpants. You're cussing the rotten fucking weather in this anus of a worm-eaten town for the snowy reception, trying to swivel the coat hangers twisted into vague rabbit-ear shapes and jammed down into old antennae holes as if a working angle existed. If it did, you could see which compadres were being led off amid the forty-odd dope fiends picked up in the county's biggest drug bust.

Is that Meredith's little boyfriend? your mother says.

How would I know? you say. Am I psychic? Do I look like the Great Mesmer? The coat hanger you're wrangling comes loose in your hand.

In the process of ramming it back in, somehow a blip of clarity is raised: you can see a ponytailed Frog Johnson looking all hangdog while some highway patrolman cuffs his hands behind his back. Three other boys enter the frame similarly cuffed when the snow blows back in.

You had it there, Mother says.

You turn to deliver your cold flat look full force, for there is no scorn greater than that of a sixteen-year-old girl for her mother, particularly if the task at hand is being performed with one lick of competence while the mother stares sleepily on.

You say, I had it when you were standing over by that end table. Go back over there.

Lemme get my cigarette lit. Goddamn, you're bossy, she says. She sets down her coffee cup, on which Bitches of the World Unite is emblazoned in red type.

You edge the coat hangers gingerly now, trying to coax the picture, and sure enough Skip Deslatte's face appears outside the Burger King on Gulfway Drive. Then blizzard and rolling.

She says, I know your daddy has a transistor radio somewhere from the last hurricane. Maybe they'd say their names on there. (It doesn't occur to you that your mother has not batted an eye over your pals being marched through a drug bust.)

You know for a legislative fact they wouldn't say the names of juveniles on the radio (when did you learn stuff like this?), but you prefer to blast your sister. You say, Lecia ran the batteries down last week tanning out in the yard.

Don't you miss her? Mother says, a dreamy look on her face.

Like you miss smallpox, you say. Like you miss a cyst or a goiter. In truth, you miss her so bad that you sometimes cry going to sleep at night. She gave you a surprise party for your sixteenth birthday, making pans of lasagna for the odd gaggle of heads gathered at your house. But when you call her apartment, either the line's busy or she says she's just walking out the door. Go by her house, she flounces around in hot pants with her roommate and some pair of muscle guys they're dating. Big pinheaded fellows with razor-cut hair and sharp creases ironed into their jeans. They drive Corvettes and wear senior rings the size of half dollars.

The phone rings, and Mother says, I'll get it.

You sigh and stretch, and for an instant the reception clears. It clouds again when you go back to your normal stand. You lift an arm at a right angle from your body, and the rolling stops. Suddenly you can see Clifford James and Cooter Dupris walking out of some liquor store. They're hiding faces under their shirts, but they're unmistakable.

It's for you, Mother says.

Tell them I'll call back, you say, for your outstretched arm seems the only antenna that can pick up this broadcast.

It's Meredith, she says. Then your mother stage whispers, She sounds upset.

Mother, do you mind standing here with your arm out?

For how long?

Just till I'm off the phone. She looks wearily at you until you say please. Then she assumes your post by the TV, arm outstretched. But the rolling snow comes back anyway in a blizzard.

Meredith says, Michael got busted. She's not crying, but her voice is thick with having cried. Her brother Michael always led your panoply of crushes, being lean with long fair hair loosely curled around gray eyes.

What for? you say. It's odd that your question sounds (in memory) so flat, no spike or terror in it, but Michael's cool demeanor always suggested to you that no blatant tragedy could touch him. Also, this police and jail stuff that's been edging steadily closer to your immediate circle still rings of fantasy. Bang, bang, shoot-'em-up.

Your mother whaps the set hard on one side, and you wave at her to shush. She gives you the finger, and you give it back. Jeez.

They say he was dealing drugs, Meredith says. Which is stupid. He'd have had money if he dealt. There's also this weird conspiracy thing. They knew he opposed the war, and they're saying he was gonna blow up the state capitol. (The SDS to which Michael belonged—Students for a Democratic Society—was rumored to be the public arm of the terrorist Weather Underground, which had members on the FBI's most wanted list.)

Why? Where'd they get that? you say. None of this has touched you yet. Inside, you're daydreaming how sometimes, sleeping over at the Brights', you roll over and press your ear against the cold plaster to better hear him playing on his unplugged electric guitar delicate arpeggios.

I don't know, Meredith says. They found some cherry bombs or blasting stuff in the house.

Hell, Daddy's got old cherry bombs rolling around his sock drawer, or he used to anyway.

I know, she says in a voice that's clearing, as if she's washed her face and had a long gulp of clear water.

And I'm way more likely to blow something up than Michael.

Tell that to the pigs, Meredith says.

But you're picturing some witness stand to rush onto. How you'll plead tearily to the judge till the bailiff unlatches Michael's handcuffs, and he briefly rubs his wrists before sweeping you into his arms. In this way, you take the seeds of cold fact to grow the scenario you need to focus on. (In retrospect, in light of Michael's plight, such self-absorption will boggle your mind.)

You know who else got picked up? you say.

No, she says, then goes quiet. If she was grieving when she called, now she's neatly packaged that up and backed off it. The flat tone of her voice is reassuring to you. (How stupid this comfort level is doesn't hit you till decades later.)

Are you all right? you ask, knowing she'll say nothing but sure. Which is a relief, a button she can press to return your world to normal. That Meredith's world may well have spun irreversibly past that point may never enter into it. (In those years if you were fine, everyone you cared about was fine by extension.) In the background, you hear Mrs. Bright's call.

I gotta go. Aunt Wilhemina's here, she says.

Where are y'all going?

Could you find out if there's a study sheet for chemistry? Talk to Stacy. I guess we'll be at the courthouse. Root around in my locker if you need to.

You manage to blurt out, Tell Michael I say hey—before the dial tone starts moaning at you.

You wish you could boast of having hurried to the courthouse to stand by Meredith. Or that you fried up a chicken for when they got back. Wrote a note. Offered to drive somebody somewhere. You didn't. Such a thing would never have occurred to you, and Meredith would never have asked. If her hair was on fire, as the saying goes, she wouldn't ask for a glass of water. Such requests were beyond her ken. Neither did you expect from your parents basic showing up at track meets or school plays. The one time Lecia dared ask for such a thing (back when she had the lead in ninth grade), Mother vanished into a three-day binge. The not-asking reflected the great powerlessness you were all mired in.

In fact, Meredith's placid guise of bearing up remarkably well means you're losing her.

You put the phone in its notched cradle and see that your mother has managed to noodle the TV into some watchable form. But the local news is long past. It's just fat old Gus Remus poking at the greaseboard weather map with a stick. Your mother is staring at you in a way that makes you want to run. Finally you say, What? What is it? Why are you looking at me?

Her hazel eyes are bright with tears. She says, Reckon they're gonna pick you up. I mean, should we hide you or something?

Oh for chrissake, Mother. Come here, you say. When you hug her, she feels oddly pliable in your hands. She draws back to look at you with that abstracted expression she brings to her sculpture. She tucks a strand of hair behind your ear, pinching a caress along your jawline like it's clay she's shaping. But she's not shaping you anymore. She long ago asked you to shape yourself, occasionally tossing out a shard of worry for you to dismiss.

From the first, you handle Michael's arrest as you handled most troubling events—you ignore it. Meredith helps by vanishing into appointments with the court-appointed attorney, or spending hours at the central library checking out books to bring up to the jail. While none of your close pals get indicted in that first round, plenty of peripherals you'd smoked joints with made the arrest muster.

Somebody must have fingered Doonie and his cohorts though, for in subsequent weeks a patrol car emerging from behind a billboard or hedgerow with siren flailing becomes common, as do elaborate car searches. Once two fairly clueless Bubba-type cops pull a carload of you over, then need help from the longhairs in unbolting the backseat so they can survey the floor with a magnifying glass in search of a pot seed or crumb of indictable substance while all of you stand around making Sherlock Holmes jokes under your breath. You hear about but never see pot-sniffing dogs used to search cars, though Doonie claims to carry a flip-top can of Alpo to steer hounds off the dope.

No one knows anymore where Donnie's stash is, but he's cocky enough to tell the cops as they pry the hubcaps off his tires, You got the right guy, officer, just the wrong day.

One night you're all bouncing along the beach road toward home in Doonie's packed Torino when a siren starts rotating red through the back window. You turn around and can almost feel the red blade's swipe across your throat. You've been stoned all weekend, so you have the vague sense of your body's having melted down entirely, leaving only your head afloat on your neck stem like an ungripped balloon. Everyone pats around to see who's holding, but it's Sunday night. Everything that could be smoked or snorted or eaten has been.

Doonie pulls over. The brakes take hold, and you feel your bodies start to fly forward through the car hull, then you snap back as if from rubber bands on your backs. Four or five flashlights beam in, bobbing like unfettered suns to obscure the dark cop shapes that hulk behind them, but on their shirt pockets and collars, brass stars and badges flicker and gleam.

You're rousted out into the night damp, all silent, all straining to give off the acquiescent affability of the law-abiding teen. IDs are asked for and agreeably proferred. A cop's sausage-fingered hand is beaming a flashlight into the eyes of the photo on your driver's license. Doonie's talking so fast he must be concealing a random tab of acid in his pocket or something. But Lord he can talk. (Before he's twenty-one, he'll hawk for a strip club, then briefly open a car lot called S&M Motors with the unlikely motto, "If we can't spank you, no thank you.") *How fast was I going, sir? Gosh, if I don't get my geometry done tonight Mama's gonna ground me. I know she's making some of that good cream gravy right now. Does your mamma always cook a chicken after church?...*

Despite his repartee, you all get jacked up alongside the Torino. Somebody jokes about a body-cavity search, and the cops seem to consider this—a prospect that sets you alternately giggling like a fiend, then trying not to fall to your knees and beg mercy. While you're spread-eagled alongside the car like this, limbs starting to shake, a few cops talking football sluggishly pat you all down.

The mood shifts radically when—from thirty or so yards behind you—a patrol car hurtles fast to a dusty stop. Out leaps this scrawny uniformed guy, yelling something indecipherable. The dazzling headlights you look back into still swirl with hallucinated star galaxies, but there appears to be in his hand a raised pistol, held aloft like a talisman. Somebody in your lineup hollers, Hit the dirt (later nobody would 'fess to it), so you all dive down onto the sand-gritty road.

It turns out this kind of massive synchronized movement from a line of prospective felons jogs the average small-town peace officer into unholstering his weapon. The noise of metal whipped fast from soft leather conjures the gunfight scene from some movie about the O.K. Corral. You can actually sense the blind muzzles fix on your skull and spinal column—dozens of empty little zero imprints. You squirm in the sandy shoulder like a slug, hands still pressed obediently to your head, eyes squeezed shut. (Some superstitious creature inside still believes if you can't see them, you're officially not there.) An interval ten thousand years long snails by, until the cops start reholstering their weapons, going, *Aw hell,* and *Goddamn, Leon.*

Turns out this Leon held up nothing more explosive than a tiny whisk broom he'd been sent to Kmart for, the better to sweep up the Torino's carpet nap. Which he does on his knees while everybody but you sits on the car hood devouring tiny square hamburgers from White Castle the cops ultimately fetch and pass around as compensation for how their pal scared you all sick. You say you're vegetarian, but in truth, your hands have begun to shake as if palsied. You fear if you touch the bag it will rattle loud enough to reignite suspicion. You're fighting to hold this tremble in check when some fellow ambles over and shoves his hat back with an index finger to ask, Aren't you Pete Karr's daughter? Baby, lemme bring you home. Your daddy'll kick my ass if he thinks I let you sit around out here with these sorry old boys.

Thus you walk away, not looking back at your compadres to give any it's-okay-I'll-get-bail sign. You've been differentiated from them and are glad for the patrol car ride home—a trip marked by your near constant uttering of the word *sir.* Your daddy isn't home (thank God), but you promise the officer you'll say hey and let's get after them bass sometime soon.

You retell Meredith this adventure on the phone or at lunch with amusement. But she's not the audience she once was—absorbed partly by her extremely whacky boyfriend (whom you mostly ignore, perhaps hoping he'll vanish so you can reclaim her full attention). Or she waits for disclosures and judge's rulings, for lawyer's vacations to end and calendars to clear so Michael can be exonerated and come home.

Talk of his arrest seems to weave and circle through school via low whispers and pointed looks. The two times someone openly flings these mentions at her, the only shift in her stoical bearing is that she flushes crimson.

For a while in civics class, the coarse, tobacco-spitting Mr. Wright makes daily cracks about her brother the jailbird, till a kind guidance counselor gets her transferred out. Then during some mock trial for another civics class, this born-again Christian girl playing prosecutor and thus interviewing Meredith as a possible juror says, It's common knowledge you have a brother in prison. Do you think you could be an impartial juror? At which Meredith just returns to her seat in silence. No response. Nobody says a word, teacher included.

Later that same week, this prosecutor girl is flouncing through the lunch line, when Meredith says—quietly but with great force—*Bitch!* And the aforementioned counselor, who overhears this exchange, leans in to whisper, Good for you, Meredith. I didn't know you had it in you. (Only in Leechfield could this kind of frontal attack draw kudos from educational authorities.)

Mostly you manage to believe Michael's fine, for in every Texan's mind there sleeps some genetically wired pathway that makes running afoul of the law okay. Justified in a lot of cases. In local parlance, some people just need shooting, and fistfighting to the point of arrest is an accepted sport with unofficial rankings known countywide. Everybody knows who all the badasses in town are, your daddy being one of them.

What with the civil rights movement, certain arrests hit the moral high ground. Your mother had marched with Dr. King in Selma, Alabama and just missed going to jail. The Jesuit Berrigan Brothers destroyed federal draft records, and the paper carried daily drawings of the Chicago Seven (or was it Eight?), who'd prompted riots to disrupt the Democratic convention. You could buy T-shirts in Houston with pictures of Bobby Seale bound and gagged during the proceedings. For these activists, jail was a plausible if undesirable interruption in an implausible world.

But as months drag by, some cloud of truth about Michael's fate condenses inside you. The Brights remain stranded the way each family of an arrested boy seems to be. They're entirely alone in watching Michael's legal fate unfold. He warrants no audience, no potluck supper, no rally. No fiery lawyer will fly down to take up his cause pro bono, as Gregory Peck did in the movie of *To Kill a Mockingbird*.

Even knowing this, you fail to go to the trial. You couldn't, for part of you wants to disbelieve there is a trial, or a jail into which you and your pals might conceivably be thrown.

Maybe that's why the verdicts so deeply shock, leaving you in a state of cold, inadequate fury, because the boys who couldn't make bail become those who pull prison terms. These are, of course, boys from the poorest families—those whose parents couldn't pull off a second mortgage or sell the extra car. The direct correlation between income and jail seems so blatant and grotesque you can't believe it doesn't make headlines. Part of you keeps waiting to uncover some other mysterious variable to explain the discrepancy. But when Michael's roommate walks with probation while Michael gets two four-year sentences—one for the bullshit conspiracy stuff, one for possession of a quantity of marijuana that, a few years later, wouldn't constitute a felony—you knew it was all about what Doonie called the Dough-Re-Mi.

Meredith tells you about the trial with less animation than one reporting live from the courthouse steps, though her cheeks flush in patches, and she speaks in a taut, breathless voice, as if she's been slapped.

Some short time after this, she leans over a peach-colored cafeteria tray saying, I think it's time for you to corrupt me. Which delights you. A sleepover is scheduled, but first she wants to sacrifice her maidenhood—as you jokingly call it—to her now ever-present boyfriend, Dan (who ironically enough was busted with her brother but managed to make bail and thus probation).

Dan's possessed of a child's abiding sweetness in a tall and storklike frame. (John Cleese of Monty Python will later evoke Dan.) But his psychedelic antics, which can drive you into giggling fits when stoned, also strike you as bizarre—bizarre being a hard bell to ding in your current crowd. This especially worries you since he and Meredith plan to marry just one year hence, after she's aced being a college freshman.

Dan likes to grab the pet parakeet in his fist and kiss it. The frantic bird will wrench its head to escape while Meredith yells at Dan to leave it alone, the bird doesn't like it. But Dan will just keep repeating in a falsetto *Baby loves Daddy, Daddy loves baby.* You've also seen him spend hours gluing empty paper towel rolls together so he can force the panicked parakeet to scuttle through as he coaxes from the far end saying *Come to Daddy, my little tube turd.*

This isn't just some act, for comparable oddities go down even when Dan feels unwatched. At a birthday party once, he went back for a second cake helping to find only an empty cake stand. He snatched up the empty doily and wadded the whole paper into his mouth to suck the last icing from it. Noticing the sudden quiet, he spit the wad into his palm, shrieked as if it surprised him, and tossed it up where it stuck to the ceiling and held fast. Then he innocently looked around as if nothing untoward had happened.

(By the end of Meredith's illustrious grad school career, Dan will be fully schizophrenic, and they'll divorce. Twenty years after that in Boston, he'll appear at your university office wearing a deerstalker hat and trying to convince you that everyone who sports a stocking cap is in the CIA conspiring to arrest him for drugs he bought back in 1970. A few years after this encounter, he'll die of the AIDS virus that'll plague other friends in this circle.)

Once Meredith's deflowered (a private event), you set her guzzling Gallo wine stolen from your parents' cupboard. Because you lack rolling papers, you wind up constructing a joint from a tampon wrapper, blowing smoke out the screen. You laugh yourself sick when she starts cussing, saying motherfucker and dickhead and shit-for-brains, because the words sound so foreign in her mouth.

Still the evening lacks the flavor of triumph you'd envisioned for Meredith's initial debauchery. For years, you'd tried to lure her into the illicit, perhaps believing it would bond you two more deeply somehow. (Maybe there was some unconscious desire to shave a few IQ points off that raging intellect so you might better keep up.)

But once she passes out, her eyelids sealing her from you, a bleak loneliness settles, cold as a winding sheet. Though you've ingested enough pot and wine to set your brain waves sloping into sleep, you stay awake, for there's some instinctual desire to guard her. The room revolves in such slow loops that her deep repose befuddles you, seems unnatural or wrong, like a sickness. Every now and then, she sighs like it's her last breath. Anyway, this urge to go for help keeps running through you. You climb out of bed a few times to tap on your parents' closed door but ultimately slide back under the covers, for what might you say is amiss? You're the one who brought her here.

Decades later, you'll know there was no cavalry to call, no ready salvation to offer. Meredith needed a kind of simple care that eluded you. That fact will leave this carved-out sense of having failed her. Not intentionally, but from being blind.

But no sooner does this rhetoric unhook you from blame than you remember the ragged-looking kid your son brought home about age eight. This kid also knew no better, but nonetheless drew for you on borrowed paper various cartoons as thank-yous for all the time spent at your house. One Christmas, you pulled from your icy mailbox his rendering of two Disney pals on red paper. It was folded four times and held the following note: God loves us because we loves you. Part of you knows that with sufficient heart, you might have marshaled some comfort for Meredith other than oblivion.

Chapter Nineteen

With the aid of hallucinogens, you set off like some pilgrim whose head teems with marvels and vistas, baptismal rivers from which you plan to emerge purified. But what's longed for usually bears no resemblance to what you find.

On Independence Day, you're affably tripping your brains out at dawn in a public park when Clyde pulls up in a van painted red, white, and blue, with stars in a peace sign where the Volkswagen symbol should be. He's twenty-one, and for your sixteenth birthday made you a fringed leather purse that you stupidly left at a Who concert. Leans out the window saying those dudes over there are from Colorado. Have this amazing dope.

You turn to see three shirtless, not unlovely boys you don't know (a rarity) playing Frisbee. A yellow dog with a red bandanna around its neck flies vertically through the air to catch an orange disc in its jaws.

Clyde says, Gonna take them swimming down in Village Creek. (He gestures at various vans and vehicles.) Wanna come?

Clyde has owlish blue eyes and chews the end of a safety match; his fluttering hair is long as yours. Your mild crush on him combines with the lure of strong dope, to get you off your skinny ass and into the van. (When you hear three years hence that he's killed himself in a way and for a reason unknown, the shock of it will flare through you like lit solvent then evaporate, leaving only this day's image of Clyde.)

In the phone call you make from the Fina station en route, your crotchety-sounding daddy just hears that you're going swimming, which is truth enough though he may imagine you're calling from the town pool two blocks away.

Thus a caravan of hippie vehicles winds into the bowels of east Texas, the piney woods. After a tooth-bumping ride down a rutted logging road cut by long-gone wagon wheels in red clay, you reach the sandy-bottomed creek from which you drew catfish with a cane pole your daddy baited for you. By then the psychedelic rush kicks in, and the day's episodes start to run together as if rained on. Things happen to you, and you mostly meander inside yourself, detached.

The guys strip down for swimming right away while you sit on a warm red car hood too high to move. So many dicks dangling before you somehow look individually odd. Like space creatures. How long do you goggle at them, eyeballs popped out on hallucinated springs as you marvel at the diverse herd before you check yourself and retract your attention?

An older girl in an orange halter assembles sandwiches from an economy-size packet of bologna. You want her to verify that the boys' organs dangle in lengths and girths corresponding in no way to the size of the bearer. But her granny glasses make you flash that she's not really a hippie, only some prim goodwife imported from *The Scarlet Letter*, which you should be at home reading. Though this makes no sense whatsoever, you hold your tongue and busy yourself helping with the sandwiches, scribbling peace signs or stars on slabs of Wonder bread with yellow mustard till you suspect all the boys have submerged their accompanying dicks underwater. Only then do you look up, trying to maintain the blasé air of someone who sees flagrant-dicked boys all the damn time and cannot be ruffled by one boy's high, muscled ass or by another's shiny auburn hair falling in a curtain across his broad shoulders.

When the goodwife hands you a sandwich, it seems a gargantuan Dagwood sandwich, two feet high, and it seems rude to say that ingesting stuff while tripping makes you half nuts, for who can figure how many chews to take and when to swallow? Plus you so vividly picture the musculature of your throat and the secreted digestive acids—the mechanics of eating gross you out. Because you so don't wish to offend her pinch-mouthed self, the sandwich stays gripped in hand the whole morning till all the iceberg lettuce and meat and tomato wheels have flopped out to be set upon by ants.

Blank time gets spliced in. Next thing you know, one of the Colorado boys sits on the bank with his legs stretched out stiff before him like a doll. His feet are swollen up to twice their normal size as if snakebit, worse than the gout of an old lady in a nursing home forced into those tight, white socks. Everybody gathers around, addled over the bloated feet.

You say, They kinda look like a pair of potatoes. It's a voice so rusty you wonder if you've spoken all morning. The guy cuts you this wounded look. To reassure, you say with the authority of the rabidly high that it's probably just ant bites. But inside you recoil from the prospect of those bloated feet exploding. You even edge back a few paces as if to avoid any splatter, for you have imagined the blow-out—how his spirit will leak from ankle holes till he's empty and flat as roadkill. It makes you want to make for the road and stick your thumb out or else to fall down giggling.

What ant bite does this? the guy says, voice higher with panic.

Clyde asks Cathy to look at it since her mom's a nurse. But Cathy's naked as a jaybird and, by being solo in this, seems aggressively, savagely naked. She has a great pelt of pubic thread and globular breasts perched high on what looks like a dwarf's body. In fact, she seems so devolved and feral that Clyde's speaking to her at all strikes you as perverse.

All she says is, You might oughta stop scratching at that. Looks to be making it worse. You try not to gape at her talking, for words from the bandanna-wearing dog right then would seem no more strange.

Do you think I need to go to the hospital? the dude says, his voice in another register now, like a record played too fast. You nonchalantly wonder what evolutionary purpose this might serve—the voice rising with fear. Then suddenly, the grim prospect of the hospital rears up—the even now revolving glass door that would scoop you up and spit you out into the emergency room's atmosphere of Lysol woven through with its single fiber of death.

You want to say, Exploding feet or no, buddy, kiss that hospital's ass goodbye. To get this wagon train of sun-scorched freaks rolling toward western medicine would require something way more dire—car wreck, actual overdose with heart stoppage.

The swollen-foot dude says, I can't lose my feet.

Another girl offers up, Why don't you bury your feet in sand and see if the swelling goes down?

One of the Colorado dudes asks hopefully if that's some Indian cure, the sand stuff, and somebody answers probably while the rest of you nod.

Any nod on serious hallucinogens can become sagelike, and suddenly the group resembles some Bedouin tribe weary with ancient desert wisdom looking down on the scorpion-stung interloper whose tongue is slowly swelling his throat shut.

To calm the nearly weeping boy, joints are rolled and guitars broken out. The guys take turns at Neil Young or Bob Dylan while you pretend to read—an impossible task as high as you are. The sentences warp and bow up on the page like so many worms. In truth the paperback is a shield against the unwanted advances of this one doglike Colorado guy. He keeps saying that you're one foxy lady (a phrase which sends a sliding Hendrix *wha-wha* through your head).

Eventually, you fancy being privy to everyone's thoughts. One voice at a time they wind through you until the rambling rush chatters up your mind entirely. So you set down your book, rise up, strip down, and wade into the warm river with as much offhanded aplomb as a publicly naked person can muster. (As an adult on nude beaches in France, you'll find disrobing before such a generalized audience impossible, and so will sit resolutely in your bikini as the naked sneer past. You're not overly modest, but unless someone has a fairly vested interest in your particular nudity, you find no reason to sashay it around.)

The instant you dive under, the voices wash from your ears. You swim in a hard crawl upstream till your arms get rubbery and you're forced to wade out wobbly kneed onto a sandbank in what your head announces is the Forest Primeval.

An internal flash of Adam and Eve in the garden makes you shy. Cover yourself, some internal voice commands. Though there's no one around for miles, you roll in wet sand, caking whole handfuls on your breasts and pubis (as if any picnicking fisherman might be fooled you were clothed).

Thus clad, you lie on your back in sand baking for some unmeasured interval. It's two minutes. It's an hour. The acid is gobbling up the day. Then through the brush comes a rustle and plop in the water. You sit up to see an alligator tail, or the hallucination of one—junior size, maybe three feet in length—making its S-curve in the current. The sight starts your heart jackhammering against your rib cage. Your body reverberates with every pulse beat like a struck gong.

The poem you take up writing makes your predicament an apt allegory for the human condition. You write large, walking across the sand with a stick, half-believing this artifact will be fossilized then unearthed in some distant millennium by archeologists who, stunned by the lines' grace, will derive some aborigine ritual.

But your final product has devolved into monkey language. Now you doubt the alligator was real. Meanwhile, the sun has started falling fast through pines, having burned itself into the murky red of the rubber ball you used to play jacks with.

You wade back in and swim downstream. After a few strokes, a fish leaping nearby shoots adrenaline through you again, so your arms whirl windmill-fashion, and your feet kick up a huge wake.

In an eyeblink, you're back at the camp in cutoffs and T-shirt. The river's gone, and you've entered this heavy element. They're loading vehicles around you.

You're told but don't quite believe that in your absence some redneck appeared on the far bank with a rod and reel. He hollered over to put some damn clothes on, his wife and kids were there. To which Clyde allegedly said back, *Take yours off,* then shook his dick at the guy, who said he was going to call the law. Once he disappeared, everybody but Cathy got dressed.

So the fiesta is ending, no jugglers or Mexican trumpets, and you're crashing hard among strangers. The Colorado guys once so tanned and smartly traveled in your eyes have progressed into a fairly gnarly crew. The one who fancies you has taken from his mouth a plate holding four front teeth. You long to be home with the sand rinsed out of your crotch and wearing an eyelet lace nightgown while holding a cat on your lap.

Here's when the cops show up.

Not just a pair of cops either, but legions of cops, a tide. A swarming army comes crashing toward your now simple and slow-moving tribe. (Think: Margaret Mead's peace-loving Tribe.) Through dense brush they come—announced by branches snapping under black shiny shoes. There are highway patrol wearing flat-brimmed hats à la Smokey the Bear. Cops from the nearby burg of Kountze have donned khaki and Stetsons. A few guys in pale blue shirts and dark pants wearing flashlights instead of guns may be rent-a-cops like you see hanging around the mall. They surge in a thunderous tide—hollering and waving arms—into your midst. All foliage is whapped back and shoved aside. Then they're rousting companions into various get-arrested postures.

Your response to this is to stand stock still, a marble statue like in freeze tag. That's what most everybody does. Only the swollen-foot boy tries hilariously to cram one elephantine foot into the tiny huarache that now seems woven for a Barbie. The supremely bare Cathy also scrambles, scuttling behind a car to wiggle into her gauzy Mexican dress, which—given that she's soaking wet—you can see straight through (including but not limited to every lock of her big black beaver). Clyde and a few other guys have listed backward, actually wading into the shallows. One guy says, I'm on probation.

To which Clyde replies, See that river? I'd hit it. And the boy wades off thigh high in his long jeans as some cop with a bullhorn starts shouting ghastly mechanical orders about lying down or keeping your goddamn hands raised up.

You raise your hands and wait for somebody to notice.

No actual blows fall, but the racket creates an ambience of roughness. That you're all handled somewhat like barn animals astonishes you. You keep wanting to say, It's me, Mary Karr. Winner of the Van Buren Elementary Spelling Bee in fifth grade.

Maybe you even do say it as your hands are tugged behind and latched into metal. Then you're wedged in the caged backseat of a patrol car, your purse flung into your lap, with three other girls—including Cathy, who's loudly pissed. She screams, Fucking pigs. Then she kicks the back seat and says, What are we being hauled in for, you fat-assed slab of bacon.

When she sulls up finally, slouching down in a pout, you try to shoulder her reassuringly. To this she whispers, Don't give them your right name.

But my name's on my license, you say. In my purse right here. With a picture.

They won't know that's you, she says. Not necessarily. Then Cathy straightens herself, lets her heavy, black-lashed eyelids fall like some oracle closing up shop, retreating to the netherworld. Her body sways next to you as the car seesaws down rutted roads.

Hoping to create an atmosphere of goodwill, to make up whatever ground Cathy lost for you in her rant, you address the driver's shaved neck in what you hope are mellifluous tones, sentences autocratically constructed. You talk with the anxious cheer of a job applicant about your steadfast character. You tack fifty points onto your SAT score, and lie you're in the Honor Society. You claim to have been first in your junior high class, when it was really sixth grade and you were a notch down. You brag about belonging to the drill team, whose members still believe you procured an illegal abortion.

You look back and see that every car in this slow procession has its headlights on.

Like a funeral, you say to the shaved neck, in a coffee-klatsch kind of voice. Light-hearted. But when the driver turns around at a light—this is his first acknowledgment of your more or less nonstop patter—he reveals mirrored aviator shades and a lipless mouth that says simply, almost softly, Shut the fuck up.

Which you do, though his rebuke wounds you. You stare out the side window like some frisky dog who's gotten a swat on the nose with a newspaper. Such self pity is required to steer your awareness from the deep terror the possibility of jail sparks. Dark's come on, and the first stars seem to press down like shards of some far-off, shattered thing. The pines along the road loom through the tears you hope nobody notices, for you hate being such a pussy.

Finally, the funereal parade arrives at the Kountze County Jail, which is what William Faulkner might have called a fur piece.

For some reason, you expected a crowd for this arrival, flashbulbs or TV cameras like in the TV bust you watched. But only one unmarked Chevy with a siren stuck on top sits slantwise in the lot. Handcuffs force you to wiggle sideways out of the vehicle, a cop grabbing up your purse. Then you shuffle cowlike through a glass door held open by a skinny deputy saying, Well, hello there, ladies.

A movie will come out soon about some rednecks butt-raping some city guy they find out in the woods with his pals. The whole time they've got him down on the ground, he's screaming, and some lunatic on his back keeps hollering out, Squeal like a pig. As if sodomy is the funniest damn thing on the planet. Once you see it, you locate the bowel-deep fear of being left alone in this backwater with brusque and malign-seeming men.

Your gang lines the walls around this large, nondescript room, where three central processing tables remind you of nothing so much as kindergarten snack time. (There'd been one for graham crackers, another for milk, and a third where you selected a towel to unroll on the wood floor for nap time.)

At the first table, a man inks your fingertips, pinching each one to roll it in the correct rectangle on the white arrest card. Your own hand feels limp and foreign as he handles it, an object picked up on the roadside.

At the next, a guy at a typewriter studies your driver's license then pecks a few keys. When you ask with all earnestness what you're being charged with, the words seem to echo as if down a canyon. The guy behind the typewriter says, We'll think a something. Then he says, Hey, Ray, what all are they being charged with?

Ray's patting down the guys lined up around the wall, an indignity the girls have thus far been spared. He looks up from the well muscled bare back and blue-jeaned ass of Bert Stowe. He says, Well, disturbing the peace, for one thing. Indecent exposure for two.

I had my clothes on, you say. This is a small point of pride by now. But surely you should get credit for it. Maybe there's some Wasn't Naked list you can get on. Your eyes plead toward the typewriter dude. Again, you long to stand up and lean over the table, explain to him, conspiratorially, It's me, Mary Karr. Daughter of Pete and Charlie. Sister of the large-breasted Lecia, who's a student of physics. As if this would win you an apology or outright release.

Across the room, the guy with the mug-shot camera says, Resisting arrest would make charge number three.

I didn't resist anything, you say.

The typer guy hits the space bar. You wonder is your voice audible, for no one seems to respond.

Now from a back hallway, cops enter hauling cardboard boxes with God knows what, suitcases and knapsacks, beaded purses. They even brought in somebody's Coleman camping stove. You wonder wonder wonder what contents will come to light here. A misty sweat breaks out between your shoulder blades, condenses into a few definite beads that roll down. Latches are clicked open. Receptacles pawed through. Then some oratorio-belting choir inside you starts chanting with enormous force: Don'tfinddrugsthere! Don'tfinddrugsthere!

Yet still you assume there's honor among these thieves. So anybody actually holding dope will invariable step forward if some appears, to keep the rest from being charged unfairly.

Hours seem to have unraveled while the guy at the typewriter stares at the white card. Suddenly he comes to life long enough to read out your street address, saying, This right?

You say, Yessir.

Then with a sweep of his hand, he reaches under the table to produce your purse with all the flourish of a magician. He upends it—pens and whatnot rolling. You're embarrassed at the white tube of Maybelline mascara, the small compact of Cover Girl blush—for good hippie girls eschew such vanities, and you feel instantly like a cheater and hope Clyde doesn't see, or Bert Stowe. When your spiral notebook of poems spills out, you restrain the impulse to lunge across the table and snatch it to your chest. He sets the notebook aside, not even thumbing it. Instead he holds aloft your container of birth control pills. There's a quick grip at your core.

Hey Baxter, we got you a live one here, he says to camera-guy.

Little young for my taste, Booger, I'm gonna pass.

Across the room someone chimes in, Old enough to bleed, old enough to butcher.

For your mug shot, Baxter hands you a stiff card with numbers on it to hold under your chin. He says, Smile, you're on Candid Camera! Profile. Full front. Just like on TV.

Then you're blinking stars. Your eyes clear just when a Smokey-the-Bear guy draws from a cardboard box across the room a satchel. It's woven with Inca geometries and may as well have an I-Carry-Illicit-Narcotics label on it. From it, he draws a huge freezer bag of uncleaned pot, jagged with stems and tarry clots and dry handfuls of blossom. Maybe half a pound, you eyeball it to be.

Well well well, he says, Looky here. He holds it high, Smokey does, asking with all earnestness, Whose is this?

Come on, you think. Get on with it. Before the rest of us get in trouble.

The sheriff says, Y'all done hit the jackpot now. Number next charge would be possession of an illegal substance.

A nearby cop whistles through his teeth.

A third says, Looks like intent to distribute, Jake.

By now anxiety has driven you back into prattling, like in the car. Mostly, you ask for your phone call. I get a phone call, you say. When's my phone call? Don't I get a phone call, sir?

Baxter leads you into the line of girls—between the goodwife and Cathy, who scratches her head then studies whatever lodges under her nails. Oh this is perfect, you say aloud.

For you're thinking about how you fit between these two. What's the feminist dichotomy for roles we get forced into? Madonna and whore? You say that aloud, Madonna and whore.

What? Cathy says. The goodwife says, Come again?

You look down at your grubby feet in coral-colored flip flops and fake deafness. When they move you down the hall, caged bare bulbs at intervals along the ceiling cast grids of shadows over you. You're thinking, It's not fair. It's not fair.

The room they lock you all in is a stone dungeon lacking only wall chains and iron maiden. The cold concrete floor holds at its center a drain big around as a coffee can, nothing one could tunnel through. A hard bench lines the walls. Lidless toilet in one corner. The door swings shut. Blam. A slot in it slides open. The disembodied voice says, We'll be watching you ladies.

Cathy says, Watch my flaming white ass, oinker.

The voice shoots back, We just might.

You picture that enormous plastic baggie of pot held high under the trembling neon like some chalice at mass, and you know in your bone marrow it's sufficient to indict the lot of you.

Cathy says, They'll take us one at a time. Whatever you do, don't tell them anything.

But I don't know anything, you say.

That's right, Cathy says. That's just the look to give. Real blink-blink wide-eyed.

But I don't, you say.

Since Cathy's the only one who has, in her words, been in the joint, she somehow commandeers the room to prepare you for the atrocities that come with your certain prison sentences.

Well first off, you better learn to eat pussy, Cathy says. You can ew and goo all you want. One of those dykes ham-handles the scruff of your skinny neck, you'll think better of it. Believe me. It's way easier than getting a big old dick in your mouth.

Nobody says anything for so long, you feel obliged not to leave this statement hung out there. It stretches the edges of reason to think of women doling out a rape. Finally you say, Couldn't you just talk to them? I mean. They're women, right?

Only technically, Cathy says. Then as if she's read your mind meandering, she says, Don't read this all weird. I'm not suggesting we eat each other out in here or anything.

At this the goodwife's eyebrows jag upward. A hush comes back, heavy. Unliftable. Goodwife says, I gotta mellow over here a minute.

While everybody is stretching out on benches just wide enough for their torsos, Cathy leaps up and starts pounding on the door hollering, I need a blanket, fuckwads. Get your doughnut-eating asses down here with some blankets.

The slot slides open, but no eyes appear. The voice says, Why sure, honey, and maybe you'd like some cookies and milk and a little tuck in.

The slot has two six-inch bars welded over it, and it's to these that Cathy flies—but she continues to hang there like a gorilla, rattling the metal with her whole weight. The sliding door snaps shut. She holds the bars and eventually hops up so her soles slap flat on the door.

You crook one arm over your eyes to block out the sight, for you can no longer bear to ponder Cathy. But from nowhere an image fills your head like floodlight: Cathy at seven, at twelve, at fifteen. For the first time, it strikes you that Cathy wasn't born this way. Maybe she entered custodial care with as much humanity as any girl here.

Look what happened to Hogan. When he got paroled briefly this year, you and Doonie took him to Burger King where he bummed both a smoke from a guy and his lit cigarette for fire. Once Hogan's was lit, he thumped ash on the guy's head and dropped his lit cigarette on the ground. It happened so fast and offhandedly, you questioned the fact of it, wondering if they knew each other or some nasty exchange had gone down out of ear reach. When in the car you asked what that was about. Hogan said only, I hate all this bullshit, man. Two days later, he was arrested for breaking and entering.

And even though Meredith's brother sounded like he got some protection in prison from his barbershop job, which gave him access to razors, he'd already written home about seeing a man's throat cut ear to ear. He'd already learned to say he saw nothing. Could jail transform you like that?

Not to worry. Your mother will show up and call a lawyer and get you out. Or else your daddy will march in and kick some redneck butt. But so many secrets are kept from him, you know he'll never catch wind of this. He'll also strive not to hear about it.

For a minute jail seems an okay alternative. Malcolm X started his mission locked up. Think about the yogic meditations you could master. Or the reading you'd do.

But Meredith's brother writes that his prison's library holds only grade-school grammar books and detective crap and motor-head mags. (How long's he been in? A year? Eighteen months?) She and her mother both top out their town-library cards for books to haul up on the bus. Any weekend one can go, they scrape together money for a Motel 6 and the bus fare. Sometimes your pal Stacy even drives them. (But while you're willing to ride along, you've not once borrowed your mother's car for such forays, though you regularly ferry carloads of whooping hippie strangers stoned out of their gourds on beach runs or to concerts in Houston.)

Maybe prison could mutate you into Cathy. You can suddenly picture your body hung from that door like a simian.

The night gets long, longer, longest.

Before this arrest, you believed neither brutality nor tedium in any measure could break you, for citizens of your region receive black belts in bearing up under both. There's some contrary regional pride in withstanding it all. Some kids leave elite prep schools like St. Paul's or Choate with entry into certain colleges, mastery of certain protocols. In the same way, one leaves Leechfield with raw tales on which to dine out, a sense of having escaped, and the capacity for both pathos and pissed-off that would make for either an excellent nun or a fearless infantry soldier.

So decades from now, when your stories cause people to adjudge your personal past exceptionally barbarous or criminal—or they call you strong—you'll feel like laughing. Horrifying stories could be told by anyone from Leechfield.

Or stories about crushing tedium. The slope of boredom there is steep enough to cast the shadow of an astonishingly high suicide rate. The average Leechfield teen can wring amusement from the most parched possibility, can by-God stand it.

That boast made, less than twelve hours of limbo in a town jail nearly undoes you. Even a prison sentence has an end, but the pretrial, pre-phone-call blankness and the specter of daunting consequence would dwarf and diminish the sturdiest resolve. There's nothing to watch, nothing to read or write with, and—since the others manage sleep—no one to talk to. Even one more day, and you expect to go mad. One of your favorite poems is by John Berryman:

> *[My] mother told me as a boy*
> *(repeatingly) "Ever to confess you're bored*
> *means you have no*
>
> *Inner Resources." I conclude now I have no*
> *inner resources, because I am heavy bored. . . .*

For a long time you retell yourself this story of Hogan's about solitary confinement, what he called the Hole. How the baddest dude in Huntsville—the head of the Black Panthers there, a lifer—got slammed down for some period of months. He was left naked in a lightless concrete room with only a mattress on the floor and a slop bucket they took out twice a day when they brought food. For a while, he kept up his running regimen by jogging in place for hours until—from constant impact with the floor—bone spurs formed on the balls of his feet and stopped even that.

One day or night or day as he lay there immobile, he plucked a metal button off the mattress—one of just two left. When he flipped it away, the click of it hitting concrete was, he realized, the day's greatest novelty. He felt around the floor for the button, eventually standing up to slide his bare feet in the dark till his toe touched it. By then an hour had gone by. He was sweating. He stood there holding the button with a small rush of triumph, also wondering if he listened hard enough, could he find it quicker next time. Which he did. By dividing the floor into quadrants, he could isolate the area the button fell to and limit his search to there.

Eventually he could bend to within a square yard of it, then a square foot. So he had to jack up the ante, make the game harder—dividing the floor into smaller squares, a grid he numbered longwise from the *x* axis and heightwise from the *y*. He cut the imagined tiles smaller and smaller till he had thousands of squares burned into his memory, each just big enough to accommodate the button. Then he kept a running curve of his improvement.

As he gained expertise, he toughened the rules again to keep it challenging. So he began more complex throws with ricochets—the button bouncing from multiple walls. Over time, he learned to predict them in the same way he'd mastered bank shots in pool, which required understanding the cant of each angle.

But one day he threw the button, and it didn't come down.

He felt over each square meticulously up and down, time and again. Still the floor was bare of it. So was the slop bucket and the mattress's soft edge of piping where it perhaps—in a fluke move—balanced. He crawled the cell on his hands and knees for days, up and down like a farmer hoeing along tiny inch-wide rows.

Of course, there was another button on the mattress. He could have started over with it. But that was cheating, he told himself. Besides if there was some warp in the physical universe that could gobble up one button, why feed it two?

As time stretched vacant without the button and the game, doubts about that last throw began to erode his former confidence in memory. Perhaps he only imagined he'd thrown it. He ran the scene over and over, till doubt tore holes in his reasoning.

That's how, over time, he posited that in some deranged instant, he'd ingested the button. Just eaten it—that was the only solution. That's how he wound up mashing through his own shit every day. Why he pleaded with the guards to let him get into the septic tank and crawl through the excrement he'd passed weeks before—or was it months?

You knew as Hogan told the story where it was headed. This rock-hard man started to rave like a dog. He ripped apart the mattress thread by thread, began a systematic chewing and spitting out of its stuffing. Once done with that, unable to bear the total disintegration of his sense of control, he decided the entire game had been a child's fantasy only. If there was not now a button, then there never had been.

They found him hung by lengths of mattress ticking he'd tied together.

Where was the button? you'd said. There's gotta be a punch line.

And there was, of course. When they cleaned out the cell and hosed down the shit-smeared walls, they washed a spiderweb from the high corner. A little disc swaddled in white silk fell and lodged in the drain at the cell's center.

Chapter Twenty

KARR, THE VOICE SAYS. A nightstick raps the door. You come back with your least ironic *Yessir.*

He leads you out, saying it's two A.M. (You would have thought daylight or even two days beyond.) You'll never know if they kept you from calling till two just to fuck with you, or if they were waiting for the circuit judge to finish some July Fourth picnic. Whatever the case, you're brought into the office of a man whose clothes make him an aberration. At this ungodly hour in this unlikely place, he's wearing a three-piece seersucker suit with an honest-to-God watch fob, his silk tie held down by an American flag stickpin. He must have bought the suit about 1940 and slept in it every night since then to convey the weathered, Mr. Chips style he greets you with. He gestures to the phone, saying, Go on and call who you need to, honey.

You dial, and Lecia answers. Why she was sleeping over there, you'll never know, but without her—because your parents' room sits on the far side of the house—the call would've gone unanswered (unless, of course, someone was up roaming sleepless). But Lecia, God love her, can snap up a receiver from dead sleep in half a second, which is what she does, albeit sounding all blurry and slurry.

Lecia, don't wake up Daddy. I'm in jail in Kountze.

Fuck you, she says, and you hear her fumble to hang up. You know that if she hangs up, she'll purposely cover her head to sleep through the call back. That is, if they let you call back.

So you bay shamelessly in a voice you hardly recognize, Don't hang up! Don't hang up! This causes the judge to look up from whatever he's scribbling. You turn your back to him, cup the phone and say sotto voce, I swear to God this isn't a joke. I'm in jail. In Kountze.

Well I'm not coming to get you, you little freak. Actually, you know this bluster for horseshit: she'd be there fast if you asked, albeit chewing your ass out every mile home. You can hear her shift around. She says, Do you have the foggiest idea what time it is?

They tell me it's two-something, but they don't keep a clock in the drunk tank, you say. You feel the judge's eyes on your back and glance over your shoulder. Sure enough, his pen has ceased to move across the legal pad, and he's staring full bore at you.

You're drunk? Lecia asks.

No, I'm not drunk. I'm not anything. I'm in jail. This is my only phone call. Remember on *Dragnet* they get one phone call? This is mine. Please, Lecia. I'm begging you. Don't hang up. Sneak in there and get Mother to the phone. She's gotta drive up here and make them let me out. And don't wake up Daddy!

For fuck's sake, she says. The receiver drops into soft covers.

What your mother says you won't recall. (Lecia in the background did say as Mother closed the door on her, Now you've done it, shit-for-brains.) Ultimately, she asks to speak with the judge, who—from your end—gets downright friendly. The whole time he's talking, your hand is out, waiting for the receiver again.

The judge finally says, We'll be here, Charlie. But the phone he hands you back issues a dial tone.

Still, your mother must have convinced the judge that you were some wrong-place-at-the-wrong-time case, because after you hang up, he offers to buy you a soda (the machine being unfortunately empty of all but unpalatable root beer and Dr. Pepper). Then rather than send you back to your cell, as he calls it, he lets you sit in one of the faux oak chairs outside his office.

You've waited about thirty minutes when you glimpse two of the Colorado boys (minus Big Foot) across the room. Rather, it's only their heads you see bobbing along, above the low wall of a cubicle. It takes you a second to twig to who they are, for these disembodied heads have been shorn, electric-razored down to Marine Corps prickles. You can picture the clippers, gliding up the back of each skull—all that glistening hair waterfalling to the floor. The result is a mutation: the boys suddenly appear overtly criminal—characters from the grainy wanted posters tacked in the post office. If one of them were hitchhiking on the beach road, even in daylight, you'd lock the car doors.

An hour or so after that, a short black man comes in the front door to the counter holding a long pistol that resembles a six-shooter from *Gunsmoke.* He sets it down on the counter, saying to the deputy, I just shot my old lady. His eyes are watery and bloodshot, the whites yellowed. He's wearing a beige leisure suit that might be made of molded plastic. Like doll clothes, you remember thinking. He's ushered to a chair. Somebody even washes out a coffee mug for the fellow and brews up a fresh pot. Before they close the door where the tape recorder's already running, you catch sight of him once more. He's interlaced his fingers and carefully placed his weeping face into that mask while this stout cop stands behind him patting his back says ts'ok, ts'ok.

By the time your mother arrives, a chill has settled inside you, a slight, marrow-deep tremor. When she bends for a hug, you cling to her neck like some marsupial, and she asks one of the cops for a blanket because her baby here's freezing to death.

She winks before pulling the judge's door shut. Then you sit extra still, wrapped in the rough wool blanket straining to hear. Mostly you expect her to talk in tones of shock and outrage at your behavior, convincing the judge she plans to take you firmly in hand. Saying blah blah blah *some limits.* Saying yakkity-yak *her father!* If she persuades the judge that she'll ride down on your ass like the hound of hell, maybe he'll set you loose.

Instead, after twenty minutes or so of low tones barely perceivable through the shut door, you hear laughter, greedy bursts of it. This goes on and on until you realize they're discussing some topic wholly unrelated to your plight. In fact, they're kind of whooping it up.

The judge opens the door with your mother still laughing broadly. He's squeezing her hand in a grip that doubtless started in a goodbye handshake but which he's stayed fiercely committed to and which she's tolerating. He says, Charlie, Charlie, you're still a piece of work. In the harsh light, he suddenly looks much older than you'd thought. Maybe eighty. Under thinning white hair his shiny pate has brown spots big as quarters. His tie must sport reminders of every soup he ever ingested.

But she's treating him like some hero. She ducks her head at this kittenish angle that sets your skin crawling. Inside, you're screaming, What about me?

The judge turns to you and settles a hand on your shoulder as if you're standing on a church step after services, this far-off look in his eyes. He says, I met your mother twenty years ago when she was the police reporter for the *Gazette.* She'd been doing a lady's column, but the editor got in a bind and bingo! He sends her to cover this murder trial—big case I was prosecuting. Trial of the century and so forth. Imagine! This dame on heels yay high comes clicking up the courthouse steps!

His face wears this beatific expression—like one of Giotto's angels staring up at light from God's throne.

He says, I was a young DA then. Let me tell you, little darling, she walked through those big oak doors, and I had to catch my breath. I thought, *That's the most beautiful woman I've ever seen in my life.*

Oh horseshit, your mother says. Her grin is so self-satisfied, you imagine offering her a silver-tined fork, with which to gobble up all this slobbering praise.

And if anything ever happens to your daddy, the judge says, I'd marry her in a Yankee minute.

You old fool, Mother says. She jerks her hand back from his, adding, You just want somebody to nurse you till you die.

Mother! you say. But the old man doesn't even flinch either from the rejection or the curt mention of his mortality. If his circulation were better, he'd be blushing.

He escorts her around desks and cubicle walls while you follow, more pissed with every step at being so disregarded. This is, if anything, your deal. Only Mother could make you a minor character in it.

At the door, one of the cops who rousted you is coming in with a white sack of something and two paper cups of coffee. His presence shifts the judge's demeanor several degrees. The old man suddenly beetles up his eyebrows and turns to you to say, loudly, You'll hear from the court soon, Miss Karr, about your trial date. But the broad grin he gives to your mother as she opens the car door makes you doubt that. (None of you are even charged with anything, though you suspect the Colorado dudes, who vanished, were less lucky.)

The whole time you'd been in that tank, you'd vowed to cherish freedom if you won it, to take no breath for granted, to get into your mother's car spewing oaths to reform. Instead you're steaming. You ask what the hell happened in there.

She lights a Salem then waves the smoke out her cranked side window. She says, It's no big deal. I'm pretty sure it won't come to anything, honey. That's probably the last we'll hear of it.

This breeziness with what school authorities have trained you to view as the stone tablets of Your Permanent Record cranks your own volume higher. So you're hollering, You're pretty sure? Pretty sure? Well since it's gonna be my skinny ass going to jail if you're wrong, let's drum up a lawyer and get a little bit more sure. I like the sound of *absolutely sure.* Or *real sure.*

Don't worry about it, baby. Stop being so silly. Just trust me, she says.

Long ago—aged seven or eight maybe—you'd loosed the grip on the tether that held you to the confidence she's so glibly asking for.

Since then, you've been floating along pretty much on your own, especially since Daddy vanished into wherever Daddy goes to, and Lecia took her right-wing turn just as you hooked to the left.

None of this is consciously understood, only intuitively acted on. You can barely contain the annoyance that sweeps through when you should be happy—both to be loose and that your mother's not hopping up and down in your ass. Anybody else would sing hosanna.

Instead, you do what sixteen-year-olds girls do best. You slouch down into a glower. About halfway home, she starts talking about what she plans to do with your room when you go off to college.

If I can get into college, you say. If my parole officer'll let me go.

Oh hush. I was just saying that you won't be home that much longer, and I might move my painting stuff in your room. You wouldn't mind, would you?

Do what you want, you say. Though you do mind. You'd imagined some eternal home that waited for you post-college, your room sealed and shrink-wrapped—a museum to your exploits.

The car glides over Cow Bayou Bridge, and there's a roadhouse Lecia frequents where Jerry Lee Lewis probably hit the stage last night pounding piano.

How far apart we've grown, you think, Lecia and me. Once you did Supremes routines in your bathing suits before the long hall mirror, synchronizing every step. Now if you're home at the same time (a rarity), you pester her by playing Hendrix full volume, or the Mothers of Invention ("Suzy Creamcheese, what's got into you, nyah nyah nyah nyah nyah . . ."). Mother actually likes this stuff, and even Daddy thinks your liking it is hilarious. But it drives Lecia gaga—completely affronts her. Which is partly the idea—her ire constituting the biggest response you can draw from the whole indifferent household. Apparently, even getting thrown in jail doesn't register a jag in your mother's heartbeat. No big whoop.

You ask her how she got that judge to let you off.

Oh honey. That was his idea. I'd never presume—

Mother, the old letch was dripping all over you. Like you're not fifty-some-odd years old.

Oh I see. You mean, How does an old hag like me turn the head of anybody possessed of a pecker? The light in her eye at this instant is knifelike and slant.

Basically, you say.

Your asking advice from your mother has become so rare she doubtless wants to savor it, so she takes a minute before answering. She thumbs the butt of her cigarette out the side window so sparks whoosh behind her profile. She says, Well, baby, you either got it or you don't.

After a while, you say, Well we know Lecia's got it.

Seems like, Mother says. Definitely.

What about me? Do I 'got it'?

Absolutely. No question about it. By the boatload. By the time you're thirty—

Thirty! Christ why don't you just say by the time I'm dead?

No, I just mean. Well, you were a later bloomer—

You hold up your hand like a traffic cop, saying, Say no more—

She says, You're gonna be one of those women who's always real little. You'll stay skinny like your daddy—and you won't get any wrinkles. You'll just get skinnier and better looking without sprawling out all over your ass. Getting pones on your legs, and so forth.

When I'm thirty? You say. When I'm thirty? Fabulous. That gives me thirteen years of celibacy before I start getting any johnson. (In truth, it's not johnson you want, but you have no other vocabulary for wanting.)

Anybody else's mother would have slapped your face for talking that way, but your mother's dearth of maternal impulse permits her an ironic distance. Like you're not really her daughter, just some interesting kid she hooked up with. Oh she worries, of course, but there's no spine in it—and no threat of intervention, nor even firm opinion.

Finally, she says, Aw hell, Mary, you'll be beating them back with a stick way before then.

This will turn out not to be true. But the alacrity with which she says it feels like a longed-for pat on your greasy head.

So you ride home strangely placated. You lack the wits to acknowledge the jail cell of the previous night. If you'd glanced back even once, given that arrest one hard look, a lot of onrushing trouble might have been staved off.

Chapter Twenty-One

Stacy Ferone is the perfect friend—budding poet, volleyball star on the championship varsity you never made. She doesn't complain when you keep her John Lennon record for nearly two months. She'll always pop for French fries. Plus you can usually muscle her into skipping school even days when she has a chem test. Top student. But such perfection is costly for its bearer. Even as you celebrate her departure for a top college, you can sense some payment is coming due. Will be expected from her. Extracted.

Who saw it coming?

You two cackle overmaniacally at her house that night. Her parents are off wherever her parents went, and you two are about to consume scads of worry-obliterating dope.

Now Janis Joplin's gritty voice from *Pearl* ("Freedom's just another word for/Nothing left to lose . . .") blares grittier still from the record player's tinny single speaker. And that beep of the horn in the driveway is your daddy dropping off tacos for you both. When Stacy opens the door, he says, Don't you look like a little angel standing there.

She takes the bag and edges out on the porch a little to stand as a receptive audience for Daddy's counsel, for he cannot come within spitting distance of you without launching into nagging advice of the most nerve-wracking kind. On his way to his truck, he's saying: Put on some house shoes. You'll take sick running barefoot on that cold floor. And eat those while they warm. Chop you up a raw onion. . . .

You hide behind the door, whispering to Stacy, Come on in. You're just egging him on.

But when you tug her elbow, she shakes loose, repeating what he just said as if it's a pearl of great price while resolutely holding the bag, which darkens with creeping grease.

He climbs into his green truck saying, You girls lock those doors when y'all get ready to lay down. The truck backs out about one tire's rotation before it stops, and he leans out yelling, You look like a little girl out there in your pajamas, Miss Stacy. About ten years old.

In the tremulous neon green light of Stacy's bathroom, you watch her untwist the razor's stem at the bottom so the safety hinges on top open.

Like a magic doorway, Stacy says.

More like a crocodile mouth, you say. Isn't it the crocodile that both jaws open up on? With the gator only having flip-top action?

Stacy says, I think so. But her voice arrives as if spoken in a trance. She pinches the safe ends of the metal and draws it out, holding it up so light shines through the oddly shaped die cut in the center. (Is it really Gillette Super Blue, or is that just the brand you most used back then?) Stacy's parents leave her alone so much because she exudes some Anglo-Saxon competence that perhaps comes with being her team's power spiker. Oh, she'll mouth off now and then, but she's never actually been expelled.

She's also inordinately well read for her economic station and geographical placement. Maybe your combined respect for her intellect and physical powers persuades you that she knows what she's doing, even if you don't. Also, suicide has become integral to the jargon that you and Stacy and Meredith deal in. You all three joke about swinging off beams, or laying down on train tracks. Buying the farm.

In the bathroom's neon, she talks sagely about how serious suicide would call for wrists sliced the long way, rather than sawing lightly side to side, which she plans now to undertake. Unstitchable, the long way. This exercise is not that dark endeavor. No, this is cutting, and she claims to have perfected it. Mr. Provost in physiology always raved about her dissections. Delicate as a surgeon, he said. Your efforts to embroider blue jeans always leave a bramble of thread on both surfaces, with snags and puckers every which way.

You don't actually wonder why she invited you into this. Again, notions of suicide threaded many of your conversations. People also tend to invite you into the clandestine event, rituals that would fill most people with sweaty trepidation. You do feel a little breathless looking at her strong wrist, for the prospect of it razored and bleeding seems like butchery. But the whole scene also holds you in morbid wonder. (Maybe your mother's flirtation with suicide is evoked, and you witness this scene played out with some semblance of control, as if this time you're mastering it. You'll see it without blinking, stand resolute before it without stifling a scream. As a kid outside a locked bathroom, you lacked such self-possession.)

You say, Just promise me you won't cut the long way. Or deep. You said not deep. Then you try not to stare at the criss-cross scabs on the other wrist, which seem inflamed at the edges though Stacy swears devotion to two antiseptics. You noticed the band-aids under her cuff today. That's when she'd told you about the cutting.

On the other wrist, veins the color of bright sky are embedded. She lowers the razor's edge to that milky spot. Even this makes you wince, and she hesitates as if in deference to that. How you suck air between your teeth. It's a breach you might step into, an interval for a protest.

Finally she says, I haven't even done it yet.

You ask for the umpteenth time doesn't it hurt.

She says no, but in that offhanded way of one reading from a sheet. Then, You wanna try it? You'll see it's no big deal.

Oh hell no. I'm not doing it. It hurts me to see you do it.

(Why you were there? You'll justify it later by saying she insisted you come as witness, but you've no specific memory of that.)

Some nasty taste is globbing up your mouth—viscous and bitter. You don't move as she swipes one light stroke at her wrist, not too deep, the thin line oozing crimson in the skin. Then she criss-crosses a few times, beads of blood gathering along each slice.

That's enough, you say. It's freaking me out.

But Stacy doesn't seem to be listening. Her head has fallen forward as if she's praying.

Afterward, the wounds will foam under the sheer splash of peroxide. Then she'll dip a small glass wand in some orange medicine to swipe on. You'll help her stick the oversize band-aids to her wrists.

A decade hence, when you ask her what purpose this cutting served, she'll claim there seemed no other way to get release. By then, you'll know she suffered from what Churchill called the black dog. You all did. You'll be conversant with symptoms like blunt affect; the virtues of exercise-induced endorphins; understand how exogenous depression (caused by outward losses) opposes the endogenous (the brain you were doomed to be born with).

What you won't know—ever—is who you were at sixteen that you failed to stop one of your best friends from mutilating herself. Couldn't you have told someone? Or just left the room? Surely witness is tacit approval. What was that elegant, self-condemning sentence Michael Herr wrote in *Dispatches* about being a journalist in the carnage of Vietnam? *I was there to watch.*

Chapter Twenty-Two

In fall, remote colleges once again let swing their low-swooping scythes over Leechfield proper, harvesting the few remaining pals left in your area code. The year before, all the boys left; this fall every dear girl clears out. Those who were once leaving in a few months or weeks or days seem to vanish in an eyeblink.

Only Doonie remains. And by now, he's so swarmed on by sloe-eyed blonds and so-called business associates (read: gangsters) that you mostly see him in motion—either entwined serpentlike with some teen beauty queen in the rearview of your mother's car heading home from the concert you drove to stoned, or he's flying past in the shotgun seat of some jacked-up hot rod so fast his profile trails vapor.

Thus you're left with various snapshots of departure that you mentally fondle in the scooped out days to follow the way a film aficionado replays scenes for detail.

Like this: Stacy climbs the bus steps in the blurry stop-action that prompts you to address her first letter to "Dude Ascending the Staircase"—a joke on Marcel Duchamp so ubiquitous that someone eventually makes a postcard of it. Through smoked glass, her solid shape moves behind the heads of strangers while your throat tightens. Dan drives Meredith away from her house in afternoon scorch, while she leans her head back into the open window so her waves of copper hair trail flapping behind her like some shredded flag.

Even Clarice goes away, albeit metaphorically. When at the church altar during her wedding (you were maid of honor), she turns to hand you her waterfall bouquet of white roses and baby's breath, you'd just finished whispering how it wasn't too late to bolt, your car being just outside. But she instead turns away, promising to love, honor, and obey a young soldier who often looks at you slantwise as if he might eventually spy the horns he suspects under your hair or the scaly tip of your long prehensile tail withdrawing under your floor-length gown. (This is pure projection—he never says boo to you.)

This loneliness sets you loose on a spiritual path, for after so many goodbyes and so many hungover mornings, you long for some steady state. *Please let the boat stop rocking,* you write in your journal. That's how you wind up swearing off drugs—not as part of a conscious reform program (for you never link drug use either to your mind state or to any harrowing experience). You just sign up for transcendental meditation class (aka TM) at a local technical college. A letter you get from Raphael claims you're just looking for some self-induced buzz the pigs won't toss you in the tank for. Absolutely.

The head TM honcho asks initiates to stay dope-free for some weeks prior to the ritual induction when mantras are doled out. Dope-free, you think. No big effort.

Not smoking pot turns out to be easy if you don't leave the house. This isolated spate of clean living also prompts a Get Me into College Please God Program that involves rereading Russian novels between slaving over letters to your girlfriends, who, from their respective colleges, actually write immediately and keep the mailbox stuffed.

But you dodge and wheedle and hand-wring to avoid the one college entry task you absolutely must undertake: the college essay, a document so dreaded that you repeatedly lose application forms from every school—some more than twice. Each time you send off for a new form, you picture some malevolent clerk who actually keeps track of your requests, citing each incident in your file with the note—*Poor organizer!*

Finally you tire of the effort toward virtue, and thus you wake one Saturday to your rat's nest of hair in the smudgy bathroom mirror—in response to which you think, Fuck it, I'm going to the beach. Next thing you know, you're standing in wet sand under nail-headed stars having smoked some head-fogging hash. (In the absence of a hash pipe, somebody heated wide knife blades in the fire, pressing them together over little thumbnail nuggets of hash so smoke rises from the crossed blades in a hissing fury that you all lean over and snuff down like wolves.)

You feel vaguely guilty the day you set off for the TM initiation Lecia calls Nirvana-rama. But that hash was Your Absolute Last Time with Unprescribed Chemicals. It's fall of senior year, the last year of your long sentence in this spirit-frying inferno. The day is blue-skyed and sparkling, since in the night a freak cold snap brought an ice storm that sheathed backyard foliage with hard rime.

You'd imagined that some reverence would infuse the ritual, but the doe-eyed college boy who inducts you has set an unlikely stage with the altar he's created—a batik bedspread draped over what looks like a TV tray. It's there you lay your mother's check along with a snap-frozen azalea withering to black and a handful of Uncle Ben's Instant Rice—both of which seem inordinately paltry and last-minute as holy offerings go. But when the instructor starts chanting mumbo jumbo with his eyes rolled up in his head, you gaze around the room half embarrassed for him. (As an adult, it will stun you that most bizarre encounters with virtual strangers from this period could have ended by your simply leaving, walking away—an option you exercised by running off from various boys but that never occurred to you in real time.) You don't feel like a bodhisattva. You feel like a chump.

Still, you give meditation a go for nearly a week, morning and night for ten or so minutes (you were supposed to do fifteen or twenty). But enlightenment is coming at such a snail's pace, and your senior year is stretching out so long before you that soon you're gobbling down a black molly pre–SAT testing because you need a little boost. Then you're blowing a little boo to take the edge off, and etcetera.

By now, the streets of Leechfield are closely patrolled for unwary teens holding dope. So every time you drive under an overpass and see (surprise!) some cop car like a low-lying cobra waiting to strike at your tripping or otherwise medicated self, your own brief jail stint flashes bright inside to kickstart cardiac overdrive. You wind up eating perfectly good joints while uttering prayers that you're certain no Great Spirit of the Cosmos would venerate with attention. (Later you'll decide that desperate, self-serving prayers must surely predominate, and that foxhole spirituality is perhaps the only kind anyone gets.)

Though your romantic travails are scant, a few stray heads steer you to concerts or through dope parties.

Then Doonie introduces you to a catlike guitarist everybody calls Little Hendrix for the laid-back, willowy moves he carves out with his body onstage and for the Fender Stratocaster he can play (already, at eighteen) with his teeth. He inserts your name in enough rock songs at the strip mall's Battle of the Bands (which he of course wins) that you find yourself standing backstage any time he warms up for or jams with some headliner like Johnny or Edgar Winter. You master the disaffected, I'm-with-the-band pose that makes it extremely easy to picture yourself—resplendent in Edwardian hippie regalia—on the cover of *Rolling Stone.*

About that romance little will survive, for you both stayed fairly bleary from the abundant drugs his hangers-on doled out. You will remember he bathed in some herbal stuff that sparked fantasies of Eden and resulted in a game for making love in the shower that you would ever after call Tropical Rain Forest. When he swayed above you in bed, that same fragrance made a small curtained room that held your two faces.

You even transfer illegally to his school—the crosstown rival high where Doonie also goes. You just lie to the registrar that your family has moved, and so your checkered records are mailed from Leechfield.

Within a month of carpooling with Doonie and Little Hendrix every day, blowing joints with his entourage in the parking lot at seven A.M., he goes back to his college girlfriend. She looks like Olivia Hussey in *Romeo and Juliet,* drives a white Mercury Cougar, and has her own apartment in Austin. Bummer.

Little Hendrix's baby sister, who worshiped the ex-girlfriend, even dropped a dime on you at the registrar's, ratting you out about your parents' true address, so you were ignominiously sent packing. Double-dog Bummer.

Chapter Twenty-Three

Your crush on little Hendrix fades out in a whiff of smoke and sulfur, but he blesses you with a lingering thirst for good blues.

That's how one legendary night you travel to Effie's Go-Go, a black juke joint in the bowels of Beaumont behind the shipyards where no underage girl of any color should be granted admission. You drive there flaming so luminously on orange sunshine that dark trees on the roadside seem to rear back to let you pass, and your bare arms and hands glow in the car's hull like fine marble.

You go with the new kid in town—a boy maybe higher than you—and with his putative girlfriend, Ann. Let's call him Augustus Maurice Schuck—a curlicued moniker no less astonishing than his real name or the self behind it. Augustus is a tall and chubby-cheeked, flamboyantly gay creature (albeit not yet officially uncloseted) with brown corkscrew ringlets that are a white man's answer to a Jheri-Kurl.

Augustus strode into drama class the first day of senior year wearing hot pants held up by flag-print suspenders. The clogs on his feet clopping like horse's hooves caused every head to crane toward him.

He'd just moved there from Houston and shared an apartment with his mother and drag-queen brother, who carried his makeup in a metal box designed for fishing tackle, and who was more adroit than Lecia at gluing on the Bambi-esque false eyelashes popular in discos back then.

The fact that no redneck leapt on Augustus Maurice that day to beat the dogshit out of him testifies to his considerable size and to the innate splendor of his bearing. Some kind of schoolwide status instantly worked like a shield against the more common cruelties of Leechfield High toward the unorthodox. (By contrast, when Meredith wore combat boots to school her senior year, a football star rushed up to her at lunch to say, "Fuck your boots!")

Maybe the fact that he courted the creamy-skinned Miss Ann, who was what you then called a Jesus freak, counted as a stab at heterosexuality. So the average redneck could tell himself, Well hell, he's trying. But Miss Ann never normalized Augustus Maurice one iota, nor did his magnificence dim by a watt in her company.

His ability to travel sans butt-whipping also speaks well of the state of Texas, where attachment to personal freedom can result in tentative acceptance if not succor. A bold enough demeanor could buy certain oddballs something like prestige. In your family this was called having enough fuck-you. Augustus Maurice had scads of fuck-you, spewed fuck-you into every room he entered. This pose can also get the shit kicked out of you, but occasionally, it buys a pass.

He was the first person you ever saw whose clothing projected genuine ideology, for he was engaged in a sartorial project to overthrow the dominant social order. He could break you up just by deciding to wear a zip-up polyester jumpsuit in pea-soup green, the type favored by old war vets and pensioners. His sent an alternative message by hugging his ass so tight that you could see the rectangular label outlined on his jockey shorts, and the shoulder pads he stitched in made his upper body resemble either Joan Crawford's or a linebacker's.

It's Miss Ann's much older brother, Chick, who steers you all to Effie's. His blues band gets booked there to warm up for the rumored appearance of Lightning Hopkins and B. B. King. (Both were reputed to jam there en route to New Orleans from Houston—something you'll later have cause to doubt.) Chick even gets the cover charge waived by putting your names on this I'm-with-the-Band list.

You're hopeful that Little Hendrix will show up with the college girlfriend, Halter-Top Ho, as you call her. He'll see you are With-the-Band, while he isn't. Then you can flip filbert nuts at the back of his head, or shoot slobbery spit wads from your cocktail straw.

If you'd gotten to this sagging little shack even one dot or tittle less high—maybe fifteen minutes earlier—you might well have decided not to go in. You might have scoped the garbage-strewn streets skeined over with swamp gas and thought, Maybe not. But by the time you pull up, the acid rush has kicked in on overdrive, and objects are shivering inside their outlines. Just looking at Effie's through the windshield saps every amp of thought. You just think that such a Down With It place proves how Down With It your cracker ass is.

For a long time you clutch the wheel as the engine ticks like a time bomb and stars pulse in their screw holes. It looks like a ghost town, the bare street skittered through with this urban tumbleweed of cigarette cellophanes and the odd wrapper. You have to cling to that wheel for more than a few minutes to get your bearings, for your navigational instruments are giving up only the bluntest physical truths, i.e., My feet are down; my head is up. Or, a chair is to sit. Or, right is the hand I color with.

Outside, the proportions are already going wrong. Some streetlights rise up thin as skyscrapers to the clouds; others shrink dwarflike and cowering. Nor is any line plumb. So the curb before the bar door arcs out like a stage apron, while the door itself shrinks back in forced perspective, seeming small and edgeless as a rat hole.

Augustus Maurice says, This is what I took my party dress out of mothballs for? His top lip has a natural outward curl that keeps his face in perpetual sneer.

You say, It's a blues joint, Augustus. We're not coming to see the Jackson Five. We're not talking *ABC/Do-re-mi.*

Miss Ann thumbs a raspy Bic lighter to study by flame the map her brother drew. She looks up and cranes around for nonexistent street signs, ultimately saying, in a voice as chipper as the twittering of a bird, This is definitely it.

Though Miss Ann would be of virtually no use in an actual barroom altercation, her presence soothes someone tripping hard as you, for she gives off the joyous aura of that pink fairy godmother in Disney's *Cinderella.* Also, because of her Jesus-freak status, you're fairly sure she isn't high, so at least one of you will (allegedly) know what's going on.

While you're thinking all this, in a momentary lapse of concentration, you're all whisked across the street to the door. It's as if your feet sprouted rollers and wheeled you there like some jet-powered robot. This happens so fast that you miss the actual travel, just arrive with your head spinning.

In reference to this, you say, breathlessly, What's that?

Augustus says, That's a boarded-up place that also has bars on the windows. He is dripping sarcasm in a way that transforms him into Jack Benny when he says, Now *that's* a nice touch.

You say with some effort from your dry mouth, Least we'll be safe. All that armor'll keep the dragons out.

Or the dragons in, Augustus says. He tilts his head in puzzlement, for he is also tripping. He says, With us? Us with the dragons locked in—is that correct? Grammatically speaking?

You flash on diagramming sentences in sixth grade under the hawklike visage of Miss Clickety Clack. You're thinking it's *we* for subject, *us* for predicate. The unopened door stands before you, so tiny you imagine having to stoop to get through it.

But you pause again before going in—maybe because this is not exactly a white place. But such a motive so disturbs you that entrance is suddenly required. You now have to go in. Your pose of hands-across-the-water commands it. Besides, when you look back at the car, it sits about a thousand yards away, across a strip of desert sand. Then you notice Ann beaming serenely at the unopened door.

You remember Ann's brother is inside. Your unlikely triad won't exactly wander in unescorted, white-bread faces blaring. The band's presence will buy you safe passage. Plus look at Miss Ann glow. Whatever snakebite you suffer in these wilds, she will serve as antivenom. You hallucinate butterflies to fly figure eights around her. She is your talisman against doubt, the human equivalent of a rabbit's foot.

But once you pass through that portal and the door clicks behind you, the degree of your miscalculation is plain.

First there's the bottle-green atmosphere, for the bar air is thick as sludge with its underscent of something rotted—old Brussels sprouts maybe.

At the back of the room, there's a glaringly lit stage of planks, a structure you might find in a cowboy saloon. It holds a giant black woman dancing naked but for bra and panties. She's enormously tall, well over six feet and leggy. She wears black wraparound sunglasses, the kind with the bubbled-out, amphibian surface and just a little razor-slit to peep through, as if that thin slash were all she could bear to take in of the world.

What horrifies you more than her near nudity is the unfortunate state of those underthings. The panties are grayed-out and high-waisted, from some other era, with *Tuesday* embroidered in a circle on front, though you're fairly sure it's Friday. The elastic's torn from one leghole, and hangs down as if it's lost interest in hugging to her leg. To compensate for the underwear's lackluster cling and the fact that they're too big for her by half, she's pulled them up, the waistband stopping just shy of her rib cage. This deforms her proportions even further—shortening her torso and lengthening her legs till she resembles some ill-shaped spider.

She's also basically without breasts and yet wears an outsize push-up bra constructed to hoist boobs to one's throat. But since there are no breasts to hoist, the lace cup is scooped out, hollow. Where breasts should swell forth there's a small cup of void held out for viewing. She'd seem far less bereft dancing bare-assed, you think. She swivels her narrow hips to describe a circle first one way, then in reverse, and in that clocklike movement time as you know it begins to warp.

That's when you know: Effie's is not just another juke joint, only somewhat funkier than the joints on Highway 73 you visited with Little Hendrix. Effie's is another element, one no less foreign than ocean fathoms, with physical laws as incomprehensible.

But when you reach back for the doorknob, intending to bolt, you find it's liquefied like wax, melted into the door, which in turn has melded into the wall. There's neither knob nor door, just a seamless expanse of what looks the wall of a steel bunker. You try not to blink at this fact, for you're loath to signal terror to the bar's few occupants till you've mastered the place's rules of decorum. Best in such environs to lay low, move slow.

If I sit down, you think, the rush will wear off, and the door will materialize again. And behind that door will sit the car. And before that car will unroll the coiled road that led you here, and at the end of that will stand your unmoveable house, an icon of safety.

Or so you tell yourself.

Behind you, Augustus Maurice tugs back the hood of your sweatshirt. He says he has to leave. Now. He can't stay here. He didn't know. He has to leave. Inside his small wire-rimmed glasses, his rabbit eyes well up. His chest heaves like he's run a great distance. He is a kid facing a roller coaster, and you settle a hand on his beefy shoulder.

You say, I need to sit down a minute. Have a Coke.

Do you say this or only think it? The membrane that separates your inner world from outer phenomena such as speech has been pierced, so that imagined and real swirl together.

Ann strokes Augustus's back, whispers in a tone like a bronco buster might use to calm a cutting horse with a new bit in his mouth. In response, Augustus's facial flush begins to recede like tide.

You waver for what seems a long time as if planted there at the room's vortex, shrunken to this tiny size, a mere gnat in the bar, which is growing hollow and canyonlike. The ceiling widens and stretches away, extending far past the dancer toward an infinite horizon. Likewise, the dark floor slopes downward seemingly forever. So you stand at the hinge of a pair of yawning jaws. Plus surfaces have become mobile. The white asbestos ceiling tiles are pockmarked, and now the black holes appear to bubble and boil, while the black linoleum floor's faux marbling coils and eddies. At the center of all this, you feel like a perspective point from which all of it's drawn.

From behind you, Augustus hulks against your back. When his finger pokes between your shoulder blades, it's as if he's pushed some button to power you up. In that instant, you become—in the phrasing stolen from your friend the ex-marine—point woman for this mission. You even think of his story about some horrible place called Khe San. How on a hill there when gore was exploding around him, the voice on the radio said the same scratchy phrases over and over, words you now repeat: *Stay strong. Hang tough. Help is on the way.*

You silently repeat this refrain. Again, some unseen force, maybe what powered you earlier from car to door, suddenly whooshes you all across the room in a nanosecond. You're placed before the stage in a chair drawn up to a black cocktail table.

Before you, the Amazon dancer with the stilt-long legs and beleaguered *Tuesday* panties continues her pelvic clockwork before a blue-sparkly drum set. She swivels herself larger and larger. (Years from now, when *Star Wars* comes out, the big hairy Wookie who follows the hero around as looming sidekick will flash her to mind.)

Augustus Maurice's face has gone all pouty, his demeanor broodingly porcine. You can see his belly rise and fail. He's the terrified pig in *Charlotte's Web.* Which makes you Fern. You briefly hug his sweaty neck. Through his astringent cologne and flowery deodorant, he gives off the odor of sweat socks. He says worried things that sound like *chitter chitter chitter*, and you soothe in tones that sound like *kum-ba-ya m'Lord, kum-ba-ya . . .*

Drinks! That's it. You will go to the bar for drinks. Surely the barman will welcome the commerce in this bare place, and Lord, is he fat, a soft and sloping mountain, all curvature and camber. His form hosts not a single angle, no evidence of bone. The barstool under the spillage of him seems comically tiny. He's chewing a pickled pig's foot and is hunkered over it in a pose almost feral.

Your legs struggle toward the bar as if through thigh-high mud. He's finished the vinegary knuckle, tosses it into some unseen receptacle, and dabs at his mouth with the bar towel tucked into his shirt front like a bib. Behind him three massive specimen jars hold hot pickles and boiled eggs, cured pig's feet. The very sight of them makes a gland in your throat contract, and suddenly you smell formaldehyde, a long silver vein of it, and the giant jars hold not regular bar snacks but fetal forms you flinch away from—images you refuse to acknowledge for fear of giving them life.

You ask for sodas. He wipes each finger daintily with the towel-bib then scoops ice into three highball glasses. Grabs a jointed silver bar hose. But in his hand the spout instantly transforms into a hooded serpent's head—eyes glowing amber. He squeezes on the flared hood so its gums retract to show bared fangs, then he lowers those fangs into each glass—one, two, three. In each is hissed out a full measure of black and steamy venom.

Meanwhile, the Wookie dancer has taken a post at the end of the bar. You halfway consider her an ally, for she's a girl after all, and the kind of loose-limbed dancer you and Clarice watching *Soul Train* always aspired to be. But something in her manner makes her unapproachable—some regality in her profile, short hair burnt straight and combed back in a frazzled shock not unlike Nefertiti's headdress. The barman moves away from you to get jukebox change for her. When she turns, you can see under the amphibian glasses for the first time. How the left eye is encrusted with sores, runny as an egg, the flesh eaten by some awful infection. Surely you don't really see inside that putrefying mess to the white surface of bone, but you think you do.

In Meredith's parlance, She has suffered. Or as another saying goes: You're thinking the blues; she's living the blues.

The barman's squeezing limes in your snake venom when, to distract him from your creeping unease with your own hallucinations, you start to jabber about music. Tones exit your mouth. You sense your jaw working. Good. Your stunning insights on Albert King, Howling Wolf, Lightning.

When his eyes link with yours, you feel a flint strike of recognition you'd like to capitalize on. Connection is comfort, and you hold the instant. You order Fritos and slim jims to prove your largesse. He announces himself as Effie, and says with gruff pride, This my place.

Effie holds out change, and your hand opens to receive it. But rather than drop the coins, he clamps hold to your wrist, which feels small as a pencil in his rusty hand. Then with one finger, he lightly strokes the line that divides your palm—heart line? life line? You try to maintain your disaffected pose inside the barefaced intimacy of a light touch, but retrieving the hand would seem rude. It's become some unit of barter you're gauging the worth of when his mouth plants a moist kiss at the hand's center. Only then do the few coins fall.

In a flash, you're back at the table, lowering a drink before Augustus, who sits lumpish and still, though his face is riven with undried tears. You feel too indicted by Effie's kiss to tell of it. *(She was asking for it.)* Augustus sobs out how he needs to go to the bathroom. Bad. But he's too scared, even if you go along. He keeps saying, I know I won't come back. I know it. I won't come back.

Ann has an arm around his soft shoulder, stroking one side of his head as you would a cat's. He takes off his wire-rims, soaks two napkins in his foamy glass of venom, and places the damp wads on his eyes, pressing them into the hollows like a blind man seeking cure.

Once the drinks are settled, you remember the snacks back at the bar, paid for with the kiss that still sears your palm. To leave the snacks uncollected virtually announces your fear to Effie, your revulsion. Your mind is seesawing between the alternatives—going back for snacks or not—when you feel some new gaze graze your back. You turn back. Slow. For in these districts, quick movement might draw some lunging attack.

But there at the bar is a lividly red-haired man in a crisp white sailor suit with bell bottoms that button around the front. So overjoyed are you at his whiteness and the sparkling state of his uniform (which in normal environs would label him a filthy imperialist swine) that you cross back to the bar right away, gather Fritos and slim jims, tell him your name and lead him back to your table.

Ann tears into the Fritos and says, Hey I'm Ann.

Augustus removes the Coke-soaked compresses from his eyes and—also perking up at the sight of the sailor—waves his beringed hand like a Mouseketeer. The sailor bends to say quite lucidly, My name's Cook. You nod, and he expands it: Robert Cook.

You nod again in understanding. Augustus asks across the blaring juke box if Mr. Cook is familiar with the men's room here, and Cook leans closer to your ear—maybe because he'd have to stand and bend across the table to reach Augustus. He utters the following: Cook, Cook. Robert Cook, Robert Cook, Robert Cook. My name's Cook Cook. Robert Cook. Robert Cook's my name. . . .

Robert Cook withdraws from your ear and beams forth a sedate and blue-eyed pleasure with the introduction. How well it went by his standards.

Ann grins her fairy godmother grin.

It occurs to you maybe you fancied the repeated name, so you try again, shouting to Robert-Cook-Robert-Cook, How do you like the music?

He replies, It's a little jivey, but it's all right. A little jivey. It's a little jivey. All right. All right! All right! It's a little jivey. . . .

His words corkscrew into your ear through cranial matter till you grasp his words and sink back into fret. You haven't yet plumbed the depths of the dangers here. You don't know who the bad guys are, and who the allies. In your untouched glass, a lime is skewered on a small red sword. You slide the fruit off and think grandiloquently, If I have to do battle with this, so be it.

Robert Cook slides his chair close to yours, and you sense the nightmare quality of his brain—a structure with no lit exit signs, with sliding bookcases and trapdoors, hidden passages you instinctively know burrow into the boiling tarpits of hell.

You are so far from being able to metabolize this dosage of freakishness that you take inventory like a stock clerk. Let's see. You are boarded and barred in with a lunatic disguised as a friendly sailor, a whore whose flesh is rotting off her face, an inflated barman whose interest in you has a carnivorous edge. Augustus has digressed into a shocking state. But his fluttery panic has begun to seem less scary than Miss Ann's glib smile, which is what—after all—got you through Effie's door in the first place.

Augustus goes back to pressing soppy napkins to his stung-looking eyes, and with Ann grinning like she's won a raffle (maybe she is high after all), Robert Cook reintroduces himself all around.

The nature of your thoughts then undergoes a massive shift—an upheaval so profound as to seem volcanic. Psychically speaking, sub-continental rivers move. Your whole cosmological fundament is reshaped. Time ceases to follow normal rules of progression. Instead it blinks on and off like a strobe light. Moments actually vanish while you occupy them, as if some switch on your cranium is suddenly flipped to pause, then mysteriously restarted.

During these gaps, you are picked up like a dollhouse figurine and lowered into different places on the game board that is Effie's. So one instant you feel yourself spiraling into darkness; the next, light streams down on a whole new stage set, with characters whose faces display the comfort of having been at your table a while.

In the first of these, you snap to beside a gray-headed black man who wears green suspenders and a derby hat like a honky-tonk pianist. Robert Cook's on his other side talking into the man's ear, which is cupped to better take in Cook's jack-hammered repetitions. The man's brow under his hat brim strikes a deep furrow. Augustus and Ann are absent from their chairs. (Where are they? gone how long?) A tower of shot glasses a foot high sits at the table center, and the coppery taste in your mouth doesn't reveal whether you imbibed any of those shots, or who paid for them, or if you're owing.

There are people in the bar and at tables around you. The stage is occupied not by the Wookie dancer, but by an athletic woman maybe five feet tall in flowery blue bikini panties and matching bra. She's muscled up like a gymnast with a mismatched wig of coarse streaming hair you can see the plug-holes of, like doll hair. She possesses the hypnotizing ability to shimmy every inch of her body at once, as if the skin were some casing she could detach from and vibrate independent of muscle.

Robert Cook continues to meet and greet phantoms approaching your table while the old man says to you, What wrong with him?

You say, I don't know. Honestly. He didn't come with us.

He says, I never seen nothing like it. Say the same thang over and over like a record with a scratch.

I know, you say. He seems pretty messed up. Maybe he's on something.

He got a screw loose. Done drop the cheese off his cracker.

Can't imagine what made him like that.

The old man rears his head back, says, What you call me?

You say, I didn't call you anything. I just said, we don't know him.

He draws back further still, affronted, puts both hands on his shirt front. Beside him Robert Cook's trapped voice rises and falls in cadence. The derby man says, You don't like black folks do you?

This question has no correct answer, but your mind still scuttles in search of one. If you check the box that says, Sure I do, I like black folks fine—then you're denying both his perception and the white world's innate racism. And if you say, Much as anybody—then you're being glib about slavery's legacy. And if you say, Not this red hot second, you're essentially robing yourself in a sheet with white pointy hood from which eyeholes are scissored. What you say instead is: Where are my friends?

He says, They long gone.

Which causes the room to list slightly, like it's some bottle filled with heavy fluid at a tilt. If you were tramped down by internal uncertainties before, now you are paralyzed, welded in place.

The old man rises and levels his hat brim with great dignity, smoothes his shirtfront so even Robert Cook stops his parrotlike prattling and gazes up the height of him. The old man says, in an oracular tone, You be gone too directly.

This enigmatic goodbye sets your internal continents adrift again.

You click back to life at the same table in the midst of a tune played by a white band that must include Ann's brother: "Before you accuse me/Take a look at yourself." The presence of these guys starts your foot tapping. Your head slides back and forth on its gliding track. Augustus and Ann sit across from you. But they've been transformed. Ann's radiance has dimmed considerably, a lantern in which the wick has been turned too low. Her small smile seems tight. Augustus is pale as salt. He gnaws his right thumbnail with such vigor you half expect him to start spitting out small chunks of flesh. It's all you can do to crank out a single sentence. You say, Where were you guys?

But the black-coned speakers blare, and the blue sparkly drums go thumpata-thumpata-thumpata—a pulse with a trill in it. For a long time, the melody spirals in and out of tone and measure, as if the band is being rushed backward and forward fast enough to deform the sound. Finally, Ann says, by way of explanation, Just don't use the bathroom. When you ask why, she shakes her head.

The room blinks dark again, and you come to on the other side of the table facing the old man in the derby. He sits between two large-breasted women who seem to take turns hollering vehemently at him. He seems literally to be holding onto his hat with both hands as if the wind of their shouts could set it tumbling out some nonexistent window.

The women wear what can only be called church dresses—one royal purple with a great white pilgrim collar; the other tomato red with even rows of yellow flowers. But it's their giant sun hats that transfix you. Each is the size of a small end table and might well serve in some city apartment as a patio garden or window-box ecosystem. The purple one features lavender morning glory blooms sipped at by hummingbirds floating in place from green wires. The red hat has what appears to be the fluffy tails of rabbits rooting under the thickets of twisted foliage. Each lady takes her turn volubly berating the old man, and he bears the weight of this like somebody who has it coming.

You're absorbing all this, trying to figure out who the women are to fall so fiercely on this man (his sisters? wife and girlfriend? disappointed business partners?), when with virtually no warning, the tomato-red lady draws up a patent leather bag from the floor and whaps the guy.

All your life, you've heard the phrase—whapped upside the head—but this is the first time you've seen it executed. It's a variation on what was once called a pimp slap, for it punishes without marring the face or body. With a weighted object (the purse) and her considerable body mass behind the blow, she connected flatly against his temple with a cartoon whump. The man's head flies to the other side like a ball batted from a tee. He's thrown leaning into the large purple bosom on the opposing side, his derby now orbited by cartoon stars but still firmly clamped down with two hands.

The purple lady lets fly on the other temple, smashing two fingers. The man puts these in his mouth as if to whistle up a pack of dogs. The ladies are instantly watching the band again like nothing odd transpired.

Then you're pitched again into blankness, an interval scored through by some demonic pencil lead. Minutes or hours elapse.

You snap awake and into a state of bladder-brimming urgency, like a kid sitting up befogged from dream just an instant before she wets the bed. Your bladder must be the size of a basketball. *Don't go to the bathroom*, they said. No if ands or buts. Not a qualifier. Just don't go. Like *Don't go in the attic*, in a horror movie, or *Don't move or I'll shoot.*

You think, Between the dilemma and the deep blue devil. Between pissing my pants sitting here and braving the outback of the bathroom with neither pistol nor machete.

On the dance floor, unhooked pelvises work so butts pivot around their axes. In one corner, Miss Ann and Augustus even execute their stilted moves. You ponder this while admiring the crowd. You think, These are my people. You think, My country 'tis of thee.

Behind you, the purple lady is still verbally chewing out the old man. One of his eyes has sprouted what boxers call a mouse—a plum-sized bulge, pornographically blue. The tomato-red lady's drink marks the place she once sat—a martini glass filled with amorphous pink fizz.

Which can only mean one thing: The tomato-red lady has gone to the bathroom. And since she wore a church dress, she must be Baptist (aren't most black folks Baptist?), and wouldn't she intervene if somebody wanted to sidle up and ask what your cracker-white ass was doing here on a Saturday night. You feel the whole room brighten as if some distant sun has risen. You can picture the bathroom now, maybe a little run down, but hey. The tomato-red lady will lend it the requisite dignity.

The instant you stand a warm hand lands lightly on your low back. Its fingers spread like spilled syrup, settling in the curve just above your ass—familiar but not out-and-out vulgar. Rotating, you find the monumental Effie bowing slightly and gesturing to the dance floor, arm crossed where a waist should be. It's an attitude almost gallant. So while you'd rather chew linoleum than dance with Effie—not to mention the fact your bladder is aslosh—a refusal would open the door to interpretation. Maybe it would be another nick in the racist tally sheet the old man in the derby started by claiming you didn't like black people. You look at Effie and think—in the clichés that have begun to string the loose rolling instants together—We shall overcome. You think, Give peace a chance.

That's how you allow yourself to be drawn (as so many girls do and will and shouldn't) into a set of arms you'd prefer to stay out of. The luxurious heat that enfolds you instantly suffocates. Effie is damp and smells like a sour beer rag. Plus Effie delivers the night's largest and least predictable surprise, a massive *gotcha.*

It turns out Effie has breasts.

You're not talking about the flabs men sometimes get from too many servings of pork chop and cream gravy. These are homegrown, Effie-generated boobs, each easily the size of your head. Which means that hand the size of a waffle iron on your lower back belongs to a female.

This betrayal tears a final rent in the already shredded fabric of the evening, for it casts doubt on the identity of every extant human. The room is instantly set whirling slowly around the pegged center of your discovery. You try to box out your feet as if under a basketball hoop—an attempt to gain foundation in the midst of the slow spinning.

In one orbit, you again glance at the derby man's table and see the tomato-red lady—is she a lady?—is still absent. And the lure to the bathroom is now undeniably powerful, for even if Tomato Red happens to be a man, there's still the fact of that Baptist church-dress to which you continue to attach some moral stamina. Plus she's still in the ladies' room, even now, waiting to act as your sponsor. The room reserved solely for ladies.

You say, I gotta use the bathroom.

Effie says *whisper whisper whisper, Baby-doll.* There's no spiked insistence in her tone, but she draws you closer, actually wedges your narrow body in the deep fissure between her Macy's-balloon tits. You manage to shove back hard and make excuses not unlike those Cinderella must have gabbled forth near the stroke of midnight.

Then in a wisp of time, you're shoving through the bathroom door convinced you'll find Tomato Red in a lush feminine lean over the sink, her net veil raised so she can apply her Billie Holiday lipstick.

The door creaks on its rusty spring, and you find the bathroom as expected. There's the predictable faucetless sink—maybe a little grubbier than you'd planned for. In fact, it seems urine-streaked. But the bent elbow you jar with the door belongs to the Wookie lady, who leans into a rust-freckled mirror. She says, I'm doing something here.

Both her hands are working on the far side of her head—maybe pinning her hair back or putting in an ear stud—some fairly delicate operation. Normally you'd turn back, but you've already undone your top button, thus announcing to your bladder that relief's at hand. Your bladder will have nothing less, so you shove past her toward the doorless stall, which holds only a bucket of the type you once fed pigs from. With each of your few steps, your rubber soles crunch down on what feels like kids' chalk or crayons underfoot, and you wonder what idiot would bring a child in here just as you manage to squat hovering above the bucket for blessed, if somewhat fiery, release.

That's when you see what the Wookie is up to. She's not adorning herself or ministering to her abscessed eye, which is indeed scabby and running with pus. She's holding a syringe at a delicate tilt, injecting its contents into the vein along her neck. You stepped not onto crayons or chalk pastels, but onto vials and glassine envelopes. Maybe a dozen glitter up from the concrete floor like so many spent shell casings.

While you hang stranded in midair, held hostage by your own pissing, you hear her body weight slump down as if she's been thrown. She's mumbling a kind of chant, so you know she's alive, not that you'd check her pulse if she lay still. Your only hope is for yourself—that she not touch you, and that no urinal spatters will send eager little spirochetes or venereal what-all splashing up to unfairly infect your skinny ass.

Outside the stall, you find the woman curled up, one arm instinctively covering the ruined eye. The syringe hangs from her neck like a miniature spear. She's still saying something incoherent, over and over in mournful cadence.

You don't run. Nor do you ask yourself why you're lingering if you've no intention of helping. *(I was there to watch. . . .)*

In that breach, she transforms into a child you've been hired to pull a quilt up over or fetch a glass of water for. She's in that fetal posture assumed by the dying. The long incline of her back shows rear rib bones rippling down ever smaller to the soft hill of hip. How elegantly made she is, you think, we all are.

Then an unbidden image surfaces, an illustration from your old zip-around white Bible—Jesus's back bent over into the exact same curve, the cut flesh awaiting another lash.

When she rolls over suddenly, you startle and dash out. But in that instant of her turning, you made out what she'd been saying over and over, that litany of disappointed longing: *Effie say I can sang. Effie say I can sang . . .*

You fly across the maze of tables and bodies with Ann and Augustus in tow to find the steel bunker wall that once sealed you in has again melted, so the door to the outer world has reassembled, its knob in place. It's there the old man with the battered derby calls out with a raised finger, Hold up a minute. He's followed by the ever fresh Robert Cook, still stalled in that endless train of introduction.

The old man says, He fixing to drive me nuts. Y'all need to take him on outa here.

We don't know where he lives, you say. He didn't come with us.

This fact finally draws the man's face into a pucker under his hat brim. He says, He ain't y'all's?

No sir. We never saw him before in our lives.

Well, whatever wrong with him?

Augustus Maurice says with no small parcel of pique, Do I look like a medical professional? It's not some white people's disease we can diagnose! Then he huffs outside with Ann.

The derby man touches your arm one last time, says in a voice far too mournful for you to bear just then, Please don't call the po-lice on us. We ain't bothering nobody.

No sir, you say. We got no intention of calling anybody. We just want to go home.

He pats your back as you leave, saying, Thank you, darling, thank you. Y'all have a good evening.

In the yellow station wagon, you find the highway unfurling of its own accord under headlights. Augustus and Ann sit in the backseat. She's again become a fairy godmother, smiling so sweetly you see her draped in lavender organza and rosy veils. He tilts his head against her breast, but his eyes behind his wire rims are wide-staring.

He says, I'm fried.

You say, Crispy critters.

Then silence floods the car, for on nights like this the greatest truths can't be uttered. Certainly not right off, maybe never.

Chapter Twenty-Four

At home, alone in your room, you will scribble several notebooks with hieroglyphic nonsense in hopes of finding that single unutterable truth. You know it's there somewhere, skating just outside your field of vision. About four A.M., you wander naked and somewhat deranged by thirst into the kitchen, where the season's first cut watermelon is covered in plastic wrap. You hoist it to the floor and squat above it like the noble savage you've fantasized you are. It's not quite ripe yet, but you scoop the stiff fruit out with both hands, shove globs of it into your mouth so it spills down your arms and breasts and on your thighs while the Siamese sniffs and tentatively laps at the edge of the rind. The mantra chugging through your head chants, *Effie say I can sang, Effie say I can sang . . .*

At some point your mother will appear in the doorway—a colossus in flannel pajamas. She says quite foggily, What're you doing, Mary? The question will reverberate for a million miles, colliding off planets, zipping by satellites while your mind gins up the four thousand possible answers. You'll eventually find the wherewithal to say, Eating watermelon.

At that, she looks glancingly satisfied, says only, in gratuitous admonishment, Be sure and clean up that mess before you go to bed.

At dawn in an instant of psychic stillness that can only come to a badly scrambled mind, the single true sentence finally comes to you bristling with sparks. The sentence is stolen, but that doesn't diminish the force of your pounce upon it, or the cometlike brilliance with which it streaks through you.

You write it in six-inch letters on a poster board you thumbtack to the wall, as if it's a formula on par with relativity theory. Then you slip into shorts, a T-shirt and flip-flops.

The morning is dew-washed and lustrous, the inside of a pearl. In the garage, you haul out the rusty Schwinn you haven't ridden since sixth grade. Your body weight flattens its split tires, but it's the mode of transport closest to a galloping horse, which is what this type of message requires. Riding it's like plowing through swamp muck. It takes all your thighs' might to pedal on the flat rubber and aluminum rims to Meredith's house. She's home for Easter weekend. You drop the bike at her window and scratch on the screen so as not to wake her mother.

Her round face appears shining, framed by the copper waterfall of hair. The pink yoke of her nightie is cross-stitched with *x*'s.

You rant out the events at Effie's in a single gust. While you sense as you speak that your hair is standing straight out from your skull in a three-foot corona, touching your head proves every time that it's in place. The sentences unspool from your mouth of their own accord and at some velocity. Meredith listens through the screen with head bowed like a confessor.

You tell her how all this led you to unearth the ultimate sentence, the endlessly resonant snippet of language with implications no one can ignore. Before you actually let Meredith hear it, you bow your head and hear an internal drum roll. You finally look up to say, There's no place like home.

She freezes in place holding onto her grin. Mockingbirds bounce on the chinky-pin branches in the next yard. Some seconds go by. She says, That's it?

You add, Well, basically, yeah. I mean. I have to work out a few kinks.

You do remember it's from *Wizard of Oz?* she asks. Her eyebrows are raised.

You say, But the context of Effie's totally overhauls it. I mean, we were in this place where all the love had been sucked out of people, but the husks of them kept staggering around and trying to take stuff in, and there were these black ladies I guess were whores. One was this giant Amazon wearing Tuesday panties. I found her in the bathroom shooting up in the neck. . . .

Meredith listens again with the placid repose of untrammeled acceptance. Finally, she says, Sounds like wicked strong acid.

Maybe it's a little less than revelatory, you say, in the cold light of day. Plus I haven't written it up right yet.

Guess you kind of had to be there, Meredith says, coming close enough to the screen that you can finally see how she's struggling to keep her sea green eyes placid, holding down some gust.

That's when the idiocy of your insight—the treasured scrap you've rescued from your descent and meandering through Effie's—flames over you in a noxious internal backdraft.

You say, It's a completely dipshit idea, isn't it? You're deflating now notch by notch like one of those whoofed up cakes laden with frothy egg whites. Taken from the oven too soon, one'll just sag down to a puddle of nothing.

Did I say that? she says. You can sense her laughter's held back by a single breath.

Well your face is awful pink, you say. Which indicates effort.

She says, Don't feel bad. What was Doonie's big revelation that time? I wrote it down somewhere but can never remember it.

When we'd done all that crystal at the surf thing? you say. With that girl he liked.

The scene blows over you—a campsite in Mexico at dusk. You've been awake seven straight days snorting crystal, and Doonie comes scampering along the beach in his Hawaiian print baggies waving a strip of paper bag he'd written this sentence on.

You repeat it now to Meredith, 'She was thinking fucking, and I was just fucking thinking.'

That lets the laughter out. Its bursts are rib-rattling and purgative. They take your breath for some minutes. A bakery truck flies by trailing hot cinnamon. In your encyclopedia there's a photo of a cinnamon tree, guys peeling the bark with these odd tools.

You say, I want to live somewhere where there are cinnamon trees.

I thought you wanted to live in New York City.

There too.

Meredith's mother stirs around inside the next window, hollers who's out there, and you say you and hey, and she heys back.

You should leave. It's only proper, since they're not even dressed, not to mention Meredith's been away and having you descend like a harpie probably isn't Mrs. Bright's first plan. You say, I gotta go before my parents find my sign.

Sign?

With the sentence writ large, you say, shaking your head. Big letters. Yay big. They'll send the posse out looking for me. Guys with the long-armed coats.

They'll see your door closed and think you're snug down in your Barbie dream bed.

The refinery shift whistle lets go its wolf howl to end the graveyard shift. You wonder is your daddy in bed or stepping into his truck to come home? Maybe your mother's brewing up coffee. They seem smaller somehow than they once did.

You say, I wouldn't mind a little bowl of something.

Are you still hallucinating?

I can hear a Mexican mariachi band, trumpets and so forth.

That's benign enough, she says, as hallucinations go. But can you face Miz Francine in her pink sponge curlers?

Bring her on. Hell, I'm the iron maiden, woman of steel. If I can make it through Effie's, she's a cakewalk.

At the front door, Meredith is grinning, holding out a Mickey

Mouse bowl full of Froot Loops and milk. Taking it feels like accepting some blessing.

You're inside at the kitchen table wolfing cereal when she says, You have accomplished a great thing.

And what would that be, Bwana? you ask, mouth full.

You're your Same Self.

The truth of this flickers past you gnatlike. For years you've felt only half-done inside, cobbled together by paper clips, held intact by gum wads and school paste. But something solid is starting to assemble inside you. You say, I am my Same Self. That's not nothing, is it?

Meredith nods one of her gypsy fortune-teller nods. She whammy-waves her hand over your cereal, says, I see big adventures for Mary. Big adventures, long roads, great oceans: same self.

Like I'm chocolate through to the center, you say. Same self.

That oddball catchphrase will serve as a touchstone in years to come, an instant you'll return to after traveling the far roads. Like everything else, Meredith thought it up. You were there solely for embellishment and witness. You were there to watch.

At the table, your chair slips into the bolt hole left by the old examining table, and it rips some jittery giggles from you. But wrung out as you are from the acid, you're not overjangled. It's as if some substantial cloak now drapes over you, some reward for escaping the dragon's lair.

As for the actual validity of the notion, an immoveable self ever firm, you're there only by half at best. But half's still a good measure more than some people ever get. You'll spend decades trying to will Same Self into being. But you'll keep shape-shifting. Probably everyone must, so long as a body's treading sod or drawing breath.

What's unalterable as bronze, though, is the image of your radiant friend that morning barefoot on the porch with suns in her rampant hair. She's holding out that bowl of Froot Loops and touching your shoulder as if to bestow the right name upon you, the one you'll bear before you through the world, each letter forged into a gleaming shield.